Women of Taste

RECIPES AND PROFILES OF FAMOUS WOMEN CHEFS

BEVERLY RUSSELL

WILEY

JOHN WILEY & SONS, INC.

NEW YORK   CHICHESTER   WEINHEIM   BRISBANE   SINGAPORE   TORONTO

Women of Taste

Executive Publisher: Katherine Schowalter
Senior Editor: Claire Thompson
Managing Editor: Diana Cisek
Editorial Assistant: Maria Colletti
Recipe testing: Molly Siple and Lissa De Angelis
Graphic design: Gillian Redfern Rones
Book packaging: Beverly Russell Enterprises
Cover photography: Cole Rigg
Cover design: Roberta Ludlow

This text is printed on acid-free paper

Library of Congress Cataloging in Publication Data:
Russell, Beverly.
Women of Taste: Recipes and Profiles of Famous Women Chefs/Beverly Russell
Includes index.
ISBN 0-471-17943-4 (cloth : alk. paper)
1. Cookery, American. 2. Women cooks - United States   1. Title.
TX715.R963 1997
641.5'082'0973--dc21   97-13168

Printed in the United States of America
10 9 8 7 6 5 4 3 2 1

*To Tatianna and working women
everywhere who embrace the challenge*

Contents

Women in the Kitchen:

A NEW BREED OF PROFESSIONAL PERFECTIONISTS

In waging the battle for their independence, for decades women strived to get out of the kitchen and away from routine domestic chores. Stirring the pot, nurturing a family by cooking and serving food, symbolized the elementary role of the housewife. When I started out on this book, I found the older guard in the strict feminist camp thought the idea of celebrating female chefs a contradiction in terms of professional accomplishment. But if women can ride the Space Shuttle and put their lives in the danger zone in the military and police forces, then obviously the expectations of what professional women can do have expanded. Becoming a professional chef, in fact, is a way of contesting the long-accepted machismo in the hotel and restaurant kitchen and joins the list of professions successfully and joyfully pursued by many women in search of equal status.

It's true that a natural skill - rooted in hereditary instinct perhaps - has led most of the women chefs profiled in this book to their achievements. Many of them never went to culinary school, and some never even had a formal cooking lesson in their lives. They mastered the art by apprenticeship and hands-on experience. At the Culinary Institute of America, considered the foremost culinary institution in the country graduating professional chefs, with 2000 students on campus, women are still in the minority - about 26 per cent in the highest-enrolled, 21-month program for an Associate Degree. In pastry and baking,

however, the student ratio is about fifty-fifty. This is because pastry hours in a restaurant kitchen run from early morning to early evening, allowing women to be at home with their children in the evenings. Executive chefs work longer hours up until midnight which means that the job becomes their life. You either marry a man who stays home with the kids, decide not to have children or never get married at all. This is the reality that all these women have dealt with, each in their own way, to make their lives satisfying and fulfilling.

As in many of the professions (law, architecture, medicine) in which women have caught up with the opposite sex in the past few decades, this generation of women chefs is the first to make it to the top. Throughout the 50s and 60s, a restaurant was more likely to be identified with its maitre d' or owner in the front of the house, than its chef at the back of the house. In the 70s and 80s, French nouvelle cuisine, and the masterchefs associated with it, introduced a cultural and gastronomic revolution. At the same time, women's liberation gained new momentum. In this adventurous climate of sexual rights and epicurean discovery, women stepped into the professional kitchen and fitted in very naturally. Intuitive techniques that belong to the feminine psyche were required. "Plating" became a vital process, demanding an artistic touch with swirls of sauces under rather than over the dessert, or piled up architectural arrangements of salad and shrimp as a way of presenting the appetizer. Dining rooms were transformed with atmosphere created by the chef-owner in collaboration with foremost architects and interior designers. The idea was to tempt customers to book tables for the ambiance as much as the food. Women seized windows of opportunities: in the garde manger, on the line, in the pastry department. From there, it was a logical step to executive chef and restaurant owner, as these profiles demonstrate.

In the thirty-six weeks during which I interviewed these thirty-two chefs, I visited twelve cities. At the Four Seasons Hotel in Philadelphia, I lunched with Alison Barshak, one of the youngest executive chefs in the country during her stint at the three-star Striped Bass. As soon as word got around she was in the restaurant, I understood that my desire for a simple spinach salad was simply unrealistic. Chef Jean Marie La Croix was determined to fete her. I have never seen anything quite as exquisite as the two opaque glass Lalique bowls of shellfish sprinkled with two caviars that arrived on oversize chargers as a surprise between courses. At the Four Seasons Hotel in Beverly Hills, fragrant with the scent of a thousand flowers in great bouquets throughout the public spaces, I was invited to interview executive chef Carrie Nahabedian over coffee at eleven in the morning. As we talked, lunch service began and soon we were into tastings that went on until three in the afternoon. A spicy shrimp salad was followed by a tempting vegetable torte, followed by spinach ravioli in a creamy tomato coulis, followed by John Dory with spring vegetables, followed by rack of lamb with matchstick frites. Long before the meal ended I had almost forgotten where it all started.

Also in Beverly Hills, I was treated to a memorable dinner at Wolfgang Puck's Spago by pastry chef Sherry Yard, seated at the No. 1 window table in the restaurant, with a 180-degree view of the room, and surrounded by movie notables discussing megadeals while tucking into gargantuan quantities of food and wine. Sadly, Yard is not included in the book, although she definitely deserves a place in it. Her work takes precedence over publicity activities and she could not find the time to have photographs of her desserts taken. Another highly talented pastry chef in Chicago, Judy Contino, is also missing because she has no time to devote to publicity. I went to her charming cafe and bakery, Bittersweet, twice. Her team of bakers in the kitchen were all visible through a glass window, producing the one hundred different items - cookies, tarts, muffins, scones, croissants - she sells each day.

During my research, while reading restaurant trade publications I was startled to see that the advertisements come from major bulk food producers who are not doing much to enhance the healthy eating habits of the country. Aware of the national predilection for fast food coupled with an increasing tendency toward obesity, the women chefs in this book are very concerned about the general quality of food that is served to the public, setting the highest standards in their restaurants by creating dishes with only the best ingredients. Many of these women are involved in helping to raise the public consciousness about good nutrition and a healthy diet.

Susan McCreight Lindeborg, in Washington, D.C. for example, has worked with Operation Frontline which teaches low-income women how to make the most of their dollars at the supermarket and serve nutritious meals to their families. Jody Adams in Boston supports Old Ways, an institution to promote and preserve traditional ways of cooking. This organization is also collaborating with the Harvard Institute of Public Health to create new food programs. Adams is also a co-founder of Chefs Collaborative, formed to sustain small farms in the North East by ensuring markets for fresh, organic, locally-grown produce from quality restaurants in the region. In Maui, Beverly Gannon helped to create a cooperative of chefs to change the practice of eating imported frozen goods on the islands, while exporting all the great Hawaiian produce overseas!

Is it possible to tell whether a man or a woman has cooked a particular dish? There are disputes about gender identification of culinary creations. Some women chefs insist there is no way of telling who is at the stove, a man or a woman. On the other hand, Andree Abramoff, winner of the 1997 Silver Spoon Award from Food Arts magazine was described in her tribute as creating a cuisine de femme. Abramoff felt this was the highest compliment she could have received. In France cuisine de femme means cooking from the hearth. It is warm, homey, giving and nurturing.

So as in most things in life, what goes around comes around. Eons of standing at the hearth have most certainly helped women to compete with men in a super-masculine field - and gain increasing respect as they do it.

Introduction

"We have come a long way in the last thirty-five years."...says America's most celebrated culinary expert, Julia Child, in her recent book 'In Julia's Kitchen with the Master Chefs'. When her first book was published in 1961, many American cooks had never heard of a leek, had never seen or used a shallot. Fine restaurants in New York were mostly French, and the chefs in those restaurants were French and most definitely men. For years the chef was considered an artisan, not an artist. Cooking was considered menial work, not a profession.

Now chefs and cooks and American cuisine are indeed news, and Mrs. Child, with her phenomenal television series and best-selling books, has helped to encourage respect and enthusiasm for the culinary arts. She has made home cooks understand that food is a family affair, and every meal, she affirms, including breakfast, should be a joyous occasion. She believes we are here on this earth not only to be nourished by our food but to enjoy the infinite pleasure of the table, as well as the preparation of what goes on it.

As a mentor and inspiration to many of the women chefs in this book, who are taking their place beside famous men in their profession, both national and international, we invited Julia Child to provide a foreword in an interview with Molly Siple.

I am not a chef, I'm a home cook and a teacher, so I haven't had any of the problems that many of the women in this book have had, getting accepted as professional chefs. Anyway, I am big and tall, so that helps. People are hesitant to try intimidation on me.

It is still very difficult for a woman in Europe, or a woman in a European-type kitchen in this country, to be accepted on an equal level, because male chefs just don't like women in the kitchen. Professional chefs of the old school, even Jacques Pepin, don't think women belong in the kitchen. That's beginning to change, of course. But it's been a long time coming.

Now that women have their own restaurants, and their own kitchens and hire people, that makes quite a difference. It's like women lawyers. In order to get to the top, you have to have your own firm. With men of this current generation who have trained in America, however, I have observed that it doesn't seem to make a difference if the chef is a woman. But it does depend on how good she is and if she has authority as the boss.

I've had many women chefs on my television show, I've tried very hard to make it fairly even, and thank heavens there are so many talented women chefs now. Twenty or thirty years ago, of course, the culinary arts was not a profession at all. It was looked down upon. But we finally even have a master's degree program at Boston University. The Culinary Institute of America, as well as New York University are about to start four year courses, giving a bachelor's degree and eventually a doctorate. So it has become a real science, a discipline and a profession. Educated people with liberal arts and other degrees are going into food. I look upon this as very necessary, if the profession or the product is going to improve.

If you are going to be a top chef - man or woman - you should count on a ten-year training period, working in a great many places. After your formal training, you work as an apprentice. It's a long haul. It's important to work with the best chefs - to get into the best restaurants, stay about two years, and do every station. Wring them dry! Then go somewhere else and learn something more. That's the fun of it. There's always more to learn and more to observe. The more training you get, the better you will be. I'm very much in favor of the contemporary French classical training. It's a solid course with the result that anything you see, you can cook. It is essential that you know what really fine food tastes like. If you don't know it, how can you produce it?

As for me, I've been a kind of journeyman cook. Since I am a generalist, I have to do a bit of everything. After my formal training, I started out with my two French colleagues. and our own cooking school in my apartment in Paris. It was called L'Ecole des Trois Gourmandes, the school of the three hearty eaters. We had an old-fashioned French apartment, and the kitchen was on the top floor. We often invited professional chefs to teach special classes, cooking a fancy lunch and serving it formally in the dining room. We usually had guests, such as visiting friends and husbands. Teachers and students cooked together, and it was totally hands-on. An informal program of classes like ours is, of course, vastly different from structured courses like those at the CIA, the Cordon Bleu or La Varenne. But our classes served as an introduction.

The culinary arts make a wonderful profession whatever aspect one follows. It's a passionate hobby and one that is totally absorbing. When you are in it to the hilt, it's like belonging to a big family of chefs and cooks and teachers.

ANDRÉE ABRAMOFF   JODY ADAMS   SUZANNE BABY   KAREN BARNABY

ALISON BARSHAK   ANN CASHION   SUZY CROFTON   SUSANNA FOO

Andree Abramoff

CAFE CROCODILE

"Women have a very different touch with food."

Multinational Influences

Andree Abramoff never had a cooking lesson in her life, or worked in a restaurant, but for many years she has presided over one of the most highly respected restaurants in New York, attracting well-known people from the worlds of art, politics, business and society. She cooks French Mediterranean food, with recipes acquired from her mother and grandmother. Brought up in Cairo, with a French father and a Turkish/Greek mother, she was introduced to a multiplicity of cuisines as a child. She moved to Paris after the 1956 Suez Canal Crisis, where she married her husband, a chemical engineer from Alexandria. The couple moved to the United States and Abramoff at first pursued a successful career in publishing in New York, coupled with a hobby of cooking, which subsequently developed into a catering business and cooking school. Eventually the cooking took over and Abramoff opened a charming bistro in a brownstone on Manhattan's Upper East Side: Cafe Crocodile. It is so named because "crocodiles have a ferocious appetite, and the name has a bite to it," says the chef whose dishes explore the aromatic spices of the Middle East along with the classic flavors of French cuisine.

Cafe Crocodile

In 1997, Abramoff's artistry was recognized with the highly regarded Silver Spoon Award from Food Arts magazine. She has received rave reviews from many other publications, including Harper's Bazaar, Vogue, Avenue, the New York Herald Tribune. She participated in the 1985 Master Chefs series on PBS. Abramoff talked in her restaurant one afternoon.

354 East 74th street
New York, N.Y. 10022
Phone: 212 249 6619
Fax: 212 327 0350

Right:
Red Snapper
marinating in
Herbs, Olive Oil
and
Lemon Juice

Below:
Cassoulet
Toulousain

When Food Arts magazine described my cooking as a traditional cuisine, a cuisine de femme, I regarded that as the highest compliment I ever received. That means cuisine from the hearth. Women are always cooking, nurturing and simmering. Women have a very different touch with food. I'm not putting men down. Men do certain things women don't do. They have an overall view of what a dish they are cooking will look like in the end. They cook in a spectacular way. Their food is beautiful and delicious but it does not have that something that touches the heart. When a women chef cooks it is absolutely different. Not in the appearance of the dish, but in the taste and flavoring. Women seem to know the exact amount of salt and pepper to put in, exactly how much lemon juice to use to highlight a certain flavor. They do it better, whether they are professional women chefs or cooking for their family.

When I started cooking as a hobby, I began one day by saying jokingly that while Proust was looking for time lost, I was looking for flavors lost. I remembered flavors from the time I lived in Cairo when I was exposed to many cuisines of the world, French, Spanish, Turkish, Greek, Egyptian. So my mother and grandmother shared their recipes with me. The rest of my repertoire is self-generated.

Andree

For the first seven years in my restaurant, I only employed women in my kitchen. It was not deliberate, but when I placed an ad, I picked the most competent candidates and they turned out to be women. Now I have a

mixture of both men and women. But I have found women are less accident prone, less likely to suffer minor accidents. They don't break things as much. and they are cleaner. When you open a refrigerator, for example, it is not all helter skelter and a mess of things, like you will find when a man is in charge. Women put everything away carefully, they label jars and bottles so that they are easy to see. When I went to restaurant Trois Gros in France some years ago and toured the kitchen, I noticed that out of 40 people there was only one woman peeling the vegetables. French chefs are very chauvinistic, very much so. Even today.

It is hard to say what it is that makes food prepared by women so special. You can even have two sisters, like my grandmother and her sister. They both made the same jams but my grandmother's tasted better. It's a gift, and it involves having a taste. My husband is very discerning and though he can't cook or boil water, he can taste. He is my best and foremost critic. He's a Virgo. I'm a Sagittarius - you can tell from my fire.

Above:
Choc Aux Chocolat

Above Left:
Pissaladiere
with Tomato,
Olives, Anchovies
and Onions

Jody Adams

"If you work in the restaurant business, the stress is high but the reward is in the culture."

Just four months after Jody Adams and her partners opened Rialto in September 1994, the Boston Globe awarded the restaurant four stars, its highest rating. This prestigious endorsement followed a list of other achievements for Adams: Boston magazine's Best Chef de Cuisine in 1991; Restaurant Hospitality's Rising Star in 1992; Food & Wine's Best Ten New Chefs in 1993. Although Adams comes from a New England family that is passionate about good food, she entered Brown University as an anthropology student, concentrating on music, sociology and nutrition, among other subjects. Soon after taking a part-time job with professional food writer and teacher Nancy Verde Barr, Adams realized she was happier in the kitchen than in anthropology class, although her academic study tempered her understanding of male and female culinary attitudes. "Women cook from the heart and necessity and from what is available in ways that are available. Men have had the luxury to cook from their heads," she asserts. Following her nose and her heart, Adams apprenticed with Barr and learned French and Italian cooking techniques. And she read Elizabeth David and Julia Child. In 1983 she moved to Boston, to work at Seasons restaurant under chef Lydia Shire. Three years later, she became sous-chef at Hamersely's Bistro, and then moved up to executive

chef at another highly regarded Boston restaurant, Michela's. When she felt it was time to establish her own kitchen, Adams formed a partnership with Michela Larson and Christopher Myers to create a unique dining experience in Cambridge; at Rialto her singular interpretation of classic Spanish, Italian and French Mediterranean food is presented in a high-energy atmosphere that encourages customers to party. In the bar one evening, she poured a glass of premium Russian River Chardonnay and served some zesty skewered prawns while discussing her feelings about women in the restaurant business.

Rialto

The Charles Hotel
I Bennett Street
Cambridge, MA 02138
Phone: 617 661 5050
Fax: 617 497 5552

Right:
Spicy Grilled
Pork Tenderloins
with
Slow Roasted
Egg Plant

This focus on women chefs is well deserved. We still have a lot of work to do to get real recognition, as in any other profession. I try to keep my staff at a ratio of fifty-fifty men and women, always choosing the best candidates but making sure the kitchen is not dominated by either men or women. If you look through the food magazines, it seems like women represent only two percent of the people invited to do the big dinners or get the big press coverage. It's still men who get the most attention. We've got to fight always and keep plugging away, and not allow ourselves to fall into the position of victims. We are in control of our lives. If you're going to work in the restaurant business, you have to love it. The stress is high, the hours are long, and the pay is nominal. The reward is

in the culture. It's full of interesting, creative people who excel in the art of performance and making people happy. I can't imagine doing anything else. Every challenge is a step forward. I feel fortunate to have found work I love. That, for me, is the dream.

I found out by traveling in Italy, Greece and other countries in Europe and observing traditional ways with food that there is lot more to eating than just food and experiencing the immediate satisfaction that comes from eating a lot salt and fat. There is sitting at a table, savoring flavors, having conversation. My food has a warm, comfortable feeling because it is intensely flavored, honest and straightforward, with integrity and respect for tradition, seasons and fresh local ingredients. It's often more expensive to buy fresh

organically grown produce from local farms, but by doing so, you are maintaining standards of good nutrition, and helping farmers stay alive.

The fast food trend in this country and the world is frightening and insidious, but we can also have hope. Many communities are taking action against bad nutrition in school lunch programs, for example. I have a motto: eat breakfast and walk. People need to exercise and keep moving. You don't need to diet to keep healthy and happy if you exercise. If you do that you can enjoy an extra glass of wine now and again.

Suzanne Baby

THE GALLERY GRILL

"I rarely say no to a customer.
It's a people business -
this is why we're here."

The Gothic style restaurant where Suzanne Baby cooks up a storm bears some similarities with her ancestral castle, near Dijon in France. The Gallery Grill at Hart House at the University of Toronto overlooks the Great Hall, and its architecture is suitably grand with medieval touches: trussed ceilings, stone fireplace, walls hung with fine paintings and ornate chandeliers throwing light down to the tables. The foyer lounge with its wood-burning fire and soft upholstered couches contributes to a warm and relaxed atmosphere, matching Baby's particular style of rustic, comfort food. Baby credits her French Canadian parents for influencing her ultimate choice of career. They obviously made quite an impression, since two of her five brothers are chefs as well. Although she studied classical music at the Royal Conservatory in Toronto as a child and considered music as a career possibility, after graduating from high school, Baby left her native city to tour Europe, Russia and Southeast Asia for two years. To finance her travels, she took on cooking positions. This led to a formal apprenticeship in the culinary arts, beginning in a bakery in Stockholm. Baby returned to Canada, graduating with honors from the George Brown College of Hospitality in Toronto. Moving through various stages at the Windsor Arms Hotel, and some of

Toronto's top restaurants, Bistro 999, Splendido, Bower's, Lake's Bar & Grill and Acqua, (where she co-chefed with her husband), she eventually became chef de cuisine at the Gallery Grill. The restaurant received three stars in 'Taste of Canada' during Baby's first year in the kitchen. After lunch one afternoon at the Gallery Grill, she traced her story.

The Gallery Grill

Hart House
University of Toronto
7 Hart House Circle
Toronto ON.M5S 1A1
Canada
Phone: 416 978 2445
Fax: 416 978 6542

My mother died when I was quite young and my stepmother had a career as an art history teacher, so it was necessary for the children in the family to take on the cooking. My stepmother was interested in trying new things from other cultures. My father was a disciplined French Canadian and preferred more refined French cooking. But we were a foodie family. The first Baby came over from the Dijon region of France. I have visited the family chateau, Mon Teton, which still exists and is used for art retreats, ballets and stage performances.

I like to cook honestly, with my heart. I would rather spend more time developing something classic than on a trend. I think of myself as a rustic cook, serving French Canadian traditional dishes. Although I have cooked Pacific Rim and Med food in the past, I would rather do what I have inside me. There are different ways people cook. I'm interested in knowing if people had a good time and were comfortable rather than serving the more blatant in-your-face style of cooking. I'm much more concerned about making people happy. I rarely say no to a customer if they request leaving an ingredient out of a dish. I'll say I don't recommend it but I'll be happy to do it. It's not take-it-or-leave-it, this is my work. If someone isn't happy here, that bothers me a lot.

When I started out I decided I wanted to work with chefs who were excellent cooks and very good business people, such as Marc Tuet, Mark McEwan and Michael Bonaccini - chefs who treat the customer from an all-around point of view. This is a people business. This is why we're here. We eat to live and live to eat.

Above:
Tenderloins of Rabbit and Foie Gras with Sweetbread and Mushroom Ragout in Port

Right:
Cornmeal Shortcake with Ontario Peaches in Late Harvest Wine Syrup with Lavender Yogurt

Right:
Arctic Char with
Organic
Bean Salad and
Red Ginger
Essence

Below:
Summer Grill
of Guinea Hen
and Fruit in
an Eau-de-Vie
Reduction

I've been asked a lot of times whether being a woman chef has been a hardship. I worked in a hotel kitchen where there were only two women in a kitchen crew of thirty. I was well accepted because I expected to be taken seriously. Only once did a sous-chef blurt out that he had a problem with the fact that I was a woman. But I have found that women work harder for the same acceptance as men. I like to think that women - like men - feel they will do what they set out to do.

Karen Barnaby

"Food is more visceral than intellectual."

To find Karen Barnaby, you must enter Vancouver's historic Stanley Park, one of the largest parks in North America, first visited by Captain George Vancouver in 1851.

The Fish House restaurant occupies a 1930 sports pavilion in the park, renovated into a warm, clubby series of rooms pivoting around a magnificent raw bar, presided over by chef Barnaby. Born in Ottawa, Barnaby, encouraged by her two grandmothers, was making tea sandwiches and summer pudding by the age of ten. She stumbled into the profession, she says, because it was one thing she could do well. She started off in an Ottawa cafe baking carrot cake, quiches, cheesecakes - the hot items of the 1970s. Moving to Toronto, she landed a job as second chef at the Queen Mother Cafe, under chef Vanipha Southalack, whose Thai and Laotian cuisine expanded her knowledge of flavors and sensations. She learned to cook by doing and watching. After working for five years for David Wood, another important mentor, in 1991 Barnaby moved with her chef husband, Steven McKinley, to Vancouver, eventually to reopen The Fish House. Barnaby has authored two cookbooks, 'Pacific Passions' and 'Pacific Feasts.' A member of Les Dames d'Escoffier, she won the Evian Health Menu People's Choice Award in 1995 and the Critic's Choice Best Seafood Restaurant in Vancouver magazine in 1996. She talked over lunch of Flaming Rock Prawns, one of her signature dishes, sautéed with garlic roasted peppers and tomatoes, tossed with spinach and feta cheese and drizzled with fragrant ouzo.

The Fish House in Stanley Park

2099 Beach Avenue
Vancouver BC V6G 1Z4
Canada
Phone: 604 681 7275
Fax 604 681 3137

The West Coast is very different. Although the population in Vancouver is multicultural, it is very conservative. The food we do is not fancy, it's comfort food with a twist. Simple, plain, not elegant. That's my style of cooking in the

Right:
Black Cod with
Manila Clams and
Chorizo

Opposite page:
Swordfish
Carpaccio

Far right:
Grape Cobbler
with Rosemary
Crème Anglaise

Karen

restaurant and at home. Many restaurants are chef-driven but we are not. We have comment cards for customers to fill out, and we read them. It's intimidating, and you want to be defensive, but we also want to keep people coming back, so it's important to know what they like and what they don't like. I compare it to brain surgery. One slip and that person is gone. You want everyone who comes to the restaurant to have the ultimate experience. If you look at it in that way it makes a difference. I am always talking with my staff. Everyone has to believe in the product, otherwise how can they sell it? That doesn't mean that I follow every piece of customer advice. There are two camps on my calamari dish that is done in a wood oven: some like it and some don't.

Women are the natural tenders of the hearth. I'm a home cook, but I learned how to cook in quantity and how to run my kitchen while doing it. You can be the greatest cook but people won't know it if you don't have the kitchen help to share your vision. There has to be personal, full involvement. Menu engineering is what makes or breaks the business. You can have a very popular restaurant but it can go under if you don't pay attention to the food buying and the financial side. I wasn't born with this talent... it's something I had to learn.

There is no really bad food, just indifferent cooks. My food has a lot of different influences, like Indian, Thai, Italian, Spanish and French - not traditional, but New World. I love cooking fish because there are so many varieties to choose from. Meat is more limited. I like putting fish with strong flavors almost like meat. In the future, I am thinking of having my own restaurant. I already have a name for it - the Everyday Cafe. It will serve entrees under $16. It will be homey food, lamb shanks, big bowls of mashed potatoes, pasta with tomato sauce, simple good things. I think food is visceral rather than intellectual.

Alison Barshak

*"Strong women are the ones who survive.
I know I can work sixteen hours a day
and outlast everyone else
in the kitchen."*

Alison Barshak is not reticent about saying she came from a privileged family in suburban Philadelphia. When she ten years old, her parents sent her to live with a Greek family outside Athens. Since then she has traveled obsessively and learned to absorb a variety of cultures. She is a self-taught chef who learned her art in her home-town. She knew at the age of 15 that she wanted to work in a restaurant and hoped to go to the Culinary Institute of America for her training, but her parents insisted that she go to a regular college - Boston University - and study liberal arts. The lure of the kitchen, however, led her to summer jobs and eventually to work in a catering and takeout business in Philadelphia. Always ready to jump in and take a risk, she became an apprentice in a Philadelphia restaurant called Rollers, where she learned line cooking, taking the screaming fits of the chef with characteristic resilience. She worked her way up through several restaurant kitchens rising to sous-

chef and then executive chef at Apropos, after training under Aliza Green. The restaurant's cuisine, rustic Mediterranean, fit her like a glove. But for Barshak, new is always better. Next came the Striped Bass, an

Above:

Pistachio-crusted Arctic Char with Stir Fry Vegetables

extraordinary seafood restaurant where Barshak gained her reputation as the highest-paid chef in the city, presiding over the most gracious ambience for dining out. Silverware, dishes, a menu that changed every day for lunch and dinner seven days a week, a staff that worked as a synchronistic team to create the most sublime food were all under the baton of a 30-year-old, charismatic cheerleader who admittedly "never saw the obstacles but just the finish line." After three years at this pinnacle, Barshak resigned, took a break to get a life and planned her next move: opening her own restaurant. She talked enthusiastically over lunch at the Four Seasons Hotel in Philadelphia.

I'm a woman chef in a man's world, but at the same time I go clothes shopping. I love to get manicures and pedicures. When you work on the line you get food all over you. People say to me, "You're too pretty to be a chef." Would they say that to a man? They don't see me doing this as a living. They say, "You don't look like a chef." Well, what's a chef supposed to look like? Do things for no money. That's what we're supposed to do. Fifteen years ago, no women were out there. Strong women are the ones who survive. I can work sixteen hours a day, and I know I can outlast everyone else in the kitchen.

My style is always Mediterranean and Southwest. In both places the colors are similar, the textures feel the same way, they have an earthy history, like the food, flavors and smells. Southwest flavors are bolder, bigger, we're talking spice with a line of intensity. The flavors stand on their own. The food is what the food is. It's smoother on your tongue, dances in your mouth. I love cilantro. I love ethnic food. I can make up food in my head and know what it tastes like. I never see the plate. I taste the plate. Presentation for me is hard. I am not into

Above:
Redcurrant
Grilled Swordfish
with
Lemongrass

Right:
Potato Pancakes
with
Crab Mango
and
Arugula Salad

playing with food, building towers. That is not how I express myself. I am always trying new flavors and textures, something new, never predictable. It's like getting dressed. You immediately know when something works and things go together well. Shaved Parmesan - one thing - can make a dish incredible.

Philadelphia's food network is incestuous. That's good and bad. I have hired and fired people. I have turned a restaurant kitchen over twice. I've learned that women will work for men for less money. I pay on the basis of experience. I don't discriminate. But men are more aggressive about asking for money. Women don't think that they're worth more. I've learned that people need structure; not everyone is like me. I don't go to work everyday for people to pat me on the back. I am my own person. If it's something important I go for it. I always say, you don't know what you can do until you do it. You must open yourself up and go further. When I took on the job at the Striped Bass I knew nothing about fish, but I thought how hard could it be to learn? It's rare that you get a chance to specialize. So I paid to go to a three-week intensive training course.

My partner at the Striped Bass taught me an important lesson. Don't think of the food first, think of the place, then the food. I just know when the food is right, and sometimes that's hard to teach someone else.

I was the highest-paid chef in the city at $85,000. I started out at $140 a week. If I were a man, the salary would not be an issue. But as a woman, it's " Look how far she's come."

Above:
Moroccan Style
Baked
Whole Pompano

Left:
Herb-crusted
Wild Striped Bass
with Roasted Garlic
Mashed Potatoes,
Baby Vegetables

Ann Cashion

CASHION'S EAT PLACE

"In Italy so many family restaurants have women cooks, there is respect for them."

Like many of her contemporaries, Ann Cashion didn't start out training to be a chef. She was a high school valedictorian who was set on a career in education, although she often worked in motel kitchens as a teenager in her native Jackson, Mississippi, "for something to do." She went to Harvard and later started doctoral studies in English literature at Stanford University, but eventually dropped out because she was "bored with the program." She came to cooking through a love of eating (her father made a habit of taking her family out to three-star restaurants), and working with her hands. Her first job in a San Francisco bakery gave her a croissant recipe she still uses today. In search of technique, Cashion spent seven months in Florence, learning how to cook authentic Tuscan food in a family trattoria; went to Paris as a pastry chef in a bakery with cutting edge technology; and eventually moved to Washington, D.C. to work at Restaurant Nora, the Austin Grill, the South Austin Grill, and Jaleo. (This last trio of "theme" restaurants grossed $7 million annually while she was executive chef supervising the kitchens.) In 1995, she opened Cashion's Eat Place with partner John Fulchino. Although she has always steered clear of fine French cuisine and earned her Washington reputation for Tex-Mex food, Cashion's Eat Place serves food

Cashion's Eat Place

reminiscent of a French bistro, with some typical Italian trattoria dishes and a few Spanish ideas as well. With its outdoor sidewalk umbrellaed tables and neat architectural design inside, the restaurant is "somewhere you can get a good meal without getting dressed up," says the chef, who in her downtime one afternoon, took a quick cup of coffee to relate the joy of chefing her own business.

1819 Columbia Road NW
Washington, D.C. 20009
Phone: 202 797 1819
Fax: 202 797 0048

Left:
Fillet of Beef
and Black
Trumpet
Mushrooms,
Potato and
Celeriac Ravioli

Lower left:
Fresh Pea and
Fava Bean Soup
garnished
with
Whipped Cream
and Fresh Mint

Top Far Right:
Rhubarb
Strawberry Tart

Right:
Curried Mussels
with Spinach

Lower Right:
Pan roasted
Halibut with Wild
Mushrooms
in a
Vin Blanc Sauce,
Spring
Asparagus Tips

As much as I thought a job teaching philosophy would be rewarding, when I was at Stanford, I realized that I liked working with food much more and that it was time for me to do what I wanted to do. I was fortunate to get started in a small bakery in San Francisco, working for a woman of taste, because there was nothing commercial about it. I learned then that the best food is always prepared in the least commercial way. When I knew I didn't want to stay in pastry, I went back to Florence. I had taken a quarter there studying Italian when I was at Stanford and ate out practically every night. So I went back to one of my favorite spots and worked ten hours a day preparing food for Francesco Ricchi in his family trattoria. It was an unbelievable restaurant because there was no attempt to embellish old family recipes. Food in Italy, like art, is so much part of the culture. And so many family restaurants have women cooks there is respect for them.

When I came back to the United States. I spent some weeks trying to get someone interested in my Italian experience but at that time there was no Il Fornaio, no Chez Panisse. Most restaurants focused on French cuisine, and I was asked what would be the advantage of a wood grill over a gas grill, or doing pasta with a rolling pin. So I went back to work as a pastry chef and eventually opened two bakeries in San Francisco. When I went to work for Nora in Washington, I learned about low-fat spa food, cooking with impeccable organic ingredients totally free of pesticides, meats without hormones, everything with maximum flavor. It was an eye-opener, because I learned that if you have these ingredients you see great results. Today they are more accessible, and there is more interest in this type of healthy food. But it is not a religion with me like it is with

Nora. I am a little more flexible in that regard. After a year, I wanted to try to put my own place together, so I took a year off. But I fell short of my game plan and ended up going back to work, and I got in on the ground floor of the Austin Grill. I learned then how to make a restaurant work, how to control costs, how to staff, and how to create a menu that can be produced efficiently when doing volume. It was the piece of the puzzle that was missing. And it also helped me realize I wanted to cook, as opposed to being an executive chef running a number of kitchens. I wanted to create a restaurant that was not about a theme or a concept but about the food and a style of eating.

Suzy Crofton
CROFTON'S

"I think about food all the time. It's always in my stream of consciousness."

Food was a focus in Suzy Crofton's family as she was growing up in Chicago. She was one of ten children. Her mother and her grandmother both liked to cook good food from James Beard or Julia Child cookbooks. Crofton always made special cakes for birthdays. Her parents liked to dine out a lot. Crofton went to art school in Minneapolis, and like many students she earned pocket money by working in a restaurant. Finding enjoyment in the kitchen, she decided to try it out for a year in her hometown. It was the beginning of a long apprenticeship working with top chefs who became her mentors: Jean Banchet at Le Francais, Norman Van Aken at Sinclair's, Guy Petit and Mark Facklam at Crickets, Carrie Nahabedian at La Tour. Finally she made it to opening chef de cuisine at Montparnasse in Naperville, a Chicago suburb, in 1989. Crofton gained instant recognition from the critics: three stars from the Chicago Tribune, named as one of Chicago's top twenty-five restaurants in 1991 and 1992 by Chicago Magazine; DiRona awards in 1993, 1994 and 1995. Six years later Crofton moved downtown to preside as executive chef at Cassis, where she received rave reviews for her South of France menu blending North African flavors and unique culinary touches. It was

Crofton's

named among the Best of the Best restaurants by Skyline. Finally she opened her own restaurant, Crofton's in 1997. She talked over tea at the Four Seasons Hotel.

533 N. Wells
Chicago, Il 60610

Above:
Strawberry Sorbet
with Ginger
Rhubarb Compote

I was discouraged in the beginning from being a chef because of the French attitude that women weren't allowed in the kitchen. But once I got into it, I never thought I can't do it because I'm a woman. It was more like, am I up to the challenge of being a chef. I don't think age has anything to do with being successful at cooking. It is about having natural talent and experience. I like the theater and I like art, and cooking is closely related to both. The show must go on. And the garnishes and colors on the plates make it a very artistic, creative occupation. When young people are deciding whether to go to cooking school or not, I always say, why don't you work in a kitchen with a chef you like, to see if you like the life. Why make a huge investment of time and money when you don't know what it's like. It's hardly glamorous, and it's hard work. But the payoff is the great feeling you get if you are happy and you find pride in what you do. My mom was concerned when I was an apprentice because there seemed to be no end in sight. But she thought it was a great job for me and right for me.

When I went to work at Le Francais for Jean Banchet, I learned the meaning of long hours: twelve to fourteen hours a day six days a week. Now if I don't work twelve hours a day I feel I haven't worked. At Le Francais I was the saucier for a year. There were thirty-five sauces on the menu, and sometimes we would serve thirty-five in one night.
I worked on pastries and the garde-manger and presentation. Pastries are a great way to start. You have to be disciplined about ingredients and measurements. I always remember Jean Banchet saying that he had one woman in his kitchen who worked like

Opposite Top:
Grilled Quail
Salad with
Avocado,
Goat Cheese,
Croutons and
Smoke Bacon
Vinaigrette

Opposite Bottom:
Grilled
Atlantic Salmon
with Morells,
Ramps and
Pancetta

Right:
Chilled Cucumber
and
Vidalia Onion
Soup

a man and was better than all the other men in the kitchen. I felt that was the ultimate French compliment.

I have been cooking French food for fourteen years, although I didn't go to France until 1990. I was cooking Provencale food, serving bouillabaisse very successfully before visiting the country. When I finally went to Perigord and ate foie gras and truffles and saw the blue water and sun, I understood why I liked that kind of food. I love it still.

When I listened to my instincts and decided to have my own restaurant. I wanted everything to be just right from the moment you walked in the door. I want to take care of people. Treat everyone with respect. Serve good food in a great atmosphere. That's what it takes. You must go for a level of perfection.

This job is a labor of love. It can't be about money. It's the same for everyone for the most part. You have to have a passion. I think about food all the time - not just specials and promotions - it's always in my stream of consciouness.

Susanna Foo

SUSANNA FOO'S RESTAURANT

"A woman in the kitchen has more patience and is less likely to get upset."

Susanna Foo was born in Inner Mongolia, and grew up in a typical northern Chinese family in which wheat, not rice, was the daily staple. Her mother and grandmother had a keen sense of smell and taste and Foo watched food preparation done by them because, she thought, if she was going to marry, she should know how to cook. "I still remember my grandmother's skillful hands kneading dumplings and noodles," Foo recalls in her James Beard Award-winning cookbook 'Susanna Foo Chinese Cuisine.' The family moved to tropical Taiwan with her Lieutenant General father, and Foo reveled in the backyard garden, with its vegetable plot, flowers, trees and shrubs and the fresh market produce.

As her parents often entertained American military officers, the family learned to speak English, and Western culture entered Foo's life. During her college years, she took classes with Fu Pei-mei a cooking teacher equivalent to Julia Child in Taiwan, where every week a leading restaurant chef was invited to teach his specialty. Eventually Foo, her Chinese husband and his family moved to the United States and opened a Hunan restaurant in Philadelphia. The business expanded to a second restaurant in 1979 which Foo and her husband were asked to supervise. Foo took courses at the Culinary Institute of

1517 Walnut Street
Philadelphia,
PA 19103
Phone 215 545 2666
Phone 215 546 9106

Susanna Foo's Restaurant

America that exposed her to a level of professional expertise in Western-style cooking, mastering the use of Dutch ovens and nonstick skillets in addition to the traditional Chinese wok. By 1987 she was ready to open her own restaurant, with her own unique cuisine blending east and west. Foo talked there one afternoon about her love of food.

Right:
Stir Fried
Thin Rice
Noodles
with
Shrimp and
Scallops

Although I'm Chinese, I recognize that the French have the techniques that the Chinese don't. I was inspired by several French cookbooks when I was at the Culinary Institute. I had never seen so many books about food and cooking as in the Institute's library. My days began with classes at seven a.m. and ended in evenings spent poring over books. When I opened my own restaurant I decided to blend classical Chinese food made with the best and freshest ingredients in this country with the classical French stocks and sauces. I find this combination helps control the quality. I have good taste buds and when I am creating recipes in my mind, I can imagine the taste and flavor and know how it is going to work. I believe it is very important to your life to go out and have a good time. Cooking and entertaining creates a feeling of warmth and closeness. It makes people friendly. I still get excited and have a certain satisfaction cooking for people to create this special feeling. My philosophy is that people travel a lot today and know fresh things and they are very particular about quality all the time. So I have to be perfect all the time, and give better and better food service and atmosphere. I am still experimenting with ingredients and changing what I do. Confucius said: "Traveling a thousand miles is equal to reading ten thousand books." Visits to Thailand, Italy and France have inspired my cooking. Although everything I cook is based on what I remember from childhood, a good cook should be open-minded. During the years I have spent living and working in this country, I have developed and adapted many of the Chinese dishes to suit my surroundings. But the basic principles are the same: freshness, simplicity and the preservation of the unique flavor of each ingredient.

Left:
One Hundred
Corner
Crabcakes

It's hard for a woman to be in a restaurant kitchen and lift heavy pots and pans. I have about half a dozen women in my staff of twenty-five. I find a woman has more patience and is less likely to get upset. I have had eighty percent of my staff a long time, more than ten years. When I spot a good person, I usually try to keep them with good raises and bonuses.

Recipes

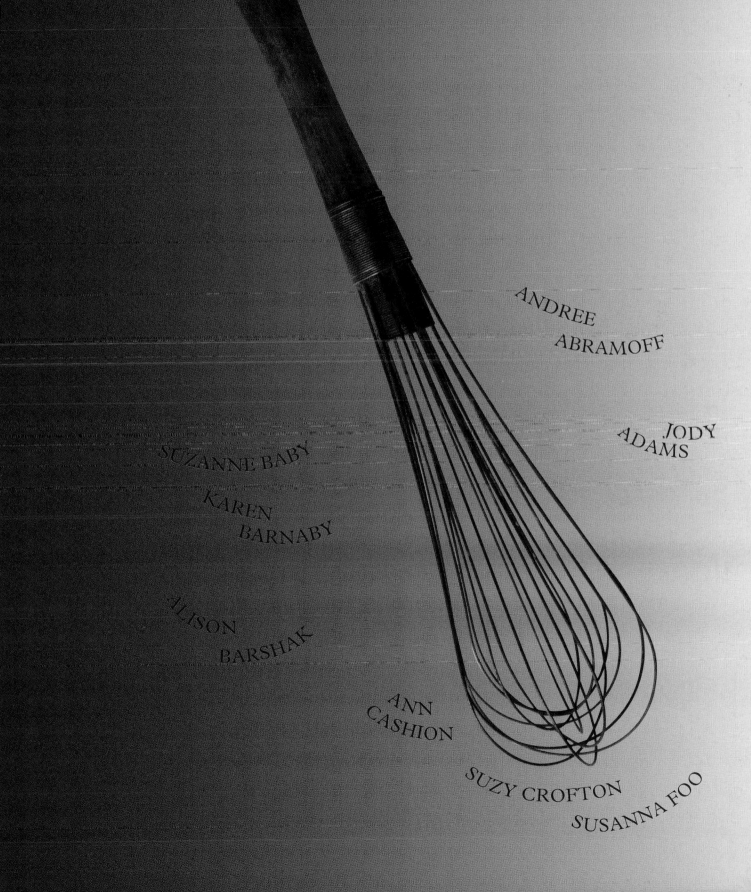

ANDREE ABRAMOFF

JODY ADAMS

SUZANNE BABY

KAREN BARNABY

ALISON BARSHAK

ANN CASHION

SUZY CROFTON

SUSANNA FOO

Bistro Dinner

Cucumber Cups
with Scallop
Seviche

Leg of Lamb
Stuffed with Wild
Rice and Porcini
Mushrooms

Provençal
Eggplant au Gratin
with Tomato Coulis

Frozen Chocolate
Charlotte
Marquise

CUCUMBER CUPS WITH SCALLOP SEVICHE

Yield: 50 hors d'oeuvre

2 pounds fresh bay scallops

1 red onion, finely chopped

1 red pepper, finely chopped

1 yellow pepper, finely chopped

¾ cup fresh lime juice

3 tablespoons finely chopped cilantro

½ teaspoon Tabasco

Salt and freshly ground pepper

10 long, slender, seedless cucumbers, cut in 1½-inch slices

Caviar as garnish

1. In a large glass bowl, combine scallops, onion, red and yellow peppers, lime juice, cilantro, Tabasco, salt, and pepper. Toss gently, making sure scallops are completely coated.

2. Cover and refrigerate at least 5 hours, or overnight. Stir occasionally while scallops are marinating.

3. An hour before serving, using a melon ball scoop, remove center portion of each cucumber cup without going through to bottom. Place cups upside down on paper towels to drain.

4. With a demitasse spoon, fill each cucumber cup with seviche. Place on paper towels to further drain. Garnish with caviar and serve.

LEG OF LAMB STUFFED WITH WILD RICE AND PORCINI MUSHROOMS

Yield: 8 to 10 servings

1 (5 to 6-pound) leg of lamb, boned with shank portion partially left on

Salt and freshly ground pepper

2 tablespoons butter

½ cup wild rice

½ pound fresh porcini mushrooms, thinly sliced

2 tablespoons fresh chopped mint

½ teaspoon fresh chopped thyme

¼ teaspoon allspice

¼ teaspoon freshly grated nutmeg

1 teaspoon grated lemon rind

Preheat oven to 375 degrees.

1. Open up the sides of the leg of lamb and remove any excess fat. Season with salt and pepper and dot cavity with 1 tablespoon butter.

2. Cook wild rice according to package directions, about 35 to 45 minutes. Drain and mix with mushrooms, mint, thyme, allspice, nutmeg, lemon rind, salt and pepper.

3. Fill lamb cavity with rice mixture. Reshape leg to look uncut. Truss openings with needle and kitchen twine.

4. Brush lamb with remaining butter and sprinkle with salt and pepper. Place on rack in roasting pan.

5. Roast in oven for 1 hour and 10 minutes, or about 15 to 20 minutes per pound.

6. Transfer lamb to serving platter and allow to rest 10 minutes.

7. Deglaze roasting pan with a little wine and pour sauce into gravy boat. Slice lamb and serve with sauce on the side.

PROVENÇAL EGGPLANT AU GRATIN WITH TOMATO COULIS

Yield: 8 to 10 servings

4 medium eggplants, cut in half lengthwise and each half cut in ½-inch slices

¼ cup coarse salt or sea salt, plus extra

Flour for dredging

Vegetable oil for frying

3 to 4 cups thick Tomato Coulis

Freshly ground pepper

1 to 1½ cups grated Gruyère or Emmenthal

Preheat oven to 375 degrees.

1. In a large mixing bowl, put eggplant and cover with water. Add ¼ cup salt and let stand for about 20 to 30 minutes.

2. Remove eggplant from water, drain and dry with paper towels.

3. Dredge lightly in flour and deep-fry in at least 1½ inches oil. Drain fried eggplant on paper towels.

4. In a heavy 13 x 9 x 2-inch baking dish, place a thin layer of Tomato Coulis, then a layer of eggplant. Sprinkle with salt and pepper and some of the cheese. Repeat layering, ending with cheese.

5. Bake eggplant for about 20 to 25 minutes, and then quickly glaze under the broiler. Serve.

TOMATO COULIS

Yield: 4 cups

3 tablespoons extra virgin olive oil

1 large onion, chopped

2 cloves garlic, chopped

5 pounds fresh plum tomatoes, or 64 ounces Italian canned tomatoes, drained

5 basil leaves

2 tablespoons chopped Italian parsley

Pinch of thyme

1. In a heavy nonreactive saucepan, heat olive oil. Add onion and garlic. Cook on medium-low heat until golden but not brown, about 10 minutes.

2. Chop tomatoes in food processor and add to saucepan. Add basil, parsley, and thyme.

3. Bring to a boil, lower heat, and cook uncovered until coulis is as thick as marmalade, about 1½ hours. Let cool and use as needed. The coulis will keep for several weeks frozen in an air-tight container.

FROZEN CHOCOLATE CHARLOTTE MARQUISE

THE ITALIAN MERINGUE:

1 cup sugar

⅓ cup water

3 egg whites

¼ teaspoon salt

¼ teaspoon cream of tartar

¼ teaspoon vanilla extract

THE CHOCOLATE MARQUISE:

12 ounces semisweet chocolate

3 ounces unsweetened chocolate

⅓ cup dark rum

2 cups heavy cream

2 dozen firm ladyfingers

Candied violets, raspberries, whipped cream, chocolate shavings or powdered cocoa, for garnish

Andree Abramoff

CAFE CROCODILE

THE ITALIAN MERINGUE:

1. Combine sugar and water in a saucepan over medium-high heat. Swirl pan slowly as mixture is coming to a boil but avoid stirring. Continue cooking until mixture becomes clear. Then cover saucepan, reduce heat and simmer while preparing egg whites.

2. Beat egg whites in the bowl of an electric mixer, first at slow speed. Add salt and cream of tartar. Increase speed until whites form stiff peaks. Beat in vanilla.

3. Return sugar syrup to a boil and cook until bubbles begin to thicken. (Droplets of syrup should form tiny soft balls.) If using a candy thermometer, the temperature should reach 238 degrees.

4. While beating egg whites, pour in boiling syrup and continue beating until shiny, white, and stiff peaks form. Set aside.

THE CHOCOLATE MARQUISE:

1. Melt semisweet and unsweetened chocolates slowly in a bain-marie. Put melted chocolate in a bowl and using an electric mixer, beat until smooth. Fold in meringue mixture. Let cool about 10 minutes.

2. Put rum and heavy cream in a mixing bowl set in a large basin filled with ice cubes. Using an electric mixer, beat until heavy cream forms soft, fluffy peaks. Fold cream into chocolate mixture and chill thoroughly.

3. Line a round 10-inch springform cake mold with lady fingers and pour chocolate mixture into mold. Cover with plastic wrap and freeze.

4. Unmold dessert onto a serving plate. Garnish top with candied violets or raspberries, or cover with whipped cream and sprinkle with chocolate shavings or powdered cocoa. Serve immediately.

Early Summer Dinner

Spicy Steamed Littlenecks with Toasted Angel Hair Pasta, Slow Roasted Tomatoes and Basil Aioli

Vesuvius Tomatoes

Aioli-Garlic Mayonnaise

Grilled Tuscan-style Sirloin Steak with Parmigiano-Reggiano, Lemon, and Truffle Oil

Peppered Peach Tarts with Ginger Caramel Sauce and Whipped Cream*

*Serving Suggestion

SPICY STEAMED LITTLENECKS WITH TOASTED ANGEL HAIR PASTA, SLOW ROASTED TOMATOES AND BASIL AIOLI

Yield: 4 servings

¾ pound angel hair pasta

2 tablespoons extra virgin olive oil

1 recipe Vesuvius Tomatoes

2 shallots, thinly sliced

3 cloves garlic, sliced

1 teaspoon hot red pepper flakes

½ cup white wine

24 Wellfleet or other fresh littleneck clams

Salt and freshly ground pepper

16 basil leaves, 8 cut into chiffonade

2 tablespoons chopped fresh parsley

¼ cup aioli

Preheat oven to 350 degrees.

1. Toss pasta with olive oil. On a baking pan, spread out pasta and roast until golden brown, about 10 minutes. Set aside.

2. In a large deep-sided pot, heat 2 tablespoons of oil from the Vesuvius Tomatoes. Add shallots and garlic, and cook over moderate heat until tender and edges begin to brown. Add pepper flakes, the rest of the Vesuvius Tomatoes, wine, and clams.

3. Cover and steam until clams open, about 10 minutes. Transfer clams to a big bowl.

4. Reduce pan juices to about one-third, or desired consistency. Taste and add salt and pepper, as needed. Pour sauce over clams. Keep covered and warm.

5. Meanwhile, bring a large pot of water to boil. Add salt and then pasta. Cook pasta until al dente, about 5 minutes. Drain pasta and pour into bowl with clams, basil chiffonade and parsley. Toss well and taste for seasoning.

6. Divide pasta and clams among four warmed pasta bowls. Top with a spoonful of aioli and garnish with basil leaves. Serve immediately.

VESUVIUS TOMATOES

Yield: 8 servings

1 large white onion, minced into ½-inch dice

6 garlic cloves, smashed and peeled

Extra virgin olive oil

24 ripe plum tomatoes, cut in half lengthwise, or 48 ripe cherry tomatoes

18 basil leaves

1 teaspoon salt

⅛ teaspoon hot red pepper flakes

Pinch of sugar

Preheat oven to 250 degrees

1. In a large frying pan, put onions, garlic, and add enough olive oil to just cover. Cook over moderate heat until onions are tender.

2. Put tomatoes in a roasting pan large enough to hold them in one layer. Add cooked onions, garlic, basil, salt, pepper flakes, and sugar. Toss well.

3. Add enough additional oil to come halfway up the tomatoes. Roast 3 hours uncovered, until tomatoes are tender, but not falling apart. Stir once during roasting. This can be made 1 to 2 days in advance.

AIOLI - GARLIC MAYONNAISE

Yield: 1 cup

2 egg yolks

1 teaspoon Dijon mustard

1 to 2 tablespoons lemon juice

1 to 2 cloves garlic, mashed to a paste with salt

½ cup vegetable oil

½ cup extra virgin olive oil

Salt and pepper to taste

Have all the ingredients at room temperature.

1. In a small bowl, put egg yolks, mustard, 1 tablespoon lemon juice, and garlic to taste. Beat together. Beat in ¼ cup vegetable oil, drop by drop. While continuing to beat constantly, add in a slow steady stream the remaining vegetable oil and olive oil.

2. Adjust seasoning with lemon juice, garlic, salt, and pepper. If the mayonnaise seems too thick, add a drop or two of water. Cover and refrigerate until ready to use.

GRILLED TUSCAN-STYLE SIRLOIN STEAK WITH PARMIGIANO-REGGIANO, LEMON, AND TRUFFLE OIL

Yield: 4 servings

4 8-10 ounce prime sirloin steaks

Salt and freshly ground black pepper

Vegetable oil

1 to 2 heads endive, separated into leaves

4 cups lightly packed arugula leaves

1 large portobello mushroom cap, cleaned and sliced ⅛-inch thick

1 lemon

4-6 tablespoons extra virgin olive oil

2 ounces Parmigiano-Reggiano, cut into shavings with a vegetable peeler

4 teaspoons truffle oil, optional

Preheat grill to high.

1. Season steaks liberally with salt and pepper on both sides. Brush with oil.

2. Cook steaks over high heat, about 7 minutes per side or to desired doneness.

3. In a bowl put endive, arugula, and mushrooms. Cut lemon in half and squeeze juice of one half over the salad. Add olive oil, ½ teaspoon salt, and ¼ teaspoon pepper. Toss well and adjust seasonings to taste. Cut second half of lemon into 4 equal wedges for garnish.

4. Distribute salad among 4 plates. Set a steak on each salad, sprinkle with cheese shavings, drizzle with truffle oil, and garnish with a lemon wedge. Serve immediately.

PEPPERED PEACH TARTS

Yield: 4 servings

6 ripe peaches

¼ cup sugar

4 teaspoons flour

1 teaspoon freshly ground pepper, to taste

1 cup freshly whipped cream

4 tablespoons unsalted butter

1 pound Sweet Pastry Dough

1. Bring a large pot of water to boil. Dip peaches into water for 10 seconds. Remove with a slotted spoon and immediately immerse peaches in ice water. Peel, cut in half and remove pit.

2. In a bowl put peach halves, sugar, flour, and pepper, and toss. Set aside.

3. Cut dough into 4 equal pieces and form into balls. Roll balls into 6-inch rounds ¼-inch thick.

4. Set 3 peach halves, skin side up, on each round of dough. Dot each peach with ⅓ tablespoon butter. Pull up edges of dough around peaches and crimp. Place on baking trays and put tarts in refrigerator for at least 30 minutes to chill.

Preheat oven to 400 degrees.

5. Bake tarts until peaches are tender and crusts golden and crisp, about 30 minutes.

6. Serve with Ginger Caramel Sauce and whipped cream.

SWEET PASTRY DOUGH

Yield: 1 pound

2 cups all-purpose flour

1 teaspoon salt

2 tablespoons sugar

12 tablespoons unsalted butter, cut into 12 pieces and chilled

5 to 6 tablespoons ice water

1. Pour flour into a mound on a work surface. Add salt and sugar, and combine well. With the fingertips, work butter into flour until butter is in pea-size pieces. Make a well in the flour mixture and add water, 2 tablespoons at a time, tossing with your fingers to incorporate the water. The dough should be crumbly.

2. Form the dough into a ball, and using the heel of the hand, push the dough away from you to flatten. Repeat until all the dough is flat, and then form the dough into a ball again and repeat the process.

3. Shape the dough into a thick, round form, wrap in plastic film and refrigerate at least one hour, to allow dough to rest.

GINGER CARAMEL SAUCE

Yield: 1 cup

½ cup sugar

2 tablespoons water

1 tablespoon finely chopped ginger

1 tablespoon butter

½ cup heavy cream

1. In a heavy bottomed saucepan, mix the sugar with the water. Add the ginger and cook over moderate heat, uncovered, until sugar is golden and caramelized.

2. Remove pan from heat and cool caramel for about 2 minutes.

3. Very carefully add butter and whisk in thoroughly. Then slowly whisk in the cream.

4. Strain sauce to remove ginger. Set aside for use with Peppered Peach Tarts.

Jody Adams

RIALTO RESTAURANT

Canadian Harvest Lunch

Poached Arctic Char with Organic Bean Salad and Red Ginger Essence

Cornmeal Shortcakes with Ontario Peaches in Late Harvest Wine Syrup with Maple Lavender Yogurt

POACHED ARCTIC CHAR WITH ORGANIC BEAN SALAD AND RED GINGER ESSENCE

Yield: serves 4

THE BEANS:

¾ cup calypso beans, soaked overnight (see Note 1)

¾ cup steuben beans, soaked overnight

¾ cup scarlet runner beans, soaked overnight

½ medium-size onion, quartered

2 carrots, peeled and cut into large pieces

2 stalks celery, cut into large pieces

4 cloves garlic, peeled

3 bay leaves

4 sprigs rosemary

4 sprigs thyme

3 quarts water

Salt and freshly ground pepper

½ cup safflower oil

1 tablespoon apple cider vinegar

½ teaspoon chopped fresh tarragon

THE RED GINGER ESSENCE:

3 quarts water

3 medium-size beets

1 3-inch piece fresh ginger, peeled and chopped

6 tablespoons fresh apple juice

Freshly ground pepper

Lemon juice

THE ARCTIC CHAR:

1 quart water

15 leeks, whites only, diced

¼ medium onion, diced

4 sprigs thyme

1 clove garlic, peeled

1 bay leaf

2 teaspoons lemon juice

4 fillets Arctic Char
(3.5 ounces each, skin on) (see Note 2)

Salt and freshly ground pepper

8 large carrots

1 medium-size fennel bulb, green tops removed

5 peppercorns

To assemble:

½ medium-size beet, finely julienned

1 carrot, finely julienned

2 tablespoons chopped chives

4 chervil sprigs

THE BEANS:

1. Strain each bean separately and discard soaking liquid. Rinse beans, and put into 3 separate pots.

2. In a bowl, combine onion, carrot, celery, garlic, bay leaves, rosemary, and thyme. Cut 3 squares of cheesecloth and into each put ⅓ of the carrot mixture. Using the ends of the cheesecloth, tie each package closed to make a bouquet garni.

3. Add 1 quart of water to each pot and one bouquet garni. Bring to a boil, covered, and simmer until done.

4. After the beans have cooked, remove bouquet garni and strain each pot. Combine all of the beans into one bowl. Season with salt and pepper.

5. In a small bowl, put oil, vinegar, tarragon, salt, and pepper. Whisk together. Pour over beans, toss and let marinate, unrefrigerated.

THE RED GINGER ESSENCE:

1. In a pot put water, beets, and ginger. Bring to a boil, covered. Lower heat and simmer beets until tender, about 30 to 40 minutes. Remove beets from pot.

2. Put beets in a bowl of cold water and slip skins off. Using a juicer, extract beet juice. Place a square of fine cheese cloth in a small bowl. Pour juice into cheese-cloth. Gather up ends and squeeze juice out, to further remove any pulp.

3. Add apple juice to beet, heat and reduce to a glaze. Season with pepper and lemon juice to taste. Keep warm.

THE CHAR:

1. In a medium-size pot put water, leeks, onion, thyme, garlic, bay leaf, and lemon juice. Bring to a boil, covered. Lower flame and simmer 10 minutes.

2. Using a fine sieve over a bowl, strain, and reserve liquid. Discard vegetables.

3. Cut char fillets on an angle, into 3 pieces each. Lightly season each piece with salt and pepper. Set aside.

4. Using a juicer, juice carrots and fennel. Add juice to the reserved leek liquid. Add peppercorns.

5. Pour liquid into a large sauté pan. Heat liquid and add char. Simmer gently uncovered, about 2 to 3 minutes.

6. Remove poached fillets from liquid, straining carefully. Keep warm.

To assemble:

1. On each serving plate, in the center, spoon the marinated beans, making a small mound.

2. On each plate, place 3 pieces of poached fish leaning against the beans.

3. Spoon beet essence around plate, but not on the char and beans.

4. Garnish top of fish with julienne of beet and carrot.

5. Sprinkle chopped chives over sauce. Garnish dish with sprigs of chervil. Serve.

Note 1: Substitute beans with canellini, Great Northern, black-eyed peas, and navy beans.

Note 2: Arctic Char has no true substitute, however Rainbow Trout can be used instead.

CORNMEAL SHORTCAKES WITH ONTARIO PEACHES IN LATE HARVEST WINE SYRUP WITH MAPLE LAVENDER YOGURT

Yield: 10 servings

THE YOGURT:

3 cups plain low-fat yogurt

¼ cup maple syrup

1 teaspoon finely chopped fresh lavender

THE PEACHES:

1 cup dessert wine such as late harvest Riesling, Muscat de Beaumes-de-Venise or Sauterne

¼ cup water

6 peaches, peeled, pitted and sliced

THE SHORTCAKES:

2 cups all-purpose flour

¼ cup cornmeal

½ cup sugar

1 ½ teaspoons baking powder

¾ teaspoon baking soda

½ teaspoon ground cardamom

½ teaspoon ground cinnamon

¼ teaspoon salt

6 tablespoons cold unsalted butter, cut into pieces

¾ cup buttermilk

1 large egg yolk

½ teaspoon vanilla extract

THE YOGURT:

1. Put a collander in a bowl, and line with several coffee filters or a large piece of cheesecloth. Pour in yogurt.

Suzanne Baby

GALLERY GRILL

2. Refrigerate uncovered for 24 hours.

3. Spoon condensed yogurt into a bowl. Discard liquid and paper or cheesecloth. Stir in maple syrup and lavender. Set aside.

THE PEACHES:

1. In a non-reactive pan, put wine and water, cover and bring to a boil. Lower heat and simmer uncovered to reduce liquid a little, about 3 minutes. Turn off flame and cool slightly.

2. Add peaches. Set aside.

THE SHORTCAKES;

Preheat oven to 425 degrees.

1. In a food processor, pulse together the flour, cornmeal, sugar, baking powder, baking soda, cardamom, cinnamon, and salt. Add butter and pulse until the mixture is crumbly.

2. In a small bowl, mix together buttermilk, egg yolk, and vanilla.

3. With processor running, add buttermilk mixture to the flour mixture, just until moistened.

4. Transfer dough to a lightly floured surface and pat out evenly, ¾-inch thick.

5. Line a cookie sheet with parchment paper. Set aside. Using a biscuit cutter, cut out dough and place on sheet.

6. Bake until pale golden, about 11 to 14 minutes. Do not overbake.

7. With a metal spatula, remove shortcakes from cookie sheet and place on a wire rack to cool, about 2 minutes.

To assemble:

1. Using a serrated knife, slice shortcakes in half around the diameter. Place bottoms on individual serving plates.

2. On bottom half, put yogurt and peaches. Top with second half of biscuit. Spoon wine and peach juice mixture around shortcake. Serve.

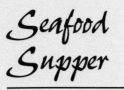

Seafood Supper

Swordfish Carpaccio
with Capers and
Shaved Parmesan

Alaskan Black Cod
with Clams and Orzo

Grape Cobbler
Rosemary Crème
Anglaise

SWORDFISH CARPACCIO WITH CAPERS AND SHAVED PARMESAN

Yield: 4 servings

¾ pound fresh swordfish fillet, thinly sliced into 12 pieces

1 clove garlic, cut in half

2 tablespoons lemon juice

½ teaspoon salt

½ cup extra virgin olive oil

1 tablespoon capers

1 wedge Parmesan cheese

Freshly ground pepper

1. On a large platter or 4 individual plates, arrange swordfish slices, and cover swordfish with plastic wrap. Refrigerate while preparing topping.

2. Spear both garlic halves on the tines of a fork. In a small bowl, put lemon juice and salt, and whisk with the fork and garlic until salt begins to dissolve. Slowly beat in olive oil.

3. To serve, remove fish platter from refrigerator and unwrap. Drizzle dressing over fish and sprinkle with capers. Using a vegetable peeler, hold the cheese over the platter and shave off long strips of cheese, about 20 total. Grind pepper over platter and serve.

ALASKAN BLACK COD WITH CLAMS AND ORZO

Yield: 4 servings

4 1-inch slices good, sturdy bread

1 clove garlic, peeled

Extra virgin olive oil

½ pound smoked Portuguese chorizo sausage

1 cup white wine

2 tomatoes, peeled, seeded and finely chopped, about 1 cup

1 pound fresh Manila clams

4 4-ounce Alaskan black cod fillets or sea bass fillets

Salt and freshly ground pepper

1 to 1½ cups cooked orzo

¼ pound spinach, stems removed

Preheat oven to 400 degrees.

1. Grill or toast bread on both sides. Rub one side of toast with garlic and drizzle with olive oil. Place a slice in individual deep pasta bowls.

2. Peel off sausage skin and cut into ½-inch pieces. Put in a large stock pot with wine. Bring to a boil. Add tomatoes and clams. Cover, lower heat, and steam clams until they open, about 10 minutes. Remove from heat.

3. Oil a baking dish and put in cod. Brush fillets with oil and season with salt and pepper. Bake until fish is cooked, about 12 minutes. Remove from oven. Cover loosely with aluminum foil to keep fillets warm.

4. To the clam mixture, add the orzo and spinach. Cover and bring to a boil. Stir once or twice and remove from heat.

5. To assemble, place a cod fillet on top of toast in each bowl. Distribute clam mixture evenly among the four bowls and serve.

Karen Barnaby

THE FISH HOUSE IN STANLEY PARK

GRAPE COBBLER

Yield: 6 to 8 servings

1 cup red seedless grapes

1 cup green seedless grapes

1 cup black seedless grapes

¾ cup brown sugar

½ cup sliced almonds

2 tablespoons Grappa

1 tablespoon lemon juice

½ teaspoon cinnamon

4 tablespoons butter, melted, plus extra for buttering the pan

1½ cups all-purpose flour

1 cup granulated sugar

2 eggs, lightly beaten

½ cup milk

2 teaspoons baking powder

1 teaspoon vanilla

¼ teaspoon salt

Preheat oven to 350 degrees.

1. In a medium-size bowl, combine red, green, and black grapes, brown sugar, almonds, Grappa, lemon juice, and cinnamon. Set aside.

2. Generously butter a 9x13-inch baking dish.

3. In a large bowl, combine flour, sugar, eggs, milk, melted butter, baking powder, vanilla, and salt. Mix together until smooth. Do not overmix.

4. Pour batter into baking dish and evenly spread grape mixture over batter. Bake for 40 minutes. Serve warm with Rosemary Crème Anglaise.

ROSEMARY CRÈME ANGLAISE

Yield: 4 cups

4 cups half-and-half

¼ cup granulated sugar

2 tablespoons fresh rosemary leaves, coarsely chopped

1 2-inch piece cinnamon stick

8 extra large egg yolks

1. In a sauce pan, combine half-and-half, sugar, rosemary, and cinnamon. Over high heat, bring to a boil, covered.

2. While the cream mixture is heating, with an electric mixer, beat the egg yolks until well combined.

3. When the cream mixture is at a rolling boil, with heat still on high, slowly whisk in egg yolks. Remove sauce pan from heat.

4. Place a medium mesh strainer in a bowl and pour the cream mixture through. Refrigerate, whisking occasionally until cool. Serve on top of warm Grape Cobbler.

Celebration Dinner

Jumbo Lump Crab and Artichoke Salad with Toasted Caraway, Dijon Mustard and St. André Cheese

Tonarelli with White Clam Sauce

Corn Crème Brûlée with Blueberry Polenta Cake

JUMBO LUMP CRAB AND ARTICHOKE SALAD WITH TOASTED CARAWAY, DIJON MUSTARD AND ST. ANDRÉ CHEESE

Yield: 4 servings

1 ½ small fresh artichoke hearts, diced

1 tablespoon blended oil

¼ cup white wine

8 ounces jumbo lump crabmeat

3 tablespoons Dijon mustard

3 tablespoons finely diced shallots

3 tablespoons finely diced roasted red pepper

1 tablespoon caraway seeds, toasted and crushed

3 tablespooons finely diced St. André cheese

Salt and freshly ground pepper

12 bouquets of mâche

¼ cup Caraway Shallot Vinaigrette

12 artichoke leaves deep-fried

12 small quenelles of St. André cheese (see Note)

1. In a saucepan saute artichoke hearts in oil until soft, about 5 minutes. Remove artichoke to a bowl.

2. Add wine to pan and deglaze.

3. To the artichoke, add wine from the pan, crabmeat, mustard, shallots, red pepper, caraway, and diced St. André. Season with salt and pepper.

4. In a bowl dress the mâche lightly in 2 tablespoons vinaigrette.

5. Divide the artichoke mixture equally among 4 plates. Accent each salad with 3 artichoke chips. Place 3 bouquets of mâche and 3 quenelles of cheese around each plate.

6. Drizzle additional dressing on salad.

Note: To make a quenelle, use two teaspoons and mound cheese in one of the spoons. Use the bowl of the other spoon to round cheese into an oval resembling an egg.

CARAWAY SHALLOT VINAIGRETTE

Yield: 1 cup

1 tablespoon caraway seeds, toasted

1 shallot, chopped (2 tablespoons)

¼ cup sherry vinegar

¾ cup blended oil

1. In a bowl combine shallot, caraway, and vinegar.

2. Slowly whisk in the oil. Use with Jumbo Lump Crab and Artichoke Salad.

TONARELLI WITH WHITE CLAM SAUCE

Yield: 4 servings

32 littleneck or top neck clams

2 cups white wine

⅓ cup fresh lemon juice

2 bay leaves

5 whole peppercorns

2 quarts water

1 pound fresh or dried tonarelli or spaghetti

½ cup extra virgin olive oil

3 teaspoons chopped fresh garlic

¼ cup Italian parsley, chopped

½ cup freshly grated Parmesan cheese

Freshly cracked black pepper

1. Thoroughly wash and scrub clams.

2. In a saucepan, combine clams, white wine, lemon juice, bay leaves, and peppercorns. Steam clams on medium heat, covered, until open, about 5 to 7 minutes. Remove 12 clams to a bowl and set remaining clams aside to cool.

3. In a large pot, bring water to a rolling boil.

4. When clams are cool, remove meat from the 20 clams and dice.

5. Line a collander with cheese cloth and pour clam stock through.

6. Add pasta to boiling water and cook according to directions on package. Drain pasta.

7. Meanwhile, in a saucepan combine stock, oil, and garlic. Bring to a boil, uncovered, lower heat and simmer, about 5 minutes.

8. Remove saucepan from heat and add parsley and diced clam meat.

9. Put cooked pasta in four individual plates or bowls. Place 3 whole steamed clams on top of each plate of pasta, and pour clam sauce over pasta. Serve with Parmesan and pepper.

CORN CRÈME BRÛLÉE WITH BLUEBERRY POLENTA CAKE

Yield: 6 servings

THE POLENTA CAKE:

¾ cup all-purpose flour, plus 1 tablespoon

½ cup yellow cornmeal, plus 1 tablespoon

2½ teaspoons baking powder

1⅔ cups unsalted butter

1 cup granulated sugar

3 eggs plus 6 egg yolks

1 teaspoon vanilla extract

1 cup blueberries

THE CORN CRÈME BRÛLÉE:

1 ear fresh sweet corn, kernals removed

1 quart heavy cream

10 egg yolks

¾ cup granulated sugar, plus extra

2 cups blueberries

Preheat oven to 350 degrees.

THE POLENTA CAKE:

1. Line the bottom of a 9-inch square baking pan with parchment paper and grease.

2. In a bowl combine flour, cornmeal, and baking powder. Set aside.

3. Using a food processor, cream butter and sugar until light and fluffy.

4. In three stages, add eggs, egg yolks, and vanilla to butter mixture. Scrape bowl after each addition.

5. Add flour mixture and mix well.

6. Fold in blueberries.

7. Pour batter into prepared pan and bake until cake springs to the touch or a knife inserted comes out clean, about 45 minutes. (This recipe makes extra cake.)

Alison Barshak
VENUS AND THE COWBOY

THE CORN CRÈME BRÛLÉE:

1. In a heavy-bottomed saucepan, put cream and corn cob. Over medium heat, scald cream, taking care not to boil.

2. In a stainless steel bowl combine egg yolks and sugar.

3. Add egg mixture to cream and whisk together.

4. Place a sieve over a bowl and pour cream mixture through. Place bowl in an ice bath to cool, about 30 minutes.

6. Fold blueberries into cream mixture. (This recipe makes enough Crème Brûlée for the cake, plus extra.

Preheat oven to 300 degrees.

To assemble:

1. Cut 6 circles of polenta cake to fit into 2 to 3-inch wide tiny pot-shaped cups. Place cake in bottom of each cup.

2. Sprinkle corn kernels onto cake.

3. Fill remainder of ramekin with Corn Crème Brûlée.

4. In a pot boil water and pour into baking pan. Put remekins in hot water bath and bake until a knife inserted comes out clean, about 20 to 30 minutes.

5. Remove from bath and cool ramekins.
6. To serve, sprinkle tops with granulated sugar and heat under broiler until the sugar melts and browns, about 1 minute. (Do not burn.) Serve immediately.

Spring Lunch

Fresh English Pea and Fava Bean Soup

Spring Vegetable Tempura with Red Pepper and Tomato Sauce

Pan-Roasted Alaskan Halibut with Morel Mushrooms

Strawberry-Rhubarb Tarte

FRESH ENGLISH PEA AND FAVA BEAN SOUP

Yield: 8 to 10 servings

1 ½ pounds English peas, or any fresh pea in the pod

1 ½ pounds fresh fava beans, in the pod

1 quart boiling water, plus additional water for stock

1 leek or medium onion, coarsely chopped

3 stalks celery, coarsely chopped

2 carrots, coarsely chopped

1 clove garlic, peeled

6 peppercorns

2 sprigs fresh herbs, such as thyme and parsley

¾ stick butter

6 shallots, finely chopped

2 to 3 fresh mint leaves

3 tablespoons finely minced chives, for garnish

Salt and freshly ground pepper

1. Shell the peas, reserving pods. Shell fava beans, discarding the pods. Blanch fava beans in boiling water for 1 minute. Drain and plunge into ice water. Slip off outer skin of fava beans. Reserve a handful of peas and blanched fava beans.

2. Prepare a simple vegetable stock, using pea pods plus the leek or onion, celery, carrot, garlic, peppercorns, and fresh herbs. Put these in a pot, adding water to cover vegetables, and covered, bring to a boil. Lower flame to simmer and cook, uncovered, for half an hour. Strain broth and discard vegetables. Place stock in the refrigerator or freezer until chilled.

3. In a soup pot, heat the butter. Add shallots and sauté for 3 or 4 minutes. Add peas and favas, except for garnish, and just enough vegetable stock to cover, about 3 cups. Add salt and pepper to taste. Bring stock to a simmer, uncovered, and cook until the peas and favas are tender, but still remain bright green, about 3 to 5 minutes. Remove from heat.

4. Using a slotted spoon, put cooked peas and favas in a blender or food processor and purée. Use as much chilled vegetable stock as required to achieve a smooth, light consistency. Add mint to one of the batches as you purée.

5. Pass soup through a chinois or medium sieve. Do not use a fine mesh sieve or the creamy solids that give this soup its consistency will be lost. Adjust seasoning.

6. Reheat soup just prior to serving. Garnish with chives and reserved peas and favas. This soup can also be served cold, though it is best heated.

SPRING VEGETABLE TEMPURA WITH RED PEPPER AND TOMATO SAUCE

Yield: approximately 8 servings as a starter course.

THE SAUCE:

Olive oil

1 small yellow onion

2 sweet red peppers

12 ripe Roma tomatoes

Salt and freshly ground pepper

THE VEGETABLES:

A variety of vegetables (see Note)

Peanut oil for frying

THE BATTER:

2 cups ice water

2 egg yolks

2 cups sifted flour

THE SAUCE:

1. Heat olive oil in a saucepan. Add onions and red peppers and sauté gently until very soft, about 10 minutes. Add tomatoes, and salt and pepper to taste. On medium heat, cook covered until tomatoes release their juices, about 15 minutes.

2. Remove from heat and pass vegetables through a food mill. Adjust seasoning and keep warm or reheat just before serving.

THE VEGETABLES:

1. Trim and cut the vegetables into finger lengths and slices (about ⅜-inch) to ready for frying. Small vegetables such as green beans and asparagus can be fried whole. Eggplant, artichokes and turnips should be thinly sliced into slabs and wedges.

2. In a wok or skillet, preheat peanut oil to near smoking, about 375 degrees. Have oil hot before making batter.

THE BATTER:

1. Using a fork or chopsticks, combine the ice water, egg yolks, and flour, mixing with only a few strokes. The batter should be lumpy with plenty of unincorporated flour showing.

4. One at a time, dredge vegetables in batter and slide into hot peanut oil. Place several vegetables in oil without overcrowding. Turn once during frying. Remove and drain on paper towels. Serve immediately with warm red pepper and tomato sauce.

Note: Almost any vegetable will do but try to choose whatever is freshest and tastiest. In the spring, look for asparagus, artichokes, small spring onions or even wild ramps, and turnips. Eggplant, squashes, green beans, and mushrooms also work well. Parsley or sage can be fried to make nice edible garnishes.

PAN-ROASTED ALASKAN HALIBUT WITH MOREL MUSHROOMS

Yield: 6 servings

8 ounces morel mushrooms

2 shallots, minced

1 tablespoon butter

½ cup dry white wine

2 cups fish stock

½ cup heavy cream

Flour for dredging, seasoned with salt and freshly ground pepper

Olive oil

6 halibut fillets, 6 to 8 ounces each

Salt and white pepper

Fresh chives or Italian parsley

1. Trim the bottom of the morels to remove stems and reserve trimmings. Sauté shallots in butter until translucent. Add mushroom stems and sauté until aromatic, 5 to 7 minutes. Do not let shallots brown. Add wine and reduce to a glaze, about 10 to 15 minutes. Add fish stock and reduce again by half, about 15 minutes. Whisk in cream and allow to cook gently until sauce coats a spoon, about 5 to 7 minutes. Strain through a fine mesh sieve and set aside. This can be done in advance.

Preheat oven to 400 degrees and warm dinner plates.

2. Coat the bottom of a large sauté pan with a small amount of oil and heat. Dredge halibut fillets in flour mixture and shake off excess. When pan is very hot, add fillets, with the side to be presented in serving placed down on the cooking surface. Cook until golden brown. Using a spatula, carefully turn fillets over. Add mushrooms to fish in pan and season with salt and pepper. Place pan in oven and cook fish for 4 to 8 minutes, until done, depending upon thickness of fillet.

3. Remove pan from oven and transfer fillets to warm dinner plates. Add sauce to pan, heat and reduce sauce slightly. Add chives or parsley. Adjust seasoning. Spoon sauce and mushrooms over each fillet and serve immediately.

Ann Cashion

CASHION'S EAT PLACE

STRAWBERRY-RHUBARB TARTE

THE FILLING:

¾ cup sugar

2 ½ tablespoons flour

¼ cup toasted hazelnuts, coarsely chopped

3 cups rhubarb, cut into ½-inch lengths

1 cup strawberries, cut in halves

THE PASTRY:

3 cups flour

⅔ cup sugar

½ teaspoon salt

¾ pound unsalted butter, cut into small pieces

1 egg yolk

½ teaspoon vanilla

¼ cup ice water

To assemble the tarte:

1 egg, beaten

Cinnamon sugar

1. For filling, combine sugar and flour and set aside.

2. For the pastry, using an electric mixer or food processor, combine flour, sugar, and salt. Add butter to flour mixture and blend until mixture resembles coarse meal. Add egg yolk and vanilla, and mix briefly. Add enough ice water to bring dough into a ball. Refrigerate 1 hour.

Preheat oven to 400 degrees.

3. Roll out dough. Line a 9-inch drop bottom tarte ring with dough. Trim and save scraps. Sprinkle hazelnuts across bottom of pastry shell. Toss rhubarb and strawberries with sugar and flour mixture. Place on top of hazelnuts.

4. Roll out remaining dough. Brush with beaten egg and sprinkle with cinnamon sugar. Cut into thin strips and form a lattice across top of tarte. Bake until filling bubbles and pastry is golden brown, about 30 minutes. Take tarte from oven and remove the outer ring of pan. Let cool. Serve slightly warm or at room temperature with whipped cream or ice cream.

Summer Weekend Soiree

Chilled Cucumber and Vidalia Onion Soup

Grilled Quail Salad with Avocado, Goat Cheese, Croutons, with Smoked Bacon Vinaigrette

Grilled Atlantic Salmon with Morels, Ramps and Pancetta

Strawberry Sorbet with Ginger Rhubarb Compote*

*Serving suggestion

CHILLED CUCUMBER AND VIDALIA ONION SOUP

Yield: 8 servings

THE STOCK:

2 to 4 tablespoons olive oil

1 leek (white part only), coarsely chopped

4 ribs celery, coarsely chopped

2 medium Vidalia onions, peeled and chopped

4 quarts water

4 sprigs fresh thyme

2 bay leaves

10 black peppercorns

THE SOUP:

4 large Vidalia onions, peeled and chopped

4 seedless cucumbers, peeled and sliced

2 cups half-and-half

2 cups buttermilk

Sea salt and white pepper

8 tablespoons diced avocado

8 tablespoons diced cantaloupe

8 grilled shrimp, optional

Chopped chives or chervil

THE STOCK:

1. In a large soup pot, add oil and sauté leek, celery, and onions until onions are soft but not brown, about 10 minutes.

2. Add water, thyme, bay leaves, and peppercorns. Bring to a boil covered, and boil uncovered until reduced by half. Strain vegetables and discard. Set aside stock.

THE SOUP:

1. Put stock in a clean pot and add onions. Bring to a boil, and simmer for 5 minutes, uncovered. Remove pot from heat and stir in cucumbers so the liquid covers them. Let stand 5 minutes, uncovered.

2. In a blender, purée cucumber mixture. Pass through a wide-mesh food mill, retaining some of the vegetable solids. Chill for 1 hour.

To assemble:

1. In a large bowl, combine half-and-half and buttermilk. Whisk in cucumber mixture. Season soup with salt and lots of white pepper.

2. In individual serving bowls, place 1 tablespoon each of avocado and cantaloupe. Pour soup over fruit. Top each serving with a shrimp. Garnish with chives, and serve.

GRILLED QUAIL SALAD WITH AVOCADO, GOAT CHEESE AND CROUTONS WITH SMOKED BACON VINAIGRETTE

Yield: 4 servings

THE SMOKED BACON VINAIGRETTE:

1 slice apple-wood smoked bacon

½ cup vinaigrette

THE QUAIL:

4 semi-boneless quail

Salt and freshly ground pepper

4 tablespoons balsamic vinegar

6 tablespoons olive oil

4 fresh quail eggs

1 tablespoon vegetable oil

THE SALAD:

½ avocado, peeled, pit removed

4 ounces fresh goat cheese

¼ cup homemade croutons

½ pound mesclun, a handful for each serving

To assemble:

½ cup reduced chicken stock

4 tablespoons chive oil

THE SMOKED BACON VINAIGRETTE:

1. Cook bacon and drain.

2. Crumble bacon and add to vinaigrette. Set aside for several hours to allow flavors to infuse.

THE QUAIL:

1. With a deboning knife, remove wings and trim ends of quail legs. Rinse under cold water and pat dry. Season inside and out with salt and pepper, and put in a shallow dish.

2. Spoon vinegar and oil over birds and toss to coat.

3. Cover with plastic wrap. Put in refrigerator to marinate at least 1 hour; several hours is preferred. Keep chilled until ready to grill.

THE SALAD:

1. Cube avocado and place in a metal bowl. Crumble in cheese. Add croutons and mesclun.

2. Refrigerate covered, until ready to assemble salad.

Preheat oven to 450 degrees.

TO COOK QUAIL:

1. Heat grill. Place quail on grill for 20 seconds and then turn over, so both sides have grill marks.

2. Put quail in a baking dish and uncovered, place in oven to finish cooking, about 4 to 5 minutes.

3. Place on a cutting board and let rest a few minutes.

4. Meanwhile put vegetable oil in a non-stick pan and fry quail eggs. Set aside.

5. On a cutting board, and preferably using an electric knife, cut quail from neck to legs in thin slices. Keep slices together so that shape of bird is retained.

To assemble:

1. Drizzle Smoked Bacon Vinaigrette over mesclun mixture. Toss gently. Divide among 4 plates.

2. Using a spatula, place 1 quail on top of each salad. Drizzle with 2 tablespoons stock. Top with a quail egg and drizzle with 1 tablespoon chive oil over egg and around salad.

GRILLED ATLANTIC SALMON WITH MORELS, RAMPS AND PANCETTA

Yield: 4 servings

1 pound fresh morel mushrooms or ¼ pound dried

2 shallots, minced

1 clove garlic, minced

10 tablespoons butter, cut into pieces

1 cup sherry or Madeira

Salt and freshly ground pepper

4 6-ounce pieces of salmon fillets, skin removed

Olive oil

16 ramps, well cleaned, cut into ¼-inch pieces (see Note)

4 generous tablespoons cubed and trimmed pancetta

Chopped parsley

1. If using fresh morels, trim stems and soak morels in a bowl of cold water for 15 minutes. Drain well and place on paper towels to absorb excess moisture. Cut larger morels in half lengthwise. If using dried morels, soak in water to reconstitute, then trim stems and proceed as for fresh.

Suzy Crofton

CROFTON'S

Preheat oven to 500 degrees.

2. Heat a small, heavy saucepan for a minute, then sauté the shallots and garlic in 2 tablespoons butter over low heat, without coloring butter.

3. Add morels, turn up heat and cook for 1 minute. Add sherry and let reduce by half.

4. Whisk in remaining butter until it is emulsified but not boiling. Season with salt and pepper. Set aside morel mixture and keep warm.

5. Heat grill. Brush with olive oil and season salmon fillets with salt and pepper. Place flesh side down on a hot grill for 10 to 20 seconds, depending on heat of grill. Turn a quarter turn to make grill marks again. Turn salmon over and grill for 20 seconds.

6. Transfer salmon to a large pan and put in oven for 5 to 10 minutes.

7. Heat a medium-size, heavy-bottomed frying pan over high heat for a minute. Add a few tablespoons olive oil and heat. Add ramps and pancetta. Cook briefly, taking care not to fry them. (Shake the pan to prevent frying.) Add morel mixture. Mix ingredients together. Season lightly with salt and pepper. Remove from heat.

8. In the center of a dinner plate place a salmon fillet and scatter with morel mixture. Spoon some over top and around sides. Garnish with parsley.

Note: Scallions may be substituted when ramps are out of season.

Chinese Dinner

Spicy Cucumbers with Sichuan Peppercorn Vinaigrette

Mandarin Pork with Brandy Infused Hoisin Sauce

Scallion Pancakes

SPICY CUCUMBERS WITH SICHUAN PEPPERCORN VINAIGRETTE

Yield: 6 to 8 servings

2 pounds cucumbers, preferably seedless (see Note)

1 tablespoon coarse or kosher salt

1 jalapeño or Italian hot pepper, cored, seeded and julienned

1 tablespoon peeled, julienned gingerroot

1 recipe Sichuan Peppercorn Vinaigrette

1. Wash cucumbers and cut off the ends. Cut each cucumber lengthwise into quarters. Scrape away any seeds with a knife or spoon. Cut cucumbers crosswise into ½-inch-wide slices.

2. Place cucumbers in a large bowl and toss with salt. Let stand for 30 minutes. The salt will draw out much of the liquid from the cucumbers.

3. Transfer cucumbers to a colander, rinse, drain and place in another bowl.

4. Add jalapeño or other hot pepper and gingerroot. Toss and set aside.

5. Pour vinaigrette over cucumbers and mix well. Refrigerate for at least 2 hours. Serve cold.

Note: Thin-skinned English cucumbers will not need peeling, but waxed and thick-skinned cucumbers will.

SICHUAN PEPPERCORN VINAIGRETTE

Yield: about ⅓ cup

2 tablespoons white wine vinegar

1 tablespoon Infused Sichuan Peppercorn Oil, strained

1 tablespoon Asian sesame oil

1 tablespoon sugar

½ teaspoon coarse or kosher salt

1. In a small bowl or jar, put vinegar, peppercorn and sesame oils, sugar, and salt. Mix well.

INFUSED SICHUAN PEPPERCORN OIL

1 cup corn or olive oil

2 tablespoons roasted Sichuan peppercorns

3 garlic cloves

1. In a small saucepan, heat the oil until very hot. Add peppercorns and garlic, cook over high heat for 2 minutes, then turn off heat.

2. When cool, strain and store in a glass bottle

ROASTED SICHUAN PEPPERCORNS

4 ounces Sichuan peppercorns

1. Heat a heavy skillet until it is very hot, then add peppercorns. Turn heat to medium-low and shake or stir peppercorns until they are dark brown and their intense smell is released, about 15 to 20 minutes. Turn off the heat.

2. Store in a tightly sealed jar. Grind the cooled roasted peppercorns in a peppermill or spice mill as needed.

MANDARIN PORK WITH BRANDY-INFUSED HOISIN SAUCE

Yield: 2 servings as a main course with rice or 4 servings rolled into Scallion Pancakes

½ pound lean boneless pork loin

1 small leek

2 tablespoons brandy

1 tablespoon soy sauce

1 teaspoon cornstarch

3 tablespoons corn oil

1 tablespoon peeled, julienned gingerroot

½ cup thinly sliced red bell pepper

2 jalapeño peppers, cored, seeded and julienned

3 tablespoons Brandy-Infused Hoisin Sauce

1 cup finely julienned jicama

¼ cup chicken or pork stock

1 tablespoon chopped fresh tarragon leaves

1. Cover the pork with plastic wrap and place in freezer for 15 minutes; the semi-frozen meat will be easier to slice and julienne.

2. Cut off the root end of the leek, and peel off and discard the tough outer green leaves. Cut the leek into 2-inch sections. Cut each section in half lengthwise, then julienne. Wash well in cold water to remove any dirt. Drain and set aside.

3. Remove pork from freezer, cut into ⅛-inch slices, then julienne. Place the julienned pork in a shallow dish.

4. In a small bowl combine the brandy and soy sauce. Pour over pork and mix well. Sprinkle with cornstarch, and using a fork or chopsticks, mix well to coat. Marinate for 15 minutes.

5. In a large skillet or wok, heat the oil until it is hot. Add the pork, along with any marinade, and gingerroot, and cook over high heat, stirring, for 2 minutes.

6. Add bell pepper and jalapeño and cook, stirring, for 1 minute. Add hoisin sauce and cook, stirring, for 2 minutes to coat the meat. Add leek and jicama.

7. Pour stock into skillet and cook, stirring, over high heat for 2 to 3 minutes, or until all ingredients are heated through and pork is cooked. Mix in tarragon and serve.

BRANDY-INFUSED HOISIN SAUCE

Yield: about 2½ cups sauce

2 tablespoons corn oil

3 garlic cloves, minced

2 cups (16-ounce jar) hoisin sauce

2 tablespoons Asian sesame oil

½ cup brandy

2 tablespoons red wine vinegar or balsamic vinegar

½ cup chicken, pork or beef stock

1. In a medium saucepan heat oil. Add garlic and cook over high heat, stirring, until golden, about 2 minutes. Be careful not to let the garlic brown.

2. Add hoisin sauce and sesame oil and bring to a boil, stirring constantly.

3. Reduce heat to medium, add brandy and vinegar and cook for 5 minutes, stirring constantly to keep sauce from sticking to pan.

4. Add stock and reduce heat to low. Cook, stirring occasionally, for 15 minutes, until sauce is well blended and thickened.

5. Cool sauce and pour into a jar with a tight-fitting lid. This sauce will keep well, covered and refrigerated, for up to 1 month.

SCALLION PANCAKES

Yield: 8 pancakes

THE BOILING-WATER DOUGH:

1¼ cups water

2 to 2½ cups all-purpose flour

THE SCALLION FILLING:

½ bunch scallions, trimmed and minced (about ½ cup)

¾ cup minced pork fat

1 tablespoon olive or corn oil

1 teaspoon coarse or kosher salt

About ½ cup corn oil for frying

THE BOILING-WATER DOUGH:

1. In a saucepan bring the water to a boil. Turn off heat and let sit for 2 minutes.

2. Sift 2 cups flour into a large bowl. Add boiling water in a slow, steady stream, mixing well with a wooden spoon to form a dough. Keep mixing until you can form it into a smooth ball. This can be done in a food processor: place the flour in the food processor fitted with the metal blade, and with the motor running, add the water through the feed tube; process until the dough forms a ball, 3 to 5 minutes.

3. Let stand, covered with a damp cloth or towel, for 30 minutes so gluten relaxes.

THE SCALLION FILLING:

1. In a small bowl, combine scallions, pork fat, oil, and salt. Mix well.

2. Place dough on a lightly floured surface. Shape into a log, cut dough into 8 portions and sprinkle lightly with flour; it should be very soft and easy to handle.

3. Roll out 1 piece of dough on a floured surface into a ⅛-inch-thick oval. Spread 1 tablespoon scallion filling in a thin layer over dough, leaving a ½-inch margin all around. Roll up the dough jelly-roll fashion.

4. Seal the ends of each piece by pinching them closed. Twirl both ends; the piece will bend a little in the middle. A little of the scallion filling may come out, but that is all right. Spiral the dough around itself, making a concentric circle. Flatten it with your palm and press it out gently with a rolling pin into a 5-inch round. Repeat, making 8 rounds in all.

TO COOK THE PANCAKES:

1. Heat a heavy skillet over medium heat. Add 1 tablespoon oil to the pan, and fry the pancakes, 1 at a time, for 2 to 3 minutes on each side, or until golden in color, adding more oil as needed. Drain on paper towels and serve hot.

Susanna Foo

SUSANNA
FOO'S
RESTAURANT

RENEE FOOTE   DIANE FORLEY   GALE GAND   BEVERLY GANNON   MONIQUE

GAUMONT LANVIN   ROZANNE GOLD   ALIZA GREEN   JOSEFINA HOWARD

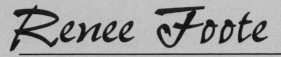

Renee Foote

MERCER STREET GRILL

"If you embrace this life you have to have the passion for leading a crew."

With African American and Irish Canadian parents and a restaurateur who persuaded her to cook Asian fusion food, Renee Foote's adventurous melange of ingredients and colorful dishes results in a totally unique cuisine, which has won her praise from many gastronomic critics. Recognition for her culinary prowess was quite unpredictable. As a teenager growing up in Toronto, Foote wanted to be nurse for a long time, but while in high school she got into a co-op cooking program and worked at a local restaurant. This experience directed her final choice of a career. She graduated from the George Brown culinary program in Toronto, and began her way up the kitchen ladder, moving from one top restaurant in the city to another: Hazelton Lanes, Glossups, the Sutton Place Hotel until she wound up as the pastry chef at North 44, where the head chef and mentor Mark McEwan taught her how to manage people in a twenty-person kitchen. As chef de cuisine at Byzantium, and then Nemo's, her flamboyant style of cooking and passionate menus of fresh market cuisine finally led her to Simon Bower's Mercer

Street Grill, where she has received rave reviews ever since. "Must go there this minute," was the verdict from Food Arts magazine. "This kitchen sings and dances," reported Joanne Kates from the Toronto Globe and Mail.. Toronto Life magazine gave it three stars in 1996. The Toronto Sun noted that the restaurant demonstrated "how far women have come in this industry." A recipient of many accolades, Foote is most proud of a Consumer Gas Competition award which she won at the age of 23, coming out ahead of ten other seasoned Toronto chefs with a frozen Ontario strawberry parfait and a crisp filo wafer. She took time out to discuss her success story and her motto, "Think first, speak second," one morning at the Mercer Street Grill.

Mercer Street Grill

36 Mercer Street
Toronto, ON M5V 1H9
Canada
Phone: 416 599 3399
Fax 416 923 1973

Above:

Grilled Tenderloin Steak with Steamed Lobster Rice Roll and Gingered Greens

Right:

Hot Nori Roll and Quail with Sweet Pepper and Rosemary Relish

I am happy to say that you can be young and make it in this business. I have never experienced anything like female prejudice simply because in most instances, the kitchens I have worked in were headed by a male chef de cuisine with a female crew. I know you hear many different types of stories about the struggles of women chefs and this will continue until more people coming into the food business are women. I feel very empowered now that I run my own kitchen. I am not a pussycat, but I think I am giving to my staff. I manage people as I would wish to be managed. I spend a lot of time teaching them to believe in what I believe in, organizing them, checking up on them and being motherly to them. When you embrace this life, you have to have the passion for leading a crew. From my point of view they must be as driven and passionate as I am. They don't just want a job. Things should run as you expect them to. If they don't, I tell them why this is my vision.

One reviewer said that people who like meat and potatoes won't enjoy my cooking, but foodies love it. I started Asian fusion food because we wanted to have a restaurant cuisine that would last. Those big Italian restaurants with lots of people lasted until the end of the '80s, but then it became easier to get goat cheese and roasted peppers and different pastas and coffees in the local supermarket. Now everyone is able to cook Italian food at home. When Simon Bower opened the Mercer Street Grill he wanted to offer a cuisine that would be appropriate for the '90s and into the year 2000. Today lots of people like Asian cuisine because it is low in fat and healthy, and the combination of flavors is unusual. We take authentic Asian dishes, but we have to use North American ingredients and techniques that make an interesting intertwining of tastes. My style of presentation is quite architectural, some- times wildly cut and shaped.

Below:
Japanese
Bento Box of
BBQ Duck

I know that I will go after my own restaurant in the end. You can't cook at the stove all your life. But I am thankful to be where I am, at the age that I am. I am constantly reading cookbooks at home, making notes, sometimes at three or four o'clock in the morning. I don't find it too mind-boggling to look at this work from a financial point of view. For example, if something costs $24 I must turn around and sell it for a profit. Creating food is a personal expression but if you spend too much time on your art, you lose the profit. You must produce quality, but you must be sensitive to the time it takes to do so.

Right:
Chocolate Sushi

Far Right:
Grilled Sea
Scallops and
Steamed
Vegetable Crepe

Diane Forley

VERBENA

"There is a very competitive atmosphere in a professional kitchen for men and women, a lot of testing going on, but once tested, then you are okay."

Grains, Greens and Fragrance

Verbena's food was instantly acclaimed for its originality when chef-proprietor Diane Forley opened the garden restaurant in a character-filled brownstone in Gramercy Park. The innovative menu arises partly from Forley's own extremely eclectic heritage: a mother born in Bombay and brought up in Guatemala, a grandmother born in Yemen, a father from Hungary. She brings all these ethnic influences to the table, along with her own individuality as a New Yorker who has worked in some of the most prestigious kitchens in the city. Although she pursued a conventional education, graduating from Brown University with a degree in literature, Forley's natural interest in the culinary arts is reflected in her honors thesis 'The History of Gastronomy in 19th-Century France, Examined Through the Works of Balzac and Flaubert.' Chef Michel Fitoussi, "a crazy Frenchman determined to be the best," was an early mentor. Forley became an apprentice to him at the Palace restaurant at the age of 16 and rejoined him at 24 Fifth, after finishing college. In 1986, chef Alfred Portale offered her the pastry chef position at the newly opened Gotham Bar and Grill. A year later she joined Jacques Chibois and Jean Michel Diot at Adrienne, and in 1989, Forley moved to the River Cafe, broadening her training and refining her culinary skills under American

Verbena

54 Irving Place, New York, N.Y. 10003
Phone: 212 260 5454 Fax: 212 260 3595

chef David Burke. Then it was off to France to work under three superchefs, Michael Guerard, Jose Lamreia and Alain Passard. In Paris she also studied bread baking at the Lenotre School.

Back in New York, Forley worked at Petrossian, Park Avenue Cafe, and Oggi Domani before taking the plunge and opening her own place. She discussed her decision to go solo in Verbena's summer dining room, a tented courtyard garden planted with hibiscus, bougainvillea and, of course, fragrant verbena.

Right:
*Layered Salad
of Sliced
Tomatoes,
Arugula and
Tapenade Toast*

Below:
*Angel Hair
Pasta in
Mushrooms*

It's great having my own place. It was not my ambition when I was cooking. I just wanted to learn the next step and be a better cook. When it came time to think about the next step, it became a step to do. Running your own restaurant presents different challenges from one day to the next. I have a staff of thirty-five and we are open six days a week. But when you have experienced the lifestyle for a number of years, you know what is expected of you in this career. When things get overloaded, I will take day or two off. It all comes down to line management. A professional kitchen is a very competitive atmosphere for a man or a woman. There is a lot of testing going on. But once tested, you are okay, accepted, and part of the group as another hard worker.

The East Coast and the West Coast have very different mentalities about women in the kitchen. Women chefs are less visible on the East Coast, but in San Francisco, about 50 percent are men and 50 percent are women. In my kitchen it might be 60 percent men and 40 percent women, but it could be half-and-half - it varies at any one time.

The '90s moved into different food choices from the '80s I have tried to take an approach that fits into the contemporary food style. I feel today there is more earthiness to cooking. I don't like the fusion style, giving unexpected flavors to food, which can get the taste buds confused. I use flavors that are classically meant to be together. I am offering seasonal American food, grounded in French traditional techniques with some ideas from the Mediterranean region. I use a lot of ingredients from the green

Left:
Saltwater Shrimp
with Artichoke
Griddle Cake

Below:
Poached Halibut
in Lemon Nage

Bottom:
Bittersweet
Chocolate Savarin

market. People are veering toward vegetables as an alternative in the way they like to eat. Food is simpler, less flamboyant, less architectural in presentation. I give smaller portions. People always want their money's worth and good value, but they are concerned about healthy eating, cutting back here and there on calories. Desserts are more fruit-based. I definitely try to take note of health aspects in my menu, including grains, greens and vegetables.

I chose the name Verbena for my restaurant because it stands for more than just an herb. It is also used as a digestive tea, and as an ingredient in perfumes and soaps. It is one of my favorite herbs and I make a crême brûlée infused with lemon verbena as a signature dish. I tried to make a parallel to this plant with my restaurant. It has a simplicity, it is down to earth, true and honest. There are no facades. No unnecessary show. It is enough to feel pleasantly surprised, pleased with the surroundings, the food, the whole experience.

Gale Gand

BRASSERIE T

"In the last ten years, women have worked hard to get equal. Men had to accept us."

Gale Gand and her husband, Rick Tramonto, have opened fourteen restaurants together. They now own the bustling 210-seat Brasserie T and the nearby Vanilla Bean Bakery in Chicago. They met at the Strathallen Hotel in Rochester, New York, where they both mentored under chef Greg Broman. Their concurrent careers took them to England, France and Spain, with Gand taking formal pastry classes at La Varenne in Paris along the way, which helped turn her into an international dessert diva. Praised by some of the world's top epicurean critics and recipient of a rare red "M" in the 1991 Michelin guide, Gand is followed by accolades wherever she goes: three stars from The New York Times's Bryan Miller when she presided over pastry at the Gotham Bar & Grill in Manhattan; a four-star rating from Chicago Tribune critic Phil Vettel when she and Rick were at Trio; the Robert Mondavi Award for Culinary Excellence in 1994 along with a listing in the Top Ten Best New Chefs by Food & Wine that year.

Gand took time out on a Saturday afternoon at Brasserie T to sweet-talk over one of her signature desserts, Sticky Toffee Pudding, a recipe she found and developed while at Stapleford Park, a hotel in Leicestershire, England.

Brasserie T

Brasserie T
305 South Happ Road
Northfield, IL 60093
Phone: 847 446 0444
Fax: 847 446 0454

Right:
Assiette of
Desserts

Above:
Gale's
Blue Plate
Special

Below:
Not Your Usual
Lemon Meringue
Pie

I come from a very creative, entrepreneurial family. When I was a teenager, my mother had me take French classes instead of typing. But I remember calling home when I was at art school in Cleveland in 1975 to tell her I had found out what I wanted to do - be a chef. The result was that I was considered a lost child. I had just been thrown the chef's job in a restaurant where I was waitressing, and it was like getting a calling, or falling in love. I discovered cooking involves all the senses - sight, sound, touch, taste and smell - and is more encompassing than the fine arts, which lack smell and taste. Suddenly, painting, or design or ceramics didn't have as much depth. Line, color, shape and spatial relationship all apply to food, as well as contrasting flavors, and you display your art on a daily basis. You can't do all that in a painting, and you can't always get into an art show.

I was obsessed by food, restaurants and chefs. In those days, cooking was a blue-collar job, and my parents didn't think that I was doing anything worth while. To be the talk of the town and a famous chef, you had to be French. And you had to be one of the few. Ironically, those French lessons were useful in the end. Now I am the good daughter, and it's funny to see the turnaround in people's attitudes. It is understood that cooking is

something you do because you love it, not because you can't do anything else.

When I first applied to be an apprentice in Lyons, France, the restaurant owners read my letter and accepted me because they thought I was a man. When I arrived, I said "I'm Mr. Gand," and they almost shut the door in my face. They were stunned but eventually they took me on for a month.

A lot of times I've been the only woman on the kitchen staff, and that's how I established my kitchen manner. I was allowed to function in a male world, provided I was independent physically. You have to learn a few tricks, like how to haul a 120-pound sack of flour, pivoting it along a counter so you don't need help. You have to get down pots from high places willingly. You have to get the rest of the kitchen staff out of their perception of you as a needy woman. Then there's the language. It is brutal. It's the male locker-room approach. The main thing is learning their language and being comfortable with their language. I have always been the pastry chef, but not just a girl who plays with whipped cream. I would always jump in and do more than what I was asked. If six cases of broccoli arrived I would help chop it up, or cut down a rack of lamb. I learned to use macho tools, big knives, a big pair of tongs with skill when dealing with an open fire, and a blowtorch to caramelize my crème brûlée.

In the last ten years, women have worked hard to get equal. Men had to accept us. We're too active, and we're too good and we never, never give up.

Beverly Gannon

*"We have to work
ten times as hard as the guys -
it's definitely a man's world career."*

Born and raised in Dallas, Beverly Gannon started out in show business working as a road manager for Liza Minelli and other stars. Taking a break from that fast-paced activity one year, she took herself off to London and went to the Cordon Bleu. She found she enjoyed cooking so much, that when she returned to Dallas, she started her own catering business. When she married and went to live in Los Angeles, she and her husband, Joe Gannon, decided to make Maui a home away from home. There she started cooking for friends and before long she was catering parties, weddings and dinners from her kitchen in the garage. When the charming, historic 1929 Haliimaile General Store, located in the pineapple plantations on the slopes of the world's largest dormant volcano, Mount Haleakala came on the market in 1987, she bought it with the idea that it would be a take-out deli and catering head-quarters. How wrong she was! The day the new store opened, a hundred people were waiting outside expecting to be served a meal. Somehow Gannon turned the chaos (no waiters, no dishwashers, no tables and chairs) into an opportunity to start a new career as a restaurateur. She now serves 150-250 dinners every night from her eclectic American menu with strong emphasis on Asian seafood. The restaurant

Haliimaile General Store

Haliimaile
Maui, HI 96768
Phone: 808 572 2666
Fax: 808 572 7128

received three stars from Food & Wine, plus a cover photo of one of Gannon's signature dishes, Pina Colada Cheesecake, and excellent reviews from Bon Appetit, Zagat's Hawaii Restaurants and other publications. In 1995, Gannon opened a second restaurant, Joe's Bar & Grill, located in a more popular tourist area, serving good American down-home chickens, chops and steaks to another 150 people in the season.

By forming a cooperative of chefs and restaurateurs, Gannon has done a lot to make local produce available to Hawaiian islanders and improve the accessibility of fresh ingredients that used to be shipped out of the islands overseas. She talked one morning at breakfast time.

Below:
Paniolo Ribs
with
House Salad
and
Chocolate Roulade

I am one of the few people in this business who has learned to survive by doing. Within three years of doing it I was in national magazines, and I was always learning. So I am an exception to the rule about how to survive. I have no background, no history of working for someone else, no years of drudgery. I didn't have ten years of struggling, pleasing another chef in another kitchen. I approached it sideways and it worked. I did it from instinct. My favorite thing to do is to eat all over the world, and that gave me the basis of how I wanted to work and how I wanted my customers to be treated.

From the beginning, I approached it as if I were serving in my own home. I wanted my customers to feel satisfied. I want to make people happy from the moment they walk through the door. I want them to feel nurtured before they even get to the food. I am ahead of the game if someone feels homey and comfortable. Instead of being served by a very standoffish, perfectly-trained waiter, I have trained my staff to make people happy. The result is that I have the same waiters serving the same people almost ten years later. They know what they like, what drinks to order - and people like that personal recognition. People come to eat at my restaurant two and three times a week, because there is nowhere else to go. I keep them coming back.

My mother raised her family on canned, frozen and packaged foods. The food outside my house was always better than the food inside. I was always interested in traveling, particularly in Europe when I was in my '20s. I loved seeing fresh food and wonderful produce in the markets. I found it fun and exciting. At home, my parents entertained a lot and I would always

stay in the kitchen watching the caterer do all the food. That's how I started entertaining for my friends - I was famous for my Halloween parties.

As women chefs, we have to work ten times as hard as the guys. It's definitely a man's world career. It's still a boys' club. There are not very man of us in Hawaii, but we share and we learn from each other.

Above:
Sashimi Taco
Samples

Left:
Vegetable Tarte

Monique Gaumont-Lanvin

THE SIGN OF THE SORREL HORSE

*"I don't take any nonsense
when working with people -
women or men."*

The Sign of the Sorrel Horse, where Monique Gaumont-Lanvin presides as executive chef, is one of those Bucks County, Pennsylvania, gems steeped in history. With its heavy, time-darkened beams, massive stone walls, three fireplaces (one a walk-in), the inn was once a mill that probably supplied flour to Washington's army while it was encamped on a nearby hill on the march from Valley Forge. The first owner, John Dyer felled trees on his three hundred-acre state in 1710 for the original building. Even though the roof had caved in, and the inn had been vandalized fourteen times, Gaumont-Lanvin and her chef-husband, Jon Atkin, had their eye on the property as a possible location, and when it came on the market, they bought it and turned it into a charming, comfortable, country manor hotel. Five chintz-decorated rooms upstairs encourage guests to stay overnight after indulging in the superb food and wine served in the formal Escoffier room, where seasonal wild game is a specialty.

Born in the Alsace region of France, home of foie gras, onion tarts and fine Riesling wines, Gaumont-Lanvin became a bicultural Franco-American as a student in the 1950s, when her parents moved to New Jersey. She studied cooking as a young bride at the Cordon Bleu in Paris in order to learn how to be a gracious hostess and entertain guests for her first

Sign of the Sorrel Horse

4424 Old Easton Road
Doylestown, PA 18901
Phone: 215 230 9999
Fax: 215 230 8053

husband, an heir to the Gaumont-Lanvin perfume fortune. Later, as a divorced working mother back in New Jersey, she turned to cooking as a profession, because it was something she knew how to do. Her first restaurant, Monique's, in New Hope, Pennsylvania, opened in 1977 and served classic Alsatian cuisine. It was followed seven years later by the first Sign of the Sorrel Horse, a restaurant and guest house in Quakertown. (She retained the rights to the name when she bought the current establishment.) Written up by numerous publications, the Doylestown Sign of the Sorrel Horse won the Food & Wine Distinguished Restaurant Awards four years in a row. It was voted one of Top Six Country Inn Restaurants in the U.S. Country Inn B & B magazine. Gaumont-Lanvin talked with her particularly wry sense of French humor in the foyer lounge one afternoon.

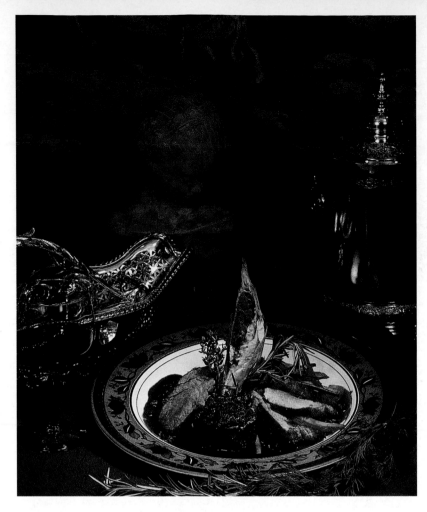

I always wanted to be a cook and have my own restaurant, ever since I was a little girl. I was stealing eggs from my mother's kitchen, although I didn't know what I was doing. I would have my menus and invite mother and father to dinner. When I was married I learned everything I know from my mother-in-law. Despite having a butler and maid, she actually cooked in the kitchen, with curlers in her hair while chain smoking. She showed me how to make a beautiful foie gras from the Bordeaux region, where she came from, and pheasant under glass. She taught me a lot of little secrets. She was very hard, very difficult, because she was a perfectionist. Everything had to be just right. She was a step beyond perfection. Everyone had to be at the table for dinner at seven o'clock, otherwise they had to eat in the kitchen. That was the standard that I was brought up with.

I have often thought of moving to a city. People say our food is so exciting we belong in Manhattan. Sometimes I think I would like to go back to France and find a nice chateau. But I do love these

surroundings. I call this place my beautiful cage. I wish I could say that there has been an evolution of American cuisine over the past thirty years but it seems to me that people are less interested in fine food and a quality of life. It's hard for me to be gracious all the time these days, when I feel we're living in the minority at this point. My most popular dish is beef Wellington. People still prefer the old standards, like steak Diane, fillet with scampi, flounder stuffed with crab. I don't serve prime rib, but I am told that it would be very popular if I did. To make our menu different, we decided to specialize in wild game. Elk comes from New Zealand, kangaroo from Australia, wild boar from Texas, caribou from Alaska. We have venison, pheasant, ostrich and even rattlesnake. My husband comes from Britain but he worked as a chef all over the place, including Germany where they do some pretty crazy things with game. These days with overnight delivery, it is possible to have anything you want.

I can say that taste in wine has definitely improved. People are no longer interested in cocktails like Manhattans and martinis as they once were. Today they would rather have a good bottle of wine and that is encouraging. It is true also that many people want to eat less and keep healthy. But I see them leave the fresh vegetables, but eat the meat and lots of bread, or drink decaf while eating a chocolate dessert.

I am a working woman because I had to be. I love the business, but I certainly would have preferred to raise children. I know that a lot of women chefs have complained about being treated unfairly in the kitchen and about sexual abuse. I don't take any nonsense when working with people, women or men. But men have trouble accepting an independent woman. Men are men and women are women.

Rozanne Gold

JOSEPH BAUM AND MICHAEL WHITEMAN COMPANY

"Chef means chief - extrapolate chief conductor, orchestrator. You take ideas and make them happen. Profitably."

As a child growing up in Queens, New York, Rozanne Gold slept with a cookbook under her pillow, little dreaming at that time that she would eventually preside over some of the most influential kitchens in the city. From organizing cheese and wine parties in her dorm at Boston's Tufts University, she moved to Manhattan to freelance as a chef and caterer. Gold, who graduated with a degree in psychology, admits to "not having a clue what the foodservice industry was all about." But word of her talent spread. Soon she was cooking for some of the city's most distinguished private dining rooms, and at the age of 24 had the distinction of being chosen by the then-mayor of New York City, Ed Koch, as the in-house chef at Gracie Mansion. A year later, she became the youngest executive chef in the country, in charge of Lord & Taylor's thirty-eight restaurants, inventing and launching the popular "demi lunch," amongst other food innovations. Finding her special niche as an advisor to elite establishments came when the renowned restaurateur Joseph Baum and his partner Michael Whiteman sought Gold out as their culinary director, putting her in charge of menu development for a multitude of their gastronomic enterprises, including the famous Rainbow Room at Rockefeller Center and Windows on the World at the World Trade Center.

An international pioneer in the food world, Gold has published two books, James Beard award-winner 'Little Meals', - "bigger than a first course and smaller than a main course," and 'Recipes 1-2-3', which demonstrates how to cook simple, yet delicious meals using only three ingredients. At her office on Fifth Avenue in Manhattan Gold gave some insights into how she maintains her level of innovation.

Rainbow Room

30 Rockefeller Plaza
New York, N.Y. 10020
Phone: 212 632 5000

Windows on the World

1 World Trade Center
New York, N.Y. 10048
Phone: 212 938 1111

FOOD CONSULTING
The Joseph Baum and Michael Whiteman Company
186 Fifth Avenue
New York, N.Y. 10010
Phone: 212 206 7110
Fax: 212 206 7114

Right:

Couscous

Chicken with

Oranges

and Almonds

Below:

Skewered

Swordfish on

Rosemary

Branches

If you want to own a restaurant and be a chef, New York is the worst place to be and the hardest place for a woman to make it. The economics of owning a restaurant are very difficult, and there is a burn-out factor, because of the extraordinary hours and hard work that goes into it. Partly because of these things, there were few women admitted to the Culinary Institute of America twenty years ago. However, the change in attitude toward women has to do with the an amazing change in the food industry. The status of the chef has changed. Food has now been added to the list of cultural things people know and care about. Everyone wants to be knowledgable, whereas thirty years ago nobody cared. Today, for example, our firm is taking over the restaurants at the U.S. Tennis Open Championships.

My path has led to a pretty singular place. I was incredibly fortunate to be in New York and to have the opportunity to work with Joe and Michael. We work in an amazing, creative environment, not by consensus but by osmosis. We have invented many things together, for instance Hudson River cuisine for the Hudson River Club - the idea of having a restaurant with food grown and farmed in New York, including the first New York state wine list.

When I was at Gracie Mansion it was a pivotal time in American cultural growth. I helped to recast the image of American cuisine. Soon after I joined Lord & Taylor, I realized my greatest ability was in menus and concepts and not cooking. My real interest was in the other part that goes into

it, the creativity, the ideas, like the demi lunch and the biscuit sandwich. I am a rainmaker. I make projects happen. I developed Pan-Mediterranean - now known as Med-Rim - cooking for the Cafe Greco in 1986. I invented American Spoon Foods, the first gourmet American foods for retail. The biggest fear you have as a food consultant is that your last idea is your last idea.

In the early days, when I first started my catering business, I was trying to experience working, which was hard to do as a woman. I took to hanging out in restaurants, and working in kitchens (Hoexter's Market, Cafe Tartuffo and Le Plaisir) when I could get the opportunity. Around that time La Colombe D'Or opened. The chef, Kai Hansen, taught me how to candy-peel potatoes, peel onions, pull the genitals off crabs, and make sauces. Everyone thought I was crazy, but it was the only way to learn. That and traveling. I was extremely impressed by one trip to Northern Italy. I read Elizabeth David and I read Julia Child, although I've more often been influenced by men than women, because it is still a business dominated by men at the front and back of the house. I have been aware of being a woman pioneer, and I have liked that. But I haven't thought of myself as a champion for women. Generally, women in the food service industry are never compensated appropriately. A restaurant owner I worked for early on once complained to me: "No one likes to be psychically indebted." I replied: "If you paid me enough you wouldn't feel like that."

Left from top to bottom:

Scallops Provencale on Olive Toast

Tabouli Salad with Melted Feta

Orecchiette with Chickpeas and Cracked Pepper

Breadspreads: Eggplant and Sundried Tomato, White Bean and Rosemary, Red Pepper Pesto

Below: Seared Salmon on Moroccan Salad

Aliza Green

ALIZA GREEN FOOD CONSULTING

*"To get from good to excellent is
a small step, but it's the point,
and you must get there often,
not just once in a while."*

Aliza Green cooked her way to the top in Philadelphia's culinary world, never having had any formal training aside from visiting Marcella Hazan's hand-rolled pastas and had radicchio flown in from Italy, or smuggled seeds in from Europe if a vegetable or herb wasn't available. After six years (and a four-star rating), Green moved to Apropos in downtown Philadelphia,

Aliza Green Food Consulting

1114 Prospect Avenue
Elkins Park, PA 19027
Phone: 215 635 0651
Fax: 215 635 3894

Left:
Iced Cucumber-
Buttermilk Soup
with Dill

cooking school in Italy, while she did stints at two Bolognese restaurants. Her career is a true case history of patience, persistence and determination. Eventually, after Green moved through several kitchens in Philadelphia, her skill and knowledge of Italian cuisine got her a job as chef at Ristorante DiLullo in Fox Chase. Green proceeded to introduce a new level of gastronomic excellence at a time when arugula, balsamic vinegar, biscotti, cappuccino, gelato and tiramisu were as yet unheard of in the United States. She demanded fresh ingredients, made

establishing what she calls American bistro cuisine with a Mediterranean rustic menu and a wood-burning oven. In her three years there, she trained chefs who were later to become Philadelphia stars and still refer to their halcyon days in Green's kitchen as Camelot. Named in the Philadelphia Inquirer's Hall of Fame as one of the city's ten most influential people in food, Green is a founding member of the local chapter of Les Dames d'Escoffier. In 1988, she made a transition into food consulting, helping restaurants improve their menus and recipes, writing a weekly food column for the Daily News, and working as a food stylist for television and magazines; the kind of life that works when you are married with children. She talked about her experiences over a breakfast omelette at the Four Seasons Hotel in Philadelphia.

Above:
Broiled
Scallops
over
Linguine
with Cherry
Tomatoes
and Basil

I have cooked as far back as I can remember. I was cooking, reading and traveling as a child of the '60s, trying to find a direction that would suit me. I dropped out of college as an honors student with a 4.0 grade average after two years of studying literature, to start my own catering business. To my family that was terrible. I was expected to go to school, get a doctorate, be a professor and teach. I never went to culinary school because there was no place that I wanted to go. At the time I started, institutional cooking was not on a high level. Most of it was very bad, and alot of cooking was straight out of the box. The culinary institutes were trade schools preparing people for management more than anything else.

It took me two years to find a restaurant job, because there were no female chefs in those days. I would walk into a French restaurant and the French chefs would laugh at me. I have always been a ground-breaker, and it has never been easy. One thing has always been important to me - that is culinary integrity. Doing things the hard way. Taking the time to clean fresh squid and cut it up - not bringing it in rings out of the freezer and into the fire. Working in Bologna gave me a benchmark of what cooking is supposed to be. In five years at DiLullo's I only had one day off, but I loved

Right:
Nantucket
Smoked
Bluefish Paté
on Rosemary
Crostini

cooking the food and was completely immersed. Altogether I worked as a chef ten years in a row, six days a week, and it was what I wanted to do. It built stamina and self-confidence. You have to prove yourself all the time to gain respect. The restaurant business is a rough business, and the hardest thing for women is the managerial thing: how are you going to get the respect from everybody. But I learned that if you spend a lot of time on endurance, you are not going to develop in a creative way. Balance is the real key.

Women are not into architectural displays of food. They think. Is it delicious? Is it simple? What does it taste like? I love working with vegetables, fruits and grains. Sometimes it's richer to have a wonderful dish of pasta made right, with mushrooms, than fancy food. To get from good to excellent is a small step, but it's the point. You must have that edge. And you must get there often, not just once in a while.

Josefina Howard

ROSA MEXICANO

"Cooking, studying and researching food you learn a lot about human behavior."

Since she opened her Manhattan restaurant in 1984, chef-owner Josefina Howard has banished the notion that Mexican food is not up to the standards of the world's other great cuisines in its approach to variety, flavors and ingredients. Real Mexican food is more than an Americanized taco, tamale, burrito or enchilada. With a repertoire of 2,500 regional dishes, Howard's versatility, coupled with an ebullient personality has made Rosa Mexicano the mecca for pomegranate margaritas, sangritas (the tequila chaser), velvety guacamole made at the table with hot peppers and cilantro, huitlacoche soup made from a Mexican fungus, creme caramel with cactus sauce and much, much more, served in the carefree atmosphere of a rose-pink, tiled hacienda.

Born in Cuba, Howard spent her childhood learning how to cook in her grandmother's manor house in the Asturias region of Spain. At the time of the Spanish civil war, her family moved to New York and Howard took courses in several different cuisines, while pursuing a career as an interior decorator. In 1956, she married an American and went to live in Mexico where she remained for twenty years, continuing to work as a decorator but learning to cook classic Mexican dishes for her family at home.

When she returned to New York, Howard gave up selecting chandeliers, mirrors, furnishing fabrics and paint

Rosa Mexicano

finishes for her interior design clients in favor of introducing New Yorkers to the real Mexican food she had learned to love. Since the day its doors opened, Rosa Mexicano has been chosen consistently by food critics as the faithful example of authentic Mexican cuisine in New York. And Howard frequently demonstrates her methods in cooking schools and department stores across the country. The patrona talked one evening at her special table, over a banquet of her colorful signature dishes.

1063 First Avenue
New York, N.Y. 10022
Phone 212 753 7407
Fax 212 753 7433

Above:
Chocolate
Mousse Cake
Accented
with Chile

I have lived many, many lives and all my life I have been in love with cooking. I was six years old when I first started cooking with my grandmother. Our family always entertained a lot. My grandmother was passionate about food. She taught me that there were two ways of cooking: in the grand manner and in the bohemian manner. I know both sides and I enjoy both.

The secret of my success is that I used to entertain a lot at my ranch outside Mexico City. Cooking for two hundred people every night in the restaurant is not that much different. I found I could follow the same routine. The system I have for cooking is a little different from other chefs. I come out in Geoffrey Beene clothes! But first I make the menu I want, and then I get the chef who works with me to cook the dishes. We work side by side, tasting as we go along.

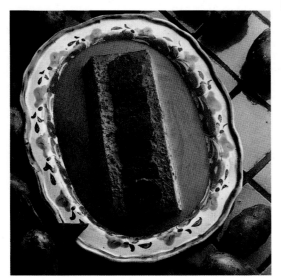

It has to taste a certain way all the time, consistency is important. After eighteen years together, he knows my palette. The next day he cooks by himself, and then he has it pretty well down. And then he teaches it to the others in the kitchen.

I don't like formality. I like customers to have a good time, enjoy food comfortably, and be able to ask a question about the menu without getting an attitude. I make sure that the kitchen staff do their thing with me out front. The restaurant is my house. I make my staff feel that this is their house, too. I train them as if they were having a party at home. You prepare the food, you clean, you set the table, you bathe, you dress, and on top of all that, you get paid, too! I tell them they are equal to the customers. I do anything to have a happy crew. This is one restaurant where no one steals anything. They are happy to come here. The most important thing is to have a happy crew.

Opposite Left:
Layered
Tortilla Pie
with a
Poblano Chile
Sauce

Opposite Far Left:
Flan
with Cactus
Pear Sauce

If I could paint, I would paint pictures of Mexico; if I could write, I would write about Mexico; if I could sing, I would sing Mexican songs. My only tool is tell people about that wonderful country through its cuisine, which is varied and has such a wide range of flavors and colors. Most ingredients are available in the United States, and you must have very good ingredients - the best you can buy. I have traveled all over the world, and I love fine French food, but I say to this day that Mexican food is second only to Chinese in variety, textures and combinations.

I'm a Virgo and people say I'm a perfectionist. I really don't know if I am or not. What is a perfectionist? If I ever had to live all over again, I would probably be an anthropologist. By cooking, studying, and researching food you learn a lot about human behavior.

Above:
Grilled Scallops
with a
Huitlacoche
Sauce

Left:
Guacamole
En
Molcajete

Recipes

RENEE FOOTE

DIANE FORLEY GALE GAND

MONIQUE BEVERLY GANNON
GAUMONT
LANVIN ROZANNE
GOLD

ALIZA GREEN

JOSEFINA HOWARD

Asian Fusion Feast

Hot and Sour Broth

Barbecued Duck

Chocolate Sushi

HOT AND SOUR BROTH

Yield: 8 to 10 servings

THE BROTH:

1 tablespoon vegetable oil

2 red onions, peeled and chopped

2 carrots, coarsely chopped

2 stalks celery, coarsely chopped

2 lime leaves

½ bunch coriander, chopped

1 to 2 Thai chilies, according to taste

1 stalk lemongrass

1 1-inch piece of galangal, chopped

1 1-inch piece ginger, chopped

10 cups chicken stock

1½ cans coconut milk, 30 ounces

*3 tablespoons tamarind paste,
dissolved in water*

*1. In a large stock pot, put oil, onions,
carrots, celery, lime leaves, coriander,
chilies, lemongrass, galangal, and ginger.
On medium heat, sauté until caramelized,
about 15 minutes.*

*2. Add chicken stock to pot and stir to
combine. Bring to a boil, uncovered.
Lower heat and cook until stock has been
reduce by one-third.*

*3. Add tamarind paste and coconut milk
to pot and bring back to a boil.*

*4. With a medium mesh strainer over
another pot, strain soup.*

5. Ladle soup into bowls and serve.

BARBECUED DUCK

Yield: 3 to 4 servings

1 whole duck, Muscovy or Brome Lake

3 pieces lemongrass, coarsely chopped

1 bunch of coriander, stems only

4 pieces star anise, broken

2 to 3 cloves garlic, coarsely chopped

½-inch piece ginger, coarsely chopped

3 ½ tablespoons 5-spice powder

8 tablespoons oyster sauce

4 tablespoons soy sauce

*1. Wash duck and pat dry. Stuff duck
cavity with lemongrass, coriander, anise,
garlic, and ginger.*

*2. With a sharp knife, score entire surface
of duck. Rub 5-spice powder into flesh.*

*3. In a shallow pan, put 6 tablespoons
oyster sauce and 2 tablespoons soy sauce
and mix together. Place duck in pan,
breast side down. Using a spoon, tip pan
and drizzle oyster sauce mixture over
duck. Marinate, uncovered, in refrigerator
for 8 hours. Turn duck over after 4 hours
and again spoon marinade over duck.*

Preheat oven to 400 degrees.

*1. In a small bowl, mix together 2 table-
spoons each of oyster sauce and soy sauce.*

*2. Place marinated duck in a shallow
roasting pan with a rack and put in oven.
Pour marinade into a small bowl and
reserve. Using a baster or brush, baste
with reserved marinade.*

*3. After 20 minutes, lower heat to 350
degrees and continue cooking until duck
juices run clear, about 1½ hours.*

*4. Remove duck from oven. Let rest before
carving, about 10 minutes.*

Note: Serving suggestion– rice and stir fried vegetables

CHOCOLATE SUSHI

Yield: 6 rolls

THE CHOCOLATE MOUSSE:

4½ ounces chocolate

4 ounces butter, melted

1½ tablespoons brandy

2 teaspoons brewed espresso/instant coffee

⅓ cup sugar

3 egg yolks

½ cup heavy cream, whipped

1. *Using a double boiler, melt chocolate. Remove top from double boiler and let chocolate cool at room temperature.*

2. *In a small bowl, put butter and stir in brandy and coffee.*

3. *In a large bowl, put egg yolks and sugar, and whisk together. Fold in chocolate, working quickly. Add the warm butter mixture.*

4. *Let chocolate mixture cool. (If refrigerated, don't allow mixture to set.)*

5. *Fold in whipped cream until well combined and there are no streaks. Set aside.*

CHOCOLATE BUTTERMILK CAKE:

1 cup brown sugar

1 scant cup all-purpose flour, plus extra

⅓ cup cocoa

1 teaspoon baking soda

½ teaspoon baking powder

Butter

½ cup buttermilk

½ cup strong brewed coffee

4 tablespoons vegetable oil

1 egg

Preheat oven to 350 degrees.

1. *In a processor, combine the sugar, flour, cocoa, baking soda, and baking powder.*

2. *In a bowl, whisk together the buttermilk, coffee, oil, and egg.*

3. *With processor running, add buttermilk mixture. Combine until a dough forms.*

4. *Using a cookie sheet, butter and flour the surface.*

5. *Spread batter over the baking sheet, making a thin layer 12x8 inches.*

6. *Bake until a knife inserted in the cake comes out clean, about 10 minutes. Remove from oven.*

7. *Cut into 3x12 inch strips and set aside.*

THE CHOCOLATE PLASTIC:

8 ounces semisweet chocolate

⅓ cup corn syrup

1. *Over a bain marie, melt chocolate. Let melt until tepid when tested on lip.*

2. *Add corn syrup all at once and stir with spatula until chocolate mixture is no longer glossy, about 4 to 5 minutes.*

3. *Wrap in plastic wrap and let sit until firm, in refrigerator if necessary.*

Renee Foote

MERCER STREET GRILL

THE COFFEE SYRUP:

1 cup sugar

½ cup water

¼ cup instant coffee

1 tablespoon brandy

1. *In a saucepan over a high flame, covered, heat sugar, water, and coffee. Boil for 2 minutes.*

2. *Remove from heat, let cool. Add brandy.*

THE FILLING:

1 pint raspberries

THE COATING:

2 cups pistachios, ground coarsely

To assemble:

1. *Line 2 baking sheets with parchment. Cut 6 pieces of parchment at least 8x14 inches and lay out on work surface.*

2. *Using a pasta machine, roll out firm chocolate plastic first on 1, then 3, and then 5, until the chocolate is almost as thin as paper. The resulting strip of chocolate should be about 4x12 inches. Place on a piece of parchment. Prepare 6 strips.*

3. *Using a spatula, place a strip of cake on each strip of chocolate, leaving equal margins. Brush lightly with coffee syrup.*

8. *Spread a thin layer of mousse on the cake, leaving a ½-inch clean border on all sides.*

4. *Down the center of the mousse, place a row of raspberries.*

5. *Using the parchment to assist in rolling the layers, pick up the side of the paper closest to you, and roll until the 2 chocolate edges meet, forming a cylinder. Squeeze slightly as you roll.*

6. *At the seam where the chocolate meets, brush on a little mousse to bind the seam.*

7. *Brush outside of roll with coffee syrup.*

8. *Put pistachios on a tray and roll chocolate sushi in nuts.*

9. *Trim edges of roll and slice in 1¼-inch pieces to serve.*

Provencale Dinner

Layered Salad of Sliced Tomatoes, Arugula and Tapenade Toast

Toasted Angel Hair Pasta with Mushroom Broth

Poached Halibut in Lemon Nage

Crème Brulée infused with Verbena Leaves

LAYERED SALAD OF SLICED TOMATOES, ARUGULA, AND TAPENADE TOAST

Yield: 5 servings

4 beefsteak tomatoes, sliced

2 shallots, finely sliced

Salt and freshly ground pepper

1 recipe Tapenade Vinaigrette

8 pieces thinly sliced peasant bread, lightly toasted

2 bunches arugula, cleaned

1. In a shallow medium-size casserole pan, place a layer of tomato slices and sprinkle with shallots, salt, and pepper. Brush with Tapenade Vinaigrette. Repeat until all tomatoes are layered and seasoned. Let marinate refrigerated 2 hours or overnight.

2. Strain marinated tomatoes. Reserve juices.

3. Dip each bread slice in the tomato juice and soak for about 10 seconds. Set aside.

4. Dress arugula with remaining vinaigrette.

TAPENADE VINAIGRETTE

Yield: about 1 cup

3 anchovies

2 shallots, minced

1 clove garlic, minced

¼ cup sherry vinegar

10 black olives, pitted

10 capers

½ cup olive oil

Salt and freshly ground pepper

1. To remove excess salt from anchovies, rinse anchovies in water, and if oil-packed, drain oil. Set aside.

2. In a small saucepan, put shallots, garlic and vinegar and cook over low heat, covered, until softened about 15 minutes.

3. Strain shallots and garlic, reserving vinegar liquid.

4. In a food processor or blender, put shallots, garlic, olives, capers, and anchovies. Process until smooth. Emulsify mixture, by adding olive oil in a slow and steady stream while continuing to purée.

5. Transfer mixture to a small bowl and whisk in reserved vinegar. Season with salt and pepper.

To assemble salad:

1. Put a slice of soaked bread on salad plate. Place 2 slices of tomato, topped with a few arugula leaves, repeat a layer of tomato and a layer of arugula. Serve.

TOASTED ANGEL HAIR PASTA WITH MUSHROOM BROTH

Yield: 4 to 6 servings

THE MUSHROOM BROTH:

2 cups white button mushrooms

4 shallots, peeled

1 sprig fresh thyme (4 inches)

½ head garlic

¼ cup olive oil

Salt and freshly ground pepper

3 cups water

THE PASTA:

1 pound dry angel hair pasta

2 tablespoons olive oil, plus additional

¼ cup sliced shallots

1 clove garlic, minced

1 cup fresh sliced oyster mushrooms

¼ cup parsley leaves

1 tablespoon chopped chives

Preheat oven to 375 degrees.

THE MUSHROOM BROTH:

1. On a baking sheet, place mushrooms, shallots, and thyme. Cut garlic in half around the diameter and add to vegetables. Sprinkle vegetables with ¼ cup olive oil, salt, and pepper. Roast about 45 minutes to 1 hour or until juices run out of the vegetables and mushrooms are well caramelized. Stir occasionally.

2. In a saucepan, put roasted vegetables and water. Bring to a boil, uncovered, and simmer until liquid is reduced by half, about 20 minutes. Strain and set liquid aside. Discard vegetables.

THE PASTA:

1. While mushrooms are baking, toss pasta with a little oil to coat.

2. Place on a baking sheet, spreading the pasta out as evenly as possible. Bake in oven until golden, about 8 to 10 minutes, turning the pan halfway through baking. Remove from oven and set aside.

3. Heat 2 tablespoons olive oil in sauce pot. Add shallots and garlic. Cook, uncovered, until shallots are translucent. Add oyster mushrooms and continue to cook, uncovered, until juices are released, 5 minutes.

4. Add mushroom broth and pasta. Cook pasta al dente, about 7 to 8 minutes, until the broth is absorbed by the pasta. If needed, add additional water.

5. Add parsley and chives to the pasta and toss. Serve immediately.

POACHED HALIBUT IN LEMON NAGE WITH YUKON GOLD POTATOES AND SOUP VEGETABLES

Yield: 6 servings

THE NAGE, OR BROTH:

Cooking oil

5 medium-size onions, sliced

1 fennel bulb, sliced

5 stalks celery, sliced

1 bay leaf

2 tablespoons fresh coriander

½ tablespoon white peppercorns

1 bottle white wine

3 quarts water

1 cup champagne vinegar

1 bunch fresh tarragon, whole

Soup vegetables: julienne of celery, carrot, fennel, and cooked beans (see Note)

6 Yukon Gold potatoes, sliced

6 6-ounce halibut filets

Salt and freshly ground black pepper

1. To make the nage, coat the bottom of a saute pan with oil and put onion, fennel, and celery, cover and cook over low heat without letting these brown, about 20 minutes.

2. Add bay leaf, coriander, peppercorns, and wine and simmer, covered, 2 minutes.

3. Add water and vinegar, and simmer, covered, for 20 minutes.

4. Remove from heat and add tarragon. Cover and allow tarragon to infuse for 20 minutes.

5. Strain nage set aside. Discard vegetables

6. In a pot, put soup vegetables. Bring to a boil and simmer 5 to 10 minutes until vegetables are soft. Follow same procedure for potatoes and cook 15 to 20 minutes. Set aside.

7. Pour the nage into a shallow casserole. Season halibut with salt and pepper, and put into nage. Cover casserole and poach fish gently until fully cooked, about 5 to 10 minutes. Using a spatula, carefully remove fish and place on a platter or individual serving plates.

8. Put soup vegetables and potato in nage to warm through, about 5 minutes. Distribute sliced vegetables over the halibut. Serve hot.

Note: The soup vegetables can be chosen according to taste and seasonal availability.

Diane Forley

V E R B E N A

CRÉME BRULÉE INFUSED WITH VERBENA LEAVES

Yield: 6 to 8 servings

3 cups cream

1 cup milk

¼ cup fresh verbena leaves (see Note)

¼ vanilla bean, split down center

1 cup sugar, plus additional for sprinkling

9 egg yolks

1. In a heavy bottomed pot, put cream, milk, and verbena leaves. Warm over low heat for 5 minutes. Turn off heat, cover and let sit to infuse flavor, about 20 minutes. Using a slotted spoon, remove verbena, and discard.

2. Scrape vanilla bean into milk mixture, and let steep on low heat. Add ½ cup sugar and bring to just under a boil.

3. In a bowl, whisk together egg yolks and remaining ½ cup sugar. Add warm cream mixture, whisking constantly.

4. Put cream and yolk mixture back in pot, and cook over medium heat until thickened, stirring constantly with a wooden spoon.

Preheat oven to 300 degrees.

5. To cool the cream mixture, prepare an ice bath with a bowl in the center. Strain cream mixture into bowl and let rest about ½ hour.

6. In a pan of hot water, place a baking dish and pour cream mixture into dish. Cover dish with foil, and bake for 1 hour. Remove from oven and cool.

7. When cool, sprinkle custard with sugar and place under broiler until sugar is lightly caramelized, about 30 seconds, and serve.

Note: Verbena, also known as lemon verbena or vervain, is an annual and medicinal herb, used as a tonic to stimulate appetite and aid digestion. Verbena can easily be grown from seed and the plant is sold at nurseries. Dried verbena may also be found in health food stores.

Dessert Buffet

Chocolate Sour Cream Marble Cake

Chocolate Almond Biscotti

Poppyseed Shortbread Cookies

Sticky Toffee Pudding

Blueberry Bread & Butter Pudding

CHOCOLATE SOUR CREAM MARBLE CAKE

Yield: 6 servings

1 stick butter

1¼ cups sugar

2 eggs, separated

1 ¼ cups all-purpose flour

2 teaspoons baking powder

½ cup sour cream

2 tablespoons half-and-half

¼ cup cocoa powder

¼ cup brewed coffee

1 pinch baking soda

Preheat oven to 350 degrees.

1. Using a mixer or processor, cream the butter and 1 cup sugar until fluffy. Add yolks, incorporating well.

2. Sift together flour and baking powder.

3. On low speed, slowly add flour mixture to butter and sugar, alternating flour with sour cream and half-and-half.

4. In a separate bowl, whip egg whites until stiff. Gradually add ¼ cup sugar and whip until glossy. Fold beaten egg whites into batter.

5. Stir together cocoa, coffee, and baking soda. Put ⅓ of batter into a small bowl and stir in cocoa mixture.

6. Using nonstick mini bundt pans, drop 2 spoonfuls of plain batter to every 1 of chocolate into the pans. Bake until firm to touch, 35 to 40 minutes. Let cakes cool in pan and turn each out onto dessert plate. Serve with warm chocolate sauce and banana-walnut ice cream.

CHOCOLATE ALMOND BISCOTTI

Yield: 24 biscotti

1¾ cups flour

1 cup sugar

⅓ cup cocoa powder

1 teaspoon baking soda

¼ teaspoon salt

3 eggs, plus 2 egg whites

¾ teaspoon vanilla extract

⅔ cup whole almonds, toasted

⅓ cup chocolate chips

Preheat oven to 350 degrees.

1. In a mixer with a paddle attachment, combine the flour, sugar, cocoa powder, baking soda, and salt.

2. In a small bowl, whisk 2 whole eggs, 2 egg whites, and vanilla extract. Slowly add egg mixture to flour mixture, blending on low.

3. Add almonds and chocolate chips to flour mixture, blending just until combined.

4. Beat remaining egg in a small bowl. On a floured surface, roll dough into 2 logs, 2 inches in diameter. Place on a greased sheet pan and brush with beaten egg. Bake until top starts to brown, about 30 minutes.

5. Allow logs to cool 15 minutes. Cut logs into ½-inch slices on the bias. Place slices on a greased cookie sheet and bake until toasted, about 15 to 20 minutes.

POPPYSEED SHORTBREAD COOKIES

Yield: 50 cookies

4 sticks butter

2 cups sugar, plus extra for sprinkling

5 cups all-purpose flour

¼ cup poppyseeds

Preheat oven to 350 degrees.

1. Using a mixer or processor, cream the butter with 2 cups sugar until light and fluffy. Add flour and mix until just incorporated.

2. Form dough into a mound, wrap in plastic film or waxed paper, and chill. Line a cookie sheet with parchment paper. On a floured surface, partially roll out dough. Place dough on cookie sheet and finish rolling out the dough to a ¼-inch thickness. Prick the dough with a fork and sprinkle with sugar.

3. Bake for 20 to 30 minutes, rotating the cookie sheet a half turn and knocking down any air bubbles in the dough after about 10 to 15 minutes.

4. Sprinkle the dough again as it comes out of the oven and cut immediately into bars. Allow the cookies to cool.

STICKY TOFFEE PUDDING

Yield: 9 generous servings

THE PUDDING:

1 cup dates, chopped

2 ½ cups water

2 teaspoons baking soda

1 stick pound butter

1 ½ cups white sugar

4 eggs

2 teaspoons vanilla extract

4 cups all-purpose flour, sifted

2 teaspoons baking powder

THE SAUCE:

2 ½ cups brown sugar, loosely packed

½ pound butter, plus 1 tablespoon butter

1 cup half-and-half

1 teaspoon vanilla brandy

THE PUDDING:

Preheat a convection oven to 300 degrees, or a standard oven to 325 degrees.

1. Put dates in a pot with water and bring to a boil, uncovered. Stir in baking soda and set aside.

2. Using a mixer or processor, cream the butter and add sugar, beating until well mixed. Continue beating and add eggs, mixing until fluffy. Add the vanilla. To this, mix in flour and baking powder alternating with dates and cooking liquid.

3. Line a medium-size baking pan with parchment paper, and pour in the mixture.

4. Bake until firm, about 40 minutes. Remove from the oven and cool the pudding in the pan, about 1 hour. Put cooled pudding in refrigerator to chill, at least 1 hour.

THE SAUCE:

1. Put the sugar, butter, half-and-half, and vanilla brandy in a medium-size pot and boil 3 minutes.

To serve:

1. Turn pudding out of the pan onto a flat platter or board and cut into triangles. Place a triangle on a serving plate and cover with sauce.

2. Heat in microwave for 1 minute to warm.

Gale Gand

B R A S S E R I E   T

BLUEBERRY BREAD & BUTTER PUDDING

Yield: 6 servings

1 loaf brioche, or 4 - 5 individual brioche

2 cups half-and-half

2 cups heavy cream

1 pinch salt

1 vanilla bean, split

6 eggs

1 cup sugar

1 pint blueberries

Powdered sugar

Preheat oven to 350 degrees.

1. Cut the the crust from the brioche and cut brioche into cubes. Toast cubes in oven until golden brown.

2. In a saucepan, heat the half-and-half, cream, salt, and vanilla bean just until boiling, uncovered. Turn off heat to allow vanilla to infuse and then remove.

3. In a stainless steel bowl, whisk together the eggs and sugar. Slowly add hot cream mixture, whisking constantly to make a custard. Strain mixture through a fine sieve and set aside.

4. Toss the brioche cubes with the custard and let soak, about 4 minutes.

5. Sprinkle berries into the bottom of 6 individual baking dishes. Divide soaked brioche among these and top with any remaining custard.

6. Place dishes in a pan of hot water and bake until set and golden brown, about 45 minutes. Remove from the oven and sprinkle puddings with powdered sugar.

Pacific Island Celebration

Duck Spring Rolls with Pineapple Citrus Sauce and Sweet Thai Chili Sauce

Island Seafood Paella

Island Strawberry Shortcake*

Serving suggestion

DUCK SPRING ROLLS

Yield: 14 spring rolls

1 duck, roasted and meat shredded

1 cup shredded green cabbage

½ cup shredded carrot

2 green onions, finely chopped

2 cloves garlic, finely chopped

2 tablespoons finely chopped cilantro

1 tablespoon toasted sesame seeds

1½ teaspoons grated fresh ginger

1½ teaspoons dark sesame oil

1½ teaspoons oyster sauce

1 teaspoon Chinese chili sauce

14 7½-inch square spring roll wrappers

1 tablespoon corn starch

4 tablespoons water

3 cups peanut oil

1. In a large bowl put duck, cabbage, carrot, green onion, garlic, cilantro, sesame seed, and ginger. Toss to combine.

2. In a small bowl put sesame oil, oyster and chili sauces. Mix and add to the duck mixture, combining well.

3. Lay a spring roll wrapper on work surface, with a corner pointing towards you. Place 3 tablespoons of filling across wrapper from one corner to the other.

4. Fold the near corner of the wrapper over the filling. When half rolled, fold in side corners to make an envelope, and continue rolling.

5. In a small bowl, whisk together corn-starch and water.

6. Using a pastry brush, seal edges of wrapper with cornstarch mixture. Set aside. Repeat procedure until all filling has been used.

7. In a heavy skillet, heat peanut oil until bubbles form around a wooden spoon inserted in oil. Gently lower spring rolls into the oil, and cook until crispy and brown, about 3 minutes. Turn to brown all sides.

8. Cover a plate with paper towels to absorb oil. With a slotted spoon, remove rolls, and place on plate. Repeat proce-dure until all spring rolls are cooked.

9. Place several rolls on each serving plate, accompanied by the Pineapple Citrus Sauce and the Sweet Thai Chili Sauce. Serve.

PINEAPPLE CITRUS SAUCE

Yield: 4 cups

2 navel oranges

1 grapefruit

1 cup fresh pineapple, diced

½ medium-size red onion, thinly sliced

½ bunch chopped cilantro, leaves only

½ jalapeño pepper, peeled, seeded and chopped

½ red bell pepper, chopped

1½ teaspoons vinegar

1½ teaspoons sugar

1. Using a knife cut off orange and grapefruit skins just underneath the pith (white part). Using a sharp paring knife over a bowl, slide blade on either side of membrane, removing the fruit sections, and letting the pulp and juice drop into the bowl.

2. Add the pineapple, onion, cilantro, jalapeño and bell peppers, vinegar, and sugar. Mix together.

SWEET THAI CHILI SAUCE

Yield: 1 cup

6 ounces rice vinegar

¾ cup sugar

¼ red pepper, finely diced

3 tablespoons red onion, diced

2 tablespoons chopped cilantro or mint

1 tablespoon grated fresh ginger

1 ½ teaspoons garlic chili sauce

1. In a small saucepan put vinegar and sugar. On medium-high heat, reduce until mixture becomes syrupy, about 10 to 12 minutes.

2. Remove pot from heat, and add pepper, onion, cilantro, ginger and chili sauce. Stir well.

ISLAND SEAFOOD PAELLA

Yield: 12 servings

THE SEAFOOD:

1¼ cups olive oil, plus extra

1 teaspoon grated lemon zest

1 tablespoon fresh lemon juice

1 tablespoon chopped cilantro

3 pounds firm white fish such as sword-fish, opah or mahi mahi, bone and skin removed and cut into bite-size pieces

2 pounds spiny lobster, tail meat only, cut into ½-inch slices

2 cloves garlic, minced

1 tablespoon Chinese chili paste

12 Molokai prawns, shells removed

1 quart fish stock

1 pound calamari tubes, cleaned and cut into ½-inch rings

THE RICE:

3 tablespoons olive oil

1 yellow bell pepper, finely sliced

½ red bell pepper, finely sliced

½ large Maui onion, finely chopped

3 cloves garlic, minced

2 cups long grain rice

3 ripe tomatoes, peeled, seeded and chopped

1 quart fish stock

2 stalks lemon grass, smashed

To assemble:

2 cups canned artichoke hearts (fresh or frozen)

1 cup sugar snap peas

1 cup chopped cilantro

THE SEAFOOD:

1. In a small bowl put ½ cup olive oil, lemon zest and juice, and cilantro. Mix together. Divide equally into two bowls.

2. Add fish to one bowl and lobster to the other. Stir each bowl, cover, and marinate 2 hours, refrigerated.

3. In another bowl put ½ cup olive oil, garlic, chili paste, and prawns. Mix together, cover, and marinate 2 hours, refrigerated.

4. In a medium-size pot on high heat, bring fish stock to a boil, covered.

5. Add calamari to pot and simmer until tender, about 3 to 5 minutes. Using a cheese cloth-lined sieve over a bowl, drain calamari. Set calamari aside.

Beverly Gannon

HALIIMAILE GENERAL STORE

6. Using paper towels, dry white fish.

7. In a sauté pan, on high heat, heat ¼ cup oil until very hot. Add white fish and brown on all sides, about 5 to 7 minutes. With a slotted spoon, remove white fish to warm platter and set aside.

8. Drain lobster. Add more oil to sauté pan if necessary, and sauté until lobster starts to turn opaque, about 3 minutes. Remove to platter with white fish and set aside.

9. Drain prawns, and sauté until prawns just start to turn pink, about 3 minutes.

THE RICE:

1. In a heavy skillet heat olive oil, and add yellow and red pepper, onion, and garlic. Cook on low heat until onions are soft and lightly browned, about 10 to 15 minutes.

2. Stir in rice and cook until translucent, about 10 minutes.

3. Add tomatoes and cook, stirring constantly, until juice evaporates, about 3 minutes.

4. Add fish stock and lemongrass. Bring to a boil and cook uncovered, until stock is absorbed, about 10 minutes. Stir occasionally.

Preheat oven to 350 degrees.

To assemble:

1. In a baking pan put half of the cooked rice and add all of the white fish and half of the lobster, and ½ cup each artichoke and peas. Add remaining rice and top with remaining lobster and all of the prawns. Make a final layer of calamari rings, remaining artichoke, and peas.

2. Cover, put pan in oven and warm until heated thoroughly, about 30 minutes.

3. Remove from oven and spoon out onto a serving platter. Garnish with cilantro. Serve immediately.

Game Dinner

Three Onion Soup
with Tawny Port

Wyoming Buffalo
in an Orange
Curry Ragout

Colorado Elk Loin
in Swedish
Lingonberry and
Cassis Sauce

Fruit Tarts

THREE ONION SOUP WITH TAWNY PORT
Yield: 10 to 12 servings

2 Spanish onions, sliced

2 red onions, sliced

2 Vidalia onions, sliced

¼ cup olive oil

1 cup good quality tawny port

1 quart chicken stock

1 cup heavy cream

Salt and freshly ground pepper

1. In a large pot, sauté Spanish, red, and Vidalia onions in olive oil on medium-low heat until caramelized, about 20 to 25 minutes.

2. Deglaze pot with half of the tawny port. Add chicken stock, and covered, simmer 30 to 40 minutes.

3. In a food processor, purée onion mixture. Pour through a fine mesh strainer.

4. Return puréed and strained soup to the pot and simmer. Add remainder of the tawny port, and the heavy cream. Bring to a simmer again, add salt and pepper to taste, and serve.

WYOMING BUFFALO IN AN ORANGE CURRY RAGOUT
Yield: 6 to 8 servings

2¼ pounds buffalo, cut into chunks for stewing

Salt and freshly ground pepper

6 tablespoons curry powder

⅓ cup olive oil

1 Spanish onion, diced

1 cup thawed orange juice concentrate

1 quart brown stock

4 or 5 fresh tomatoes, coarsely chopped (about 1 pound)

Zest from one orange

1 pound Kennett Square mushrooms, or shiitake, sliced (see Note)

1. Season the buffalo meat with salt and pepper, and 3 tablespoons curry powder.

2. In a Dutch oven or enamel casserole with a tight-fitting lid, add oil. Heat until oil just begins to smoke. Add several chunks of meat and sear on all sides. Transfer meat to a bowl. Repeat process until all meat is seared.

3. In the same pot, sauté onion briefly, 3 to 4 minutes.

4. Deglaze pan with orange juice and brown stock. Add the remainder of the curry powder, tomatoes, zest, and seared meat. Bring to a simmer. Continue to simmer, uncovered, until meat is almost fork tender, about 1½ hours, stirring occasionally.

5. Add mushrooms and cook uncovered another 15 minutes, until meat is completely tender when pierced with a fork.

Note: Kennett Square mushrooms are local to Philadelphia.

COLORADO ELK LOIN IN SWEDISH LINGONBERRY AND CASSIS SAUCE
Yield: 6 servings

THE ELK AND VEAL STOCK:

2 pounds elk bones

2 pounds veal bones

2 carrots, chopped

2 onions, chopped

2 celery stalks, chopped

3 sprigs fresh thyme

2 bay leaves

1 celery heart

1 leek, outer leaves

THE SAUCE:

1 pint elk and veal stock

1 cup cassis

¼ cup lingonberries

1 cup cassis

THE ELK:

2 pounds elk loin

Salt and freshly ground pepper

Olive oil

Preheat oven to 425 degrees.

THE ELK AND VEAL STOCK:

1. Place elk and veal bones on a baking sheet and roast until deep caramel color, about 20 to 25 minutes. Turn bones periodically for even browning.

2. In a large soup pot filled with 3 quarts of cold water put roasted bones. Bring to a slow simmer and cook uncovered for 4 hours.

3. Add carrots, onions, celery, thyme, bay leaves, celery heart, and leek. Cook for an additional 30 minutes.

4. Using a fine mesh strainer, strain elk and veal stock into a clean pot.

THE SAUCE:

1. To the elk and veal stock, add cassis. On medium heat, uncovered, reduce stock to about 2 cups.

2. Add lingonberries. Simmer for 2 minutes. Sauce should coat the back of a spoon.

Preheat oven to 425 degrees.

THE ELK:

1. Season elk with salt and pepper. Coat a skillet with olive oil. Place over high heat and when oil just begins to smoke, add elk and sear on all sides until browned.

2. Transfer elk to a roasting tray and finish cooking meat to medium or medium-rare, about 20 minutes.

3. Slice elk and divide into 6 portions. Serve.

FRUIT TART

Yield: 6 to 8 servings

THE CRUST:

2 cups flour

¼ cup sugar

1 stick cold butter, cut into pieces

1 or 2 egg yolks

THE PASTRY CREAM:

⅔ cup sugar

5 egg yolks

4 teaspoons cornstarch or flour

2 cups milk

1 vanilla bean, split

1 teaspoon vanilla extract

Butter

To assemble:

3 to 4 cups fruit of choice such as apples, strawberries, kiwi, blueberries and bananas

½ cup apricot preserves

Monique Gaumont-Lanvin

SIGN OF THE SORREL HORSE

Preheat oven to 300 degrees.

THE CRUST:

1. Using an electric mixer or processor, put in flour and sugar and add butter, mixing until crumbly. Add egg yolks and mix until combined.

2. Press into tart shell. Prick with a fork in several places and bake until golden, about 25 to 30 minutes.

THE PASTRY CREAM:

1. With a wire whisk, or an electric mixer on medium speed, beat sugar and yolks together, until mixture whitens and forms a ribbon. Gently whisk in cornstarch or flour.

2. In a saucepan, bring milk, vanilla bean, and vanilla extract to a boil. Cover and keep hot on a low flame.

3. Using a medium-mesh sieve, strain the hot milk to remove vanilla bean or remove bean with a slotted spoon. Pour into egg and sugar mixture, beating constantly as milk is added.

4. Pour egg and milk mixture back into saucepan and bring to a boil, whisking constantly so that mixture does not stick to the bottom of saucepan. Boil for 1 minute, stirring vigorously.

5. Pour cooked pastry cream into a bowl and lightly rub the surface of the cream with a lump of butter to keep a skin from forming on top as cream thickens and cools, about 1 hour.

To assemble :

1. Make a layer of pastry cream in the tart shell. Top with fresh or cooked fruit of choice.

2. Warm apricot preserves, and glaze top of tart.

Festive Feast

Mussels from Brussels

Orecchiette with Fried Chick-Peas and Cracked Pepper

Rack of Lamb with Pesto Crumbs

Tian of Eggplant and Tomato

Buttermilk Ice Cream with Strawberries in Grappa

Chocolate-Pistachio "Salami"

MUSSELS FROM BRUSSELS

Yield: 4 servings

4 tablespoons unsalted butter

1 cup finely chopped onion

⅔ cup finely chopped celery

4 cloves minced garlic

1 cup dry white wine

1 tablespoon herbs de Provence (see Note)

2 tablespoons fresh thyme leaves

1 teaspoon salt

2 pounds mussels, scrubbed and debearded

3 tablespoons heavy cream

½ cup freshly chopped parsley

1. In a large pot, melt the butter and add the onion, celery and garlic. Sauté until the vegetables are soft but not brown, about 15 minutes.

2. Add the wine, herbs de Provence and salt and bring to a boil, covered.

3. Add the mussels and cover pot. Shake the pot back and forth and cook until the mussels open, about 10 minutes.

4. With a slotted spoon, transfer the mussels to plates or flat soup bowls, discarding any mussels that haven't opened. Add the cream to the pot and cook the sauce over high heat, uncovered, until it has reduced and thickened slightly, 5 to 7 minutes. Pour over the mussels. Sprinkle with parsley.

Note: Or use a mixture of fennel seed, thyme and rosemary.

ORECCHIETTE WITH FRIED CHICK-PEAS AND CRACKED PEPPER

Yield: 4 servings

3 quarts water

¾ pound orecchiette pasta

½ tablespoon salt

¼ cup olive oil

2 cloves garlic, minced

2 cups cooked chick-peas

1 tablespoon dried whole sage leaves

1 cup chicken broth

1½ teaspoons cracked pepper, Italian-style, or mignonette

2 tablespoons unsalted butter

½ cup freshly grated Parmigiano-Reggiano cheese

1. Bring the water to a boil in a large pot. Add the pasta and salt. Cook al dente.

2. In a nonstick skillet, heat the olive oil. Add the garlic and chick-peas and cook, uncovered, over high heat until the chick-peas begin to pop.

3. Add the sage, broth and pepper. Lower the heat and let the broth reduce by a quarter.

4. Drain the pasta well. Put in a large bowl with butter. Add the chick-peas and broth and toss well.

5. Add salt to taste and half the cheese. Divide evenly into warm bowls and serve with the remaining cheese.

RACK OF LAMB WITH PESTO CRUMBS

Yield: 4 servings

2 (1½-pound, 8 ribs each) racks of lamb, trimmed, flap removed, bones exposed

⅔ cup pesto, plus more for serving if desired (see Recipe)

1½ cups bread crumbs made from fresh bread

Preheat the oven to 375 degrees

1. Season the lamb with salt and freshly ground black pepper. In a nonstick skillet, sear the outside of the lamb. Let the lamb cool.

2. Spread the pesto sauce over the surface of the meat. Coat the meat thoroughly with bread crumbs. Cover the bones with aluminum foil and place the lamb on a baking sheet. Roast for 15 minutes, remove the foil and bake 20 minutes longer.

3. Remove from the oven, let rest 5 minutes and carve, slicing into thick double chops or single chops. Serve with additional pesto sauce, if desired.

PESTO PRONTO

Yield: about 2 cups

1½ cups packed fresh basil leaves
1 large clove garlic, quartered
¼ cup grated Parmesan cheese
3 tablespoons pinenuts
6 tablespoons olive oil

1. Place the basil, garlic, cheese and pinenuts in the food processor. Blend.

2. While blending, slowly add the oil until the sauce emulsifies. Add salt and freshly ground black pepper to taste.

TIAN OF EGGPLANT AND TOMATO

Yield: about 12 portions

1 large eggplant

½ teaspoon salt

4 large yellow onions, peeled

8 ripe tomatoes

3 tablespoons dried basil leaves

1 tablespoon dried thyme leaves

6 tablespoons grated Parmesan cheese

⅔ cup fruity olive oil

1. Peel the eggplant. Slice into thin rounds and sprinkle with salt. Put in a colander and let drain 30 minutes.

2. Slice the onions and tomatoes very thin.

Preheat the oven to 300 degrees.

3. In a 12 x 8-inch rectangular or oval baking dish, place a layer of onions, top with a layer of eggplant, using half the eggplant, then a layer of tomatoes, using half of these. Sprinkle with 1 tablespoon basil and 1 teaspoon thyme. Repeat this process.

4. Make a final layer of thinly sliced onion. Sprinkle with the cheese and remaining basil and thyme.

5. Pour olive oil evenly over the vegetables and bake for 3 hours, uncovered. Several times during baking, press down the vegetables with a spatula.

6. Remove from oven and drain liquid from the tian. Serve hot, cut into squares or thick slices.

BUTTERMILK ICE CREAM WITH STRAWBERRIES IN GRAPPA

Yield: 4-6 servings

1 cup superfine sugar

Grated rind of 2 large lemons

¼ cup fresh lemon juice

⅛ teaspoon kosher salt

2 cups low-fat buttermilk

2 pints fresh ripe strawberries

¼ cup grappa

1 tablespoon granulated sugar

Lemon balm or purple basil leaves

1. Combine the superfine sugar, lemon rind, lemon juice and salt in a medium size bowl. Mix well. Add buttermilk and stir until sugar dissolves. Chill the mixture until it is very cold, 4 hours or overnight.

Rozanne Gold
JOSEPH BAUM & MICHAEL WHITEMAN COMPANY

2. Put mixture in an ice cream maker and proceed to make ice cream according to the manufacturer's directions.

3. One hour before serving, wash the strawberries and remove the stems. Cut large berries in quarters and small berries in half. Put the berries in a bowl, add the grappa and granulated sugar, and mix well. Cover and put in the refrigerator until ready to use.

4. To serve, divide the berries equally into 4 to 6 flat soup plates or large goblets. Top each with a large scoop of ice cream and garnish with lemon balm or purple basil.

CHOCOLATE-PISTACHIO "SALAMI"

Yield: 12 servings

½ cup golden raisins

10 ounces mint chocolate chips

4 tablespoons salted butter

4 tablespoons superfine sugar

¾ cup finely ground gingersnaps

2 egg yolks

½ cup chopped, sun-dried cherries

½ cup shelled pistachios

1. Soak the raisins in warm water for 15 minutes.

2. In a double boiler, melt the chocolate and butter together. Add the sugar, gingersnaps, egg yolks and drained raisins. Stirring often, heat the mixture 5 minutes until smooth.

3. Remove from heat and add the cherries and pistachio nuts. Mix well.

4. Let cool slightly, but while still warm, put the mixture on a large piece of wax paper and roll into a log that is 2" in diameter. Refrigerate until hard.

5. Slice ¼ inch thick on bias. The "salami" can be made 1 week in advance.

Country Luncheon Buffet

Chicken Salad on Rosemary Crostini

Spiced Green Olives

Gold Potato and Celery Root Cake Stuffed with Stilton Cheese

Tomato-Lovage Coulis

Arugula Salad with Roasted Beets and Garlic

CHICKEN SALAD ON ROSEMARY CROSTINI

Yield: 6 to 8 servings

2 pounds chicken breast on the bone

Kosher salt and freshly ground black pepper

½ cup mayonnaise

2 lemons, zest and juice

½ cup pignoli nuts, toasted

½ cup currants

½ cup finely chopped fennel bulb,

½ bunch scallions, thinly sliced

½ bunch Italian parsley, chopped

6 to 8 slices Rosemary Crostini

Preheat oven to 400 degrees.

1. Season chicken breasts with salt and pepper and put in a roasting pan. Put in oven, uncovered, and roast until firm to touch, about 20 to 30 minutes. Remove from oven and cool to room temperature.

2. Remove chicken meat from the bones and shred.

3. In a bowl, put mayonnaise, lemon zest and juice, and whisk. Add shredded chicken, pignoli, currants, fennel, scallions, parsley, salt, and pepper.

4. Spoon onto Rosemary Crostini.

ROSEMARY CROSTINI

Yield: 6 to 8 servings

½ cup fruity green olive oil

Leaves from 1 bunch rosemary, finely chopped

1 loaf Italian country bread

Preheat oven to 350 degrees.

1. In a bowl, put oil and rosemary. Set aside.

2. Cut bread into ¼-inch to ½-inch thick slices. Arrange on a cookie sheet in a single layer.

3. Using a pastry brush, put a light film of rosemary oil on both sides of bread. Put in oven and toast for 5 minutes. Turn slices over and toast until golden, another 5 minutes.

4. Cut slices of bread into 2-inch wide strips and place on serving plates as base for Chicken Salad.

SPICED GREEN OLIVES

1 pound jumbo-size green olives with pits

1 teaspoon ground cumin

1 tablespoon chopped fresh rosemary

1 tablespoon chopped fresh thyme

4 crushed bay leaves

1 tablespoon whole anise seeds

4 garlic cloves, smashed

½ cup sherry vinegar

2 tablespoons anchovy paste

Water to cover

1. Drain the olives, discarding liquid.

2. Using a heavy cleaver or meat pounder, lightly crush olives to break open the skins.

3. In a medium-size bowl, combine cumin, rosemary, thyme, bay leaves, anise, garlic, vinegar, and anchovy paste. Mix and add olives to marinade, mixing well.

4. Put olive mixture in a seal-jar with lid and shake olives to mix marinade and water.

5. Refrigerate olives in marinade at least 3 or 4 days before serving.

GOLD POTATO AND CELERY ROOT CAKE STUFFED WITH STILTON CHEESE

Yield: 8 to 10 servings

2 pounds Yellow Finn Potatoes, cut into large chunks

1 pound celery root, peeled and cut into large chunks

Boiling water

1 bunch leeks, washed and cut in 1-inch lengths

Kosher salt and freshly ground pepper

Clarified butter for cooking

½ pound Stilton cheese, crumbled

1. In a pot, put potatoes, celery root, and ½ cup water and steam until half-cooked, about 12 to 15 minutes.

2. Drain and cool vegetables to room temperature. Peel potato. Place potato and celery root in a bowl and put in refrigerator to chill, about 1 hour.

3. Blanch the leeks until they have begun to soften. Set aside.

4. Using a hand grater or food processor, grate chilled potatoes and celery root. Add salt and pepper.

5. In a heavy, nonstick 7 to 9-inch skillet, heat several tablespoons clarified butter. Divide the potato mixture in half and make a layer of this in the skillet, pressing down mixture. Cook at moderate heat until crispy on the bottom, 5 to 7 minutes. Do not stir.

6. Add the leeks and cheese to the skillet, evenly distributing them in the center of the cooked potato and celery root, leaving a 1-inch border.

7. Cover the leeks and cheese with the remaining potato and celery root and pat down firmly.

8. Slide a spatula under the cake to loosen. Carefully slide the cake out of the skillet onto a tray or board. Place the skillet on top of the transferred cake. Holding the skillet tightly against the tray, flip skillet over, so that the cooked side of the cake is up and the uncooked layer is at the bottom.

9. Cook cake on second side until crispy, about 5 to 7 minutes. If cake begins to stick, add more clarified butter. Serve immediately with Tomato-Lovage Coulis.

TOMATO-LOVAGE COULIS

Yield: about 1½ cups

2 large ripe beefsteak tomatoes, cut into large chunks

2 bay leaves

½ teaspoon cracked peppercorns

Zest of 1 lemon

1 teaspoon ground coriander

½ bunch lovage, leaves only, chopped

Salt and freshly ground pepper

2 tablespoons butter

1. In a nonreactive saucepan, combine tomatoes, bay leaves, peppercorns, lemon zest, and coriander. Simmer ingredients covered, stirring occasionally until mixture has thickened, about 30 minutes.

2. In a blender or processor, blend tomato mixture. Strain through a food-mill or sieve, and put purée into a clean saucepan.

3. Cook on medium heat, uncovered, until mixture is reduced and thickened enough to hold its shape in the bowl of a spoon, about 5 to 7 minutes.

4. Add lovage and butter to purée and season with salt and pepper, to taste.

Aliza Green

ALIZA GREEN FOOD CONSULTING COMPANY

ARUGULA SALAD WITH ROASTED BEETS AND GARLIC

Yield: 6 servings

1 head garlic

1 bunch beets, washed and greens removed

¼ cup balsamic vinegar

1 tablespoon coarse grain mustard

¼ cup extra virgin olive oil

½ cup rich homemade chicken stock

Sea salt and freshly ground pepper

2 bunches arugula, coarse stems removed, washed and drained

Preheat oven to 350 degrees.

1. Cut off top ½ inch of garlic, exposing cloves.

3. Place garlic and beets on a roasting pan and cook until beets are soft, about 30 to 45 minutes. Remove garlic after 25 to 30 minutes.

4. Submerge beets in a bowl of cold water and slip off skins. Cut into ½-inch dice. Separate garlic cloves and remove skins.

5. In a small glass jar with a tight-fitting lid, place vinegar, mustard, olive oil, stock, salt, and pepper. Close tightly and shake vigorously to blend dressing. Set aside.

6. Put arugula in a salad bowl and pour dressing over. Toss to lightly coat leaves. Arrange arugula on 6 salad plates. Scatter beets and garlic cloves over top and serve.

Mexican Fiesta Lunch

Cream of
Huitlacoche Soup

Guacamole

Fish Tostadas

Chile Chocolate
Truffles with
Pumpkin Seed
Praline

CREAM OF HUITLACOCHE SOUP

Yield: 8 servings

2 tablespoons extra-virgin olive oil

1 cup chopped onion

3 cloves minced garlic

1 or 2 jalapeño chilies, seeded and minced

1 cup fresh or defrosted frozen huitlacoche

2 tablespoons minced fresh epazote or cilantro

6 cups chicken or vegetable stock

1 cup cream, milk or evaporated skim milk

Fine sea salt and freshly ground pepper

1. In a large heavy pot, heat the oil and sauté the onion until golden, about 2 minutes. Add garlic and chilies, and sauté 1 minute more. Add the huitlacoche and epazote or cilantro.

2. Add 5 cups of stock, bring to a simmer and cook, uncovered, for about 10 minutes. Cool slightly.

3. Purée in one or two batches in a food processor. Add cream or milk and season with salt and pepper. If desired, add more stock to thin.

4. Serve hot in small bowls.

GUACAMOLE

Yield: 2 servings

3 tablespoons chopped white onion

1 teaspoon chopped jalapeño chilies, to taste

1½ teaspoons chopped coriander

Salt, to taste

1 Hass avocado

2 tablespoons chopped tomato, juice and seeds removed

1. In a bowl with the back of a wooden spoon, thoroughly mash 1 tablespoon onion, ½ teaspoon chilies, ½ teaspoon coriander, and ½ teaspoon salt.

2. Holding the avocado in the cup of the hand, split it in half lengthwise and remove the seed. Slice it lengthwise in approximately ⅛-inch strips, then across, forming a grid. Scoop with spoon.

3. To the onion mixture add the avocado and thoroughly coat with paste. Add the remaining onion, chilies, coriander, and tomato. Serve.

FISH TOSTADAS

Yield: 6 servings

½ cup vegetable oil

6 6 to 8-inch corn tortillas

2 packed teaspoons chopped, pickled jalapeño pepper, plus 1 teaspoon of jar liquid

12 ounces cooked hake, grouper, red snapper, or other lean white fish

1 medium onion, finely chopped

1 medium tomato, seeded and cut into ½-inch dice

¼ cup olive oil

2 tablespoons fresh lemon juice

2 tablespoons chopped fresh cilantro, plus more for garnish

½ teaspoon salt

¼ teaspoon freshly ground pepper

⅓ cup mascarpone cheese or crème fraîche

½ head romaine lettuce, finely shredded

1 ripe medium avocado, preferably Hass, cut in half and seeded

1. In a small skillet heat vegetable oil over moderately high flame until hot.

Josefina Howard

Using tongs, one at a time, fry tortillas, turning gently several times until golden all over, about 2 minutes.

2. Cover a work surface with paper towels and place cooked tortillas on them to drain oil and cool.

3. Using a large knife, chop and mash the jalapeño until it becomes a paste. Set aside.

4. Using a fork, and working over a large bowl, flake the fish. Add onion and toss gently. Add jalapeño paste, jalapeño juice, tomato, olive oil, lemon juice and cilantro stirring after each addition. Season with salt and pepper, and set aside.

5. Spread each tortilla with a heaping tea-spoon of mascarpone, then sprinkle with lettuce. Place fish mixture in center of tortilla and spread it out a little to the sides.

6. Score avocado flesh into ½-inch cubes and scoop out with a spoon. Top fish with avocado cubes and cilantro. Garnish each with a dollop of marcarpone in the middle of each tostado and serve.

CHILI CHOCOLATE TRUFFLES WITH PUMPKIN SEED PRALINE

Yield: 4 dozen small truffles

1½ pounds semisweet chocolate, broken into pieces

10 tablespoons unsalted butter

1¾ cups heavy cream

6 tablespoons Kahlúa

½ teaspoon vanilla

½ teaspoon chile de arbol powder

1 cup pumpkin seeds

⅓ cup sugar

¼ cup water

1. In a double boiler on medium flame, melt chocolate, stirring occasionally.

2. With pot on low flame, stir continuously, and add butter a tablespoon at a time.

3. In 2 or 3 additions, gradually stir in cream. Add Kahlúa and stir. Add vanilla and chili, and stir.

4. Remove chocolate from stove, cover and place in refrigerator to let cool and solidify, about 3 hours.

5. In a heavy skillet toast pumpkin seeds, shaking pan continuously. They will crackle and pop. Transfer seeds to a lightly oiled or nonstick cookie sheet.

6. In a small, heavy saucepan combine sugar and water, and stir.

On high heat, bring to a boil, and boil vigorously until mixture begins to darken and caramelize, about 5 to 7 minutes.

7. Immediately pour caramel over seeds, making sure all seeds are covered. Cool completely to harden.

8. With a spatula, remove seed mixture from sheet and break into pieces. Put in processor and process until coarsely ground. Pour onto a plate and set aside.

9. Using a teaspoon, scoop out spoonfuls of chilled chocolate, and roll in the palm of your hand to make small balls.

10. Roll balls in Pumpkin Seed Praline. Serve.

EVAN KLEIMAN   MARJORIE KLOSS   SARABETH LEVINE   SUSAN MCCREIGHT LINDEBORG

SUSAN MENDELSON   CARRIE NAHABEDIAN   NANCY OAKES   DEBRA PONZEK

Evan Kleiman

"It's possible to achieve a
camaraderie in the kitchen that
supercedes any gender issues."

Evan Kleiman was born and brought up in Los Angeles and has been chef-owner of three successful restaurants in that city: Trattoria Angeli, Angeli Caffe and Angeli Mare. Angeli Caffe, the original bistro, is still open on Melrose Avenue. One of the first of its kind in Los Angeles, Angeli offers simple Italian foods in a casual atmosphere. Entirely self-taught with a natural instinct for rustic Italian cooking, Kleiman has authored six cookbooks, including 'Cucina Fresca,' 'Pasta Fresca,' 'Cucina Rustica' and Cucina Mare.' She is an undisputed force in L.A. simply because she opened up a whole new world in restaurant style and cuisine in the early 1980s. And she introduced various olive oils and herb vinegars to a previously unknowing audience of home cooks, who have become connoisseurs about the difference betweeen "virgin" and "extra virgin."

Kleiman reminisced and talked at the family-style table at Caffe Angeli during the quiet time in the afternoon as she caught up with her bills.

Angeli Caffe

7274 Melrose Avenue,
Los Angeles,
CA 90046
Phone 213 936 9086
Fax 213 938 9873

I was an only child of a single parent in Los Angeles. There was just me and my mom. I learned to cook at an early age and I was taught to help around the house and in the kitchen. I was a latchkey kid, and so by the time I was nine or ten I often prepared dinner for my mother when she came home from work. Food was always a part of my persona. I was very shy and I used food to communicate with people. As an undergraduate major in college I began by studying Italian literature and culture. I went all over Italy in the early seventies - particularly central and southern Italy, eating everywhere. I learned to love the rustic, simple style of cooking, which is mostly olive oil-based. As a teenager I remember buying the cookbooks by Marcella Hazan.

I never apprenticed in a kitchen. In my first job cooking at a restaurant I was in charge of the kitchen after six weeks. That was in 1981. Seven months after I'd been in that restaurant, I was hired away to be an

Above:
Proscuitto,
Figs and
Angeli Bread

Right:
Spaghetti
with Gorgonzola,
Red and Yellow
Peppers

opening chef for a new restaurant. I had an executive chef underneath me who was more technically skilled, but he had to listen to me. It was very painful, because it was not what the kitchen crew thought should be the order of things. This was 1981, mind you. We were not in the dark ages, but still a single woman came up against obstacles. In my first restaurant every employee in the front of the house - from the manager, to the headwaiter and all the captains - were all men - Italian men. They told me: "We don't know why you were hired, but you'll be out of here in three weeks." I said: "As many days as you are here, I'll be here one day longer." I hung on and left when I got bored, but I wasn't fired.

When you work in a restaurant kitchen, every day is a crisis, and I began to ask: "Why am I working this hard for somebody else?" I thought that I would open my own restaurant. I was just thirty when I opened Angeli Caffe. Yes, men began to respect me after I opened this place, although there are some men who are open and some men for whom it is more of a problem, particularly Italian men, who can be rather chauvinistic. Tension arises that has nothing to do with being a boss and plenty to do with being a woman. But it's possible to achieve a camaraderie in the kitchen that supersedes any gender issue.

It's very hard to remember, but you could not get fresh herbs or simple fresh vegetables in 1984. When I opened Caffe Angeli that was the case. There was no Italian menu in L.A. before I did mine. Before that, there was just Italian food covered in a lot of sauce. Now a hundred restaurants have copied my menu and my ideas. In Italy so many women cook in bistro kitchens that home-style food is the norm. This is exactly what I brought to L.A.: fresh pastas, pizzas, pannerini. Cooking is a wonderful, earthy way to get satisfaction. I

think there is something wrong if the atmosphere in the kitchen is not volatile. It should be at a knife edge, like a ballet, coordinated, but you don't want to fall off the edge. I have never had a tantrum. That's because I have a firm expectation of exactly what's going to happen. But it's a tough profession, physically demanding, a hard life.

Above:
Pizza with
Peppers,
Olives and
Tomatoes

Marjorie Kloss

ZOCALO

I love having women in the kitchen. They are cleaner and better workers than men."

Marjorie Kloss taught grade school for a year and found she didn't like it. This was in 1984. What to do? She thought about it and realized that she liked to cook. She also determined that she did not need to study for another degree beyond her bachelor's in English to get started in this profession. She quickly learned by doing, training with different chefs, and eventually worked her way up over seven years to the chef de cuisine position at Jake's restaurant in Philadelphia, winning the prestigious Philadelphia, Delaware Valley Restaurant Association Panache Award for chef of the year in 1993.

Kloss's agility at moving from one cuisine to another is renowned in Philadelphia. She learned to love food early in her family life, when the gastronomic choices reflected the tastes of a German Irish father and a Texan mother, who cooked hominy and okra, with some local Polish dishes included. This multicultural influence enabled her to disregard culinary barriers and resist a one-track approach. Kloss has cooked Asian and Creole food and New American cuisine. As executive chef at Zocalo, Kloss now cooks contemporary Mexican food with a particularly original focus on desserts - beyond the traditional

Zocalo

3600 Lancaster Avenue
Philadelphia, PA 19140
Phone: 215 895 0139
Fax: 215 895 0140

Mexican rice pudding and flan. Her imaginative touch has won Zocalo the coveted Zagat Survey Diner's Choice Award and the Best of Philly Award. She discussed her career over afternoon tea at the Four Seasons Hotel, where she paid her dues as an apprentice at the very beginning of her career.

After I worked for chef Jean-Marie LeCroix at the Four Seasons as an apprentice, I decided I never wanted to work for another European old-guard male chef. I worked fourteen hours a day. I could tell I'd be just another pair of hands and never get past the lettuce and salad station. I didn't want to fight, so I just moved on. As a woman in the kitchen you have to be determined, you have to want it, and you have to be willing to work hard, much harder than the men around you. It's a dirty, competitive business. It's no good saying "It's too heavy for me." You can't say you don't want to clean that. You can't have staff snickering behind your back. You've got to love what you do, because it shows when you don't. The woman I replaced in the kitchen I work in now stopped liking it and got depressed. It reflected on the staff, and the state of the kitchen. I know how

she felt. She was tired. She had been cooking Mexican food for seven years. I am determined that I won't let myself get like that - tired of it. Mexican food is not a cuisine I am familiar with, but I'm learning and it's fascinating. When it stops being interesting, I'll strong-arm my husband into doing something else. A few years down the road, we may get our own restaurant. He's getting his MBA so that he can learn how to manage both the front and the back of the house.

All my mentors have been men. Sometimes they were nice and sometimes they were rude and unpleasant. It's all been good, even the not-so-good. I have found there was always something to learn. I love what I do which makes it all worthwhile. I like watching other people work. I like looking

at the plates as they go out. I've always loved to eat.

I love having women in the kitchen. Women are more meticulous. They have a different focus. They keep the kitchen cleaner than men and are better workers than men. One of the things a chef needs to do is be patient with people and bring out the best in them.

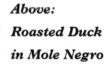

Above:
Roasted Duck
in Mole Negro

Left:
Guacamole
in traditional
Molcajete

Sarabeth Levine

"I have this perfection thing that is in my mind."

Jam Today, Jam Tomorrow

After graduating with a degree in sociology, Sarabeth Levine wanted to have a career in dentistry. But when she applied to college as a single parent, she was not considered an appropriate candidate. To help her financial situation, she started making orange-apricot marmalade and fruit preserves using her grandmother's recipes, from her kitchen on the Upper West Side of Manhattan. Soon, she was selling to Bloomingdale's and Dean & DeLuca and before long, she opened a small retail bakery and jam shop two blocks from her apartment. At the request of her customers, Levine began to serve breakfast and lunch. With its down-home, cozy atmosphere and people lining up for tables, Sarabeth's restaurant became a unique New York destination. A second bakery & restaurant opened on Manhattan's East Side, and was followed by a Sarabeth's cafe at the Whitney Museum. As a powerhouse chef in Manhattan, Levine was elected to Les Dames d'Escoffier in 1987, and in 1996 was named the James Beard Pastry Chef of the Year, a long-awaited accolade after 18 years in the profession. Levine and her husband now preside over the diverse Sarabeth enterprises, which include a thriving mail-order business selling award-winning jams, cakes, cookies and even granola, built on the principles of "putting the best fruit forward" and "smelling good." She gave more details of her route to success one morning in her sunny apartment.

Mail orders: Sarabeth's Kitchen Inc.
423 Amsterdam Avenue, New York, N.Y. 10024
Phone: 212 580 8335 or 1-800 552 JAMS

Sarabeth's

Sarabeth's - West Side
423 Amsterdam Avenue,
New York, N.Y. 10024
Phone: 212 496 6280

Sarabeth's - East Side
1295 Madison Avenue
New York, N.Y. 10128
Phone: 212 410 7335

Sarabeth's at the Whitney
945 Madison Avenue
New York, N.Y. 10021
Phone: 212 570 3670

I think I went to bed one night and God visited me and said, "She shall make jams and she shall have a restaurant." And poof! It happened. I always loved working with my hands. That was why I wanted to be a dentist - another profession that is difficult for women to break into. But when I started

Right:
Sarabeth's
Preserves

Below:
Chocolate Chip
Cookies

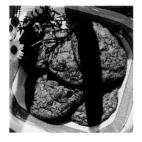

making the jams, I figured I had hit upon something good, although I don't know that there was ever a plan to get involved in cooking as a way of life. For ten years I was working eighteen hours a day, seven days a week, with three services in the restaurants. Getting up at 4:30 a.m. and baking everything from scratch, as well as running a jam factory with a baker's dozen different jams, which now produces sixty cases a day... I sometimes think there is no other crazy person on the planet. But when you are doing what you love, it isn't work. And there is no clock, no time of day when you love your work.

and yell until we get things right. My husband manages the financials of the jam factory. He's Mr. Bottom Line, and I am the creative force in the shop. I'm extravagant, Ms. Vanilla

From daily work your hands develop more feeling and dexterity and the more you cook the more your taste buds and sense of smell develop. I can smell smoke a hundred blocks away. I can imagine a flavor. Cooking is a bit like playing music: the food is there for the moment, and then it's gone. You keep creating a dish, and you never do it quite the same way twice. Temperature, quality of ingredients, rules of chemisty and speeds somehow vary, and so it comes out different. Sometimes it's perfect and that's the challenge. I have this perfection thing that is in my mind. Although the biggest challenge is to maintain consistency, maintain the same level for the customers.

I create new desserts all the time and critique menus that my chefs create at the restaurant. We taste and we play. When I created the poached pears parfait, it came out of thin air. Sometimes, I scream

Bean. That's good, because we're in balance. Where do I want to go in the future? The profit margin is so small in a restaurant, and you need good management which takes a lot of time. So I would really love to develop boxed foods, like Betty Crocker, but with great organic flavors, with dried cherries, pumpkin seeds, candied ginger. Sell them by mail-order. We've done well with the jams and cookies.

The jam is the best part of the business.

Susan McCreight Lindeborg

MORRISON CLARK INN

"Success is based on good food, and a restaurant that makes money."

As chef de cuisine at the Morrison Clark Inn, in Washington, D.C. Susan McCreight Lindeborg has turned this small, fifty-seven-room hotel's dining room into a major gastronomic destination - which is no mean feat for a self-taught woman cook from Santa Fe. Furthermore her culinary prowess has been recognized with a nomination for Chef of the Year by the Restaurant Association of Metropolitan Washington, along with numerous articles in gourmet magazines noting her original recipes and stylish food presentations. Prior to opening the Morrison Clark restaurant in 1990, Lindeborg served as pastry chef under Bob Kinkead, now chef-owner of Kinkead's an American Brasserie, a much acclaimed restaurant in the capital. She got her start in 1976 as a baker's assistant at Bishop's Lodge, Santa Fe; line-cooked at La Fonda on the Santa Fe Trail; then learned modern American and international techniques from Santa Fe chef-owners Joe and Shirley Piscane at the Periscope. On a typical sweltering day in Washington, she talked about her twenty-year career on the flower-festooned veranda of the inn, over several glasses of iced tea and a plate of butter cookies.

Morrison Clark Inn
Massachusetts Avenue and Eleventh Street, NW
Washington, D.C. 20001
Phone: 202 898 1200 Fax: 202 289 8580

I have shied away from working in a traditional classic kitchen situation because it can be very hostile to women. I can understand where the anti-woman chef attitude comes from and why. Traditionally, a young man was sold into slavery as a commis waiter. It took about five to seven years before he was able to move ahead. One of the ways of learning was to be initiated by your mistakes. They toughened kids up in brutal ways. There were a lot of hoops you had go through, learning to be a team player, following orders. It was a boys' game, and they loved it.

By contrast, most women chefs are not abusive people - it doesn't come into the equation. Women are calmer than men, less screamy than men. At the end of the day, though, you can't see a plate of food and say whether a male or female made it. No one thinks of male or female food, so the opportunities are equal for men and women. But you have to be tough. No crying in the kitchen. You have to have a passion for food. You must be crazed beyond belief, even at home you are thinking about food, dreaming about food. A day is never so great as when you made something new. A day is never so great as when a customer says "I never eat vegetables but these are really good."

Being a self-taught cook hasn't affected my career choices. Cooking schools cost a lot of money, and they accept some individuals who would never make it in a kitchen. I can develop a case for going and not going. If you want to learn, I'd say make the kitchen the classroom. Get a job in the best restaurant in town. Push yourself to be a self-starter. No restaurant chef has the time to teach someone everything they need to know. You learn by doing and by reading. I am a great purchaser of cookbooks, and read them from cover to cover. Even Paul Bocuse learned from his mother and grandmother.

I would give anything in the world to cook a highly refined French cuisine like Paul Bocuse. But I have never been associated with anyone who cooks like that. And I understand that you are best off doing what you do best and not trying to be something you are not. My mother came from a large family - she was one of twelve children and lived in Missouri. They cooked Southern style. This is the kind of food I grew up with, and even today I cook the same kind of

Right:
Chocolate Peanut
Butter Mousse
Cake

Pastry Chef Valerie Hill

food my mother made. My mother said more was always better. If you didn't have leftovers you knew you hadn't made enough. She cooked generously. Food was a nurturing experience. I have always had enormous admiration for the home cook. A lot of home kitchens are like torture chambers compared to commercial kitchens, which are designed for speed and efficiency. Home cooking has to be approached entirely differently, otherwise you can get exhausted by shopping around to find the right ingredients. I say if it's not at Gateway we're not eating it. In the restaurant, you simply pick up the phone, order and have it delivered.

I have been working for Operation Frontline, a city program that helps disadvantaged women to cook low-cost, nutritious meals. They are taught how to spend $10 on food for one or two meals for four people. They buy vegetables and fruit they have never had before, and learn to budget and eat in a healthy way. It's shocking to me that some of these women don't know how to cook - they have

never peeled a carrot, never eaten a raw carrot. But it's amazing what can be done.

Sometimes as a chef you can have a really bad day - where you want to shoot yourself. I say tomorrow is a whole new day, and anyway very few kitchens can actually say they had a perfect day. I don't think the customers in the dining room notice the little things we fixate on. I have a hard time believing that success is based on anything but good food - and a restaurant that makes money.

Susan Mendelson

THE LAZY GOURMET

"There's no throwing pans, or macho, male-dominated scenes in my kitchen."

Susan Mendelson arrived in Vancouver from Toronto as a student when she was nineteen and was drawn to the performing arts, not as an actress but as a house manager. To make extra money, she baked carrot cakes and cheesecakes and starting selling them during intermission. The food took off. "I could only make three cheesecakes a day - thirty-six pieces - but it was putting me through school." So when a local radio station called and asked for her secrets, she told them she couldn't give away her recipes, but would be glad to talk about food and give cooking hints. It was the beginning of a long and successful association as CBC's ace in the kitchen, in a drive-home show called "Three's Company" that would help her sell seven cookbooks (several co-authored with her former partner Deborah Roitberg), and create a major name for herself in the Canadian food industry. Mendelson pursued a career as a social worker while she was doing the weekly radio show and writing best-selling cookbooks. It wasn't long before her friends recommended she give up her social work and put her money where her mouth was. Soon she was catering major corporate events, calling her business the Lazy Gourmet, and serving what she calls West Coast eclectic multi-cultural food which draws from Japanese, Thai, Malaysian,

The Lazy Gourmet

Chinese and Vietnamese cuisines. "We are so close to the Pacific Rim, and this is what people want to eat today," says Mendelson. As the catering service expanded, she opened first a cafe and then a restaurant. She discussed the ongoing exhilaration of a running a business one morning in her office, while serving her trademark Nanaimo bars - a very sweet, very rich concoction of coconut and graham cracker crumbs, with a filling of butter and custard and topped with a layer of Belgian chocolate.

1595 West Sixth Avenue
Vancouver, BC V6J 1R1
Canada
Phone 604 734 2507
Fax 604 734 5877

Above:
Nanaimo Bars
and Coffee

After twenty years in the food business, I still find it fun and exciting. Especially when we get a job like the Molson Indy Vancouver, serving 20,000 meals in a three-day period with about 350 staff. This is an astonishing and thrilling event and defies all sense of the norm - creating beautiful, personalized food for corporate hospitality suites and chalets all over the track.

When I started cooking, I felt empowered. It is an incredible way to gain self-esteem. You give and share at the same time. You are personally proud as you sample your

own creativity. My mother never let me in the kitchen - she convinced me at an early age that the biggest treat in life was a TV dinner - so I didn't know I could do it. I learned everything I know from my grandmother's knee and she still shares her recipes with me. Her exuberance for cooking has never faltered and she continues to be a source of inspiration for me. She can outcook me in the kitchen anytime.

I called my first cookbook *The Lazy Gourmet* because I wanted to make it easy for people who were too lazy to follow a French cookbook step-by-step. It demystifies the traditional techniques. Then when I started catering, the idea was to offer a take-out service that looked as if you did it yourself. It very quickly became a multi-purpose catering business with valet service, flowers, everything you need to put on a major event - weddings, Christmas parties and so forth.

When I worked as a waitress when I was younger, I was often humiliated and tormented by the male chefs in the kitchen. I said never would my kitchen be like that. I try to choose nice people who are easy to get along with, and I hire both men and women.

Top Left:
Japanese
Maki Roll

Center Left:
Kiwi
Fruit Tart

Lower Left:
Truffle Torte
and White
Chocolate Mousse

Top Right:
Marinated
Salmon, Dill
and Peas

Below Left:
Mediterranean
Pizza

Below Right:
Rack of Lamb

There is no throwing pans or macho, male-dominated scenes in my kitchen. I don't want people cowering in the corner. You can get high standards without those kinds of tactics.

Food tastes have changed dramatically since I started out. Vancouver used to be a place for Swedish meat-balls. I like to think I brought good food to Vancouver, and that I was in the right place at the right time. After twenty years I thought it would get easier, but I found out not working as hard was a fantasy - you have to be sharper. A major issue is to learn to be a businesswoman. You have to be more than a cook delivering good food.

Carrie Nahabedian

FOUR SEASONS HOTEL

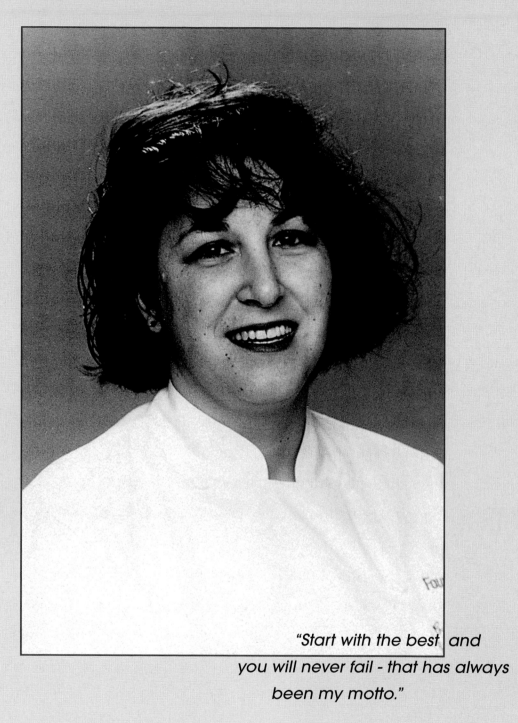

"Start with the best and you will never fail - that has always been my motto."

Carrie Nahabedian's job as executive chef at the Four Seasons Hotel in Beverly Hills puts her in the enviable position of catering to the top stars in Hollywood. Jack Nicholson, Warren Beatty, Annette Bening and other movie megapeople choose the Gardens restaurant in the hotel as one of their most preferred places, especially for the power break-

fast. With twenty years' culinary experience, Nahabedian takes it all in stride. Brought up in an Armenian family who "live and breathe food," she started out in the Ritz Carlton Hotel in Chicago while still in high school and within a year was taken on as an apprentice.

Always on the move, Nahabedian worked at Resorts International in Atlantic City, where she learned how to do volume cooking, feeding 20,000 people a day. Then at Chicago's Le Perroquet she mastered Nouvelle Cuisine. And after an extensive tour of Europe, Nahabedian became the first woman chef to cook at Le Francais, the noted Chicago restaurant, where chef owner Jean Banchet, had fourteen men in his kitchen. Then it was on to Sinclair's to act as sous-chef for Gordon Sinclair, followed by Jovan and then La Tour at the Park Hyatt Hotel. In 1988 Nahabedian joined the Four Seasons in Chicago, where she and executive chef Reto Demarmels created the look, the feel and the theme of the Seasons. She moved west to become executive chef at the Four Seasons Biltmore in Santa Barbara before joining the Beverly Hills hotel in 1995. Zagat, Travel & Leisure, Condé Nast Traveler, Wine Spectator and the American Automobile

Four Seasons Hotel

Four Seasons Hotel
300 South Doheny Drive
Los Angeles, CA 90048
Phone: 310 273 2222
Fax 310 274 3891

Association have all honored the restaurant with accolades. Typical of her generous nature, Nahabedian turned what began as a small tasting into a major multiple-course lunch in the exquisitely furnished Gardens dining room, where she talked about her career.

I credit my mother as my inspiration to go into cooking. She made tremendous meals. Her Thanksgiving dinner was legendary in its attention to detail. She knew how to make a table look great, and that's where I got my sense of entertaining. She cooked with fine ingredients and natural food. We didn't use frozen foods. I can remember her making Armenian bread, cheese soufflé, broiled white fish with almonds and onions and, despite the freezing Chicago winter, cooking leg of lamb stuffed with garlic and middle eastern grains outside on the grill. It was all very wholesome but not necessarily low cal. When my friends in high school worked in fast-food places, I chose to work in a luxury hotel - the Ritz Carlton, and I even got to meet Madame Ritz. I was so excited to be doing something I enjoyed, because I was never fond of school. I got a lot of culinary background from reading and when I graduated from high school I made a decision not to go to college but to work at the best restaurants. I wanted to break away from the pack. I didn't want to be just anyone, but the best. Start with the best and you will never fail. That has always been my motto.

I have been asked quite often if I have ever been held back because I am a woman, but I have never felt it at all. I never let it get in the way, because I work like a man. I have never said I can't do this because I'm a woman. So I was accepted wholeheartedly. But I had to know how to work with people and know my cooking skills.

Right:
Striped Bass
Trevisso
and
Sweet Currant
Tomatoes

Top:
Violet Mustard
Crusted Rack of
Lamb

Above:
Roast Ranch
Squab and
Spring Vegetables

People wonder why I left Le Francais, and it was a difficult decision. I left because I am an American. I thought I didn't know my own food - the essence of a gumbo or a clam chowder. I had failed to recognize that I am an American and proud of my heritage. So I took a job with Gordon Sinclair because he specialized in American regional cuisine. It was a great situation - we had the freshest ingredients from all over America. Los Angeles is a food city, but one that sets itself apart by the scene and the atmosphere. The clientele come here to feel comfortable, to get whatever they want, and for name recognition.

I have always chosen the places and the people I worked with very carefully. I have always believed that if you were happy it would be reflected in your cooking. It's sad if you just become a face; you need to be a player, a force in making food more than food. It has to be an experience.

Above:

Hot Smoked
and Glazed
Salmon

Nancy Oakes

BOULEVARD

*"Women tend to run a restaurant
a little differently,
like a big family."*

One alluring place in San Francisco that consistently upholds its reputation for gastronomic excellence is Boulevard, whose chef, Nancy Oakes, came to the restaurant business as a receptionist during her student years at the city's Art Institute. Oakes always thought of cooking as her hobby, but as she observed chef Rene Techninger at Nob Hill's Alexis restaurant, she decided that the culinary arts would become her career. After eight years' experience in the front of the house, a friend suggested she take over the food service at a rollicking, hamburger and beer sports bar called Pat O'Shea's Mad Hatter. Oakes felt she was ready to command a kitchen and her home-style cuisine of hearty stews, pot roasts, venison and pasta dishes won her an increasing clientele over the next nine years. By 1988, she was ready to open her own neighborhood bistro, L'Avenue, which quickly earned her the Rising Star accolade from Focus magazine - the first of many honors she has since received, including Food & Wine's list of ten best chefs in the nation. After five years at L'Avenue, Oakes and celebrity restaurateur Pat Kuleto got together to open Boulevard, a grand, turn-of-the-century Art Nouveau brasserie designed to allow the chef to spread her wings. Kuleto spared no effort to make it as opulent as his deep pockets

allowed. Hand-blown glass light fixtures and glassware, handcrafted metalwork, trompe l'oeil murals, exquisitely detailed mosaics on the floors, antique screens purchased in Paris, vaulted brick ceilings and a profusion of artwork and flower arrangements create a cornucopia of sensory experiences deliberately meant to entice Oakes into cooking the most sublime food - and the customers to keep on coming back. One afternoon between lunch and dinner service Oakes took time out to review her phenomenal success.

Boulevard

I Mission Street
San Francisco,
CA 94105
Phone: 415 543 6084
Fax: 415 495 2936

Right:
Dungeness
Crab Cake
with Spicy
Sprout Salad
and Tomato
Vinaigrette

Right:
Wood Oven
Roasted
Californian
Sea Bass
with Asparagus,
Arugula,
Morels and
Fava Beans

The restaurant business has changed and the glamour has shifted in the last fifteen or twenty years. In the old days, the maitre d' in the front of the house was the person who mattered most - or the celebrity owner of the restaurant. These were the people the public associated with the restaurant, but this is not the case so much anymore. Paul Bocuse was the first chef to change the focus. Suddenly, people switched around and learned to follow the chef, and it was no longer the maitre d' that kept the restaurant going. The days of these men are over. They came over from Europe after World War II and nobody replaced them.

In some ways I consider myself a restaurateur rather than a chef. The business of a restaurant is about hospitality combined with what is offered by the chef. Without the people in the restaurant, the restaurant doesn't exist. Success has a lot to do with food, but even more with setting up a relationship with the customer. Cooking is a chance to be generous.

I reported to enough authorative men in the front of the house to make sure that I could be my own boss. A lot of women get into trouble in the restaurant business because they become emotionally attached to their staff. They are still not guided by the cold hard facts of the profit-and-loss statement.

Sometimes when you are all cooking together in a group, working cooperatively, you may find yourself obligated to keep people. Women run a restaurant a little differently, like a big family. The most atrocious thing to have to do in this job is to fire someone. It's hard to let someone go, but I try to place a person on my staff in another restaurant if I find it's time for them to move on. It's a tough business, because the goal is zero error. That is the absolute goal, with each thing you do. If it isn't right, then you do it over without making a mistake. It's very difficult. The restaurant has to come first. There is a certain blend of workaholism required to make it all happen. I want my customers to come to a place where they don't feel intimidated. Where they can have fun and relax and make of it what they want. They can have something as simple as a salad with a glass of wine, or foie gras and pheasant with an incredible bottle of wine from our cellar. We have a well turned-out restaurant producing very high-quality food, but it's very accessible and price-conscious. It is what I call layering. It's very American, and we have attracted the rest of the world to it.

Debra Ponzek

AUX DELICES

"You don't have to be a genius, but you must have a special knack for cooking. Otherwise, you had better give it up."

'S Wonderful!

As chef de cuisine at New York's Montrachet restaurant, Debra Ponzek received three consecutive three-star reviews from The New to enroll in the Culinary Institute of America. Ponzek had learned the basics from her mother, who was schooled in French cooking, and

Aux Délices

FOODS BY
DEBRA PONZEK
1075 East Putnam Ave:
Riverside, CT 06878
Phone: 203 698 1966
Fax: 203 698 1076

York Times. This is an extraordinary achievement in itself, but was even more remarkable in this instance because Ponzek was under 30 at the time. As a result of this recognition, she was elected one of the Ten Best New American Chefs by Food & Wine magazine at the age of 28, and in 1991 was named Chef of the Year by the Chefs of America Association. In 1992, Ponzek was awarded the coveted Rising Chef of the Year accolade by the James Beard Foundation. Her career started seriously when, as a sophomore studying bio-medical engineering, she dropped out of Boston University her grand mother, who taught her traditional Polish recipes from the time Ponzek was 10. At the CIA she learned the rudiments of fine cuisine, to which she added her own special French Mediterranean touches - ideas gathered from traveling around in France from the age of 16. Ponzek's passions are described in her cookbook "French Food American Accent" and are now centered on her own gourmet food shop and cafe in Riverside, Connecticut, (designed with much charm and style by New York architect Birch Coffey) Aux Délices, where she sipped cappuccino and discussed her meteoric career.

When Drew Nieporent, the owner of Montrachet, promoted me to head chef after only ten months in the kitchen, he kept quiet for a bit and was nervous about announcing it, since I was a woman and hadn't a lot of experience. I had been cooking in a few New Jersey restaurants owned by Dennis Foy, and at a place called Mondrian in Manhattan that he owned. Dennis taught me a lot, and we are still friends today. He had a sense of taste and a passionate eye. It was interesting to work with him and adopt his techniques. These first few years of serious cooking had a great impact on me. When I joined Montrachet, the industry wasn't like it is now. Women chefs were not as acclaimed then as they are today.

I was surprised by the reaction to my leaving New York to open my own takeout food and catering business in Connecticut. It was seen as a kind of step down. But I had been at Montrachet for over seven years, and I didn't want to cook in someone else's kitchen until I was in my 50's. I enjoyed my time there and I felt that since a lot of my clientele at the restaurant lived in Connecticut, I would be able to attract them to my shop here. I wanted to get into a different aspect of food service and retail. My husband, Gregory Addinizio, and I met at the CIA and always wanted to chef together. It is great to work with him and makes the business a happy place to be. I like being in the kitchen a lot, and he's great out front with the customers, helping people do their parties.

We went combing numerous gourmet retail stores, from Fauchon in Paris to Grace's Market, Neuman & Bogdonoff, Word of Mouth, and others in New York, before we opened Aux Délices. Having this shop is actually more subtle than cooking in a restaurant kitchen. Ordering from what you see, is different from ordering off a menu. The food has to look appealing. You have to think about what looks good, for example, taking the skin off fish. If you want a customer to come in every day, you must have some simple things - pheasant, rack of lamb - and lighter, health-conscious food. We thought a lot about the decor of the store. We wanted it to be beautiful but not to feel too expensive. The colors, blue and yellow from the palette of Provençe, evoke the feeling of the landscape.

Almost every deli says "gourmet catering" on its menu. We wanted to be different from what is out there in a lot of grocery stores. We wanted people to see my food coming out from the oven directly to the customers - to create a sense of abundance, making things fresh, as fast as we can, like pastry shops and bakeries in France. We have olive oil, lavender honey, our own blend of herbs specially imported from Provençe, chocolates from Belgium, and the best smoked salmon and caviar. Eighty percent of our customers are regulars, and they know that this is a personal business and that they can rely on us. They can come here to put together a whole dinner or create a customized gift basket. We also live up to the name of the shop, which means "all the wonderful things in life." We have beautiful hand-blown glass serving pieces for the table by Andrea Zampella, Paula Estey hand-painted plates, lifestyle things, even bath products. Everything goes together in its own way. We have embraced a unique French ideology.

At the time I dropped out of college, being a chef was not really an option. You don't have to be a genius, but you must have a natural talent, a special knack for cooking, a sense of taste, style, and flavor. Otherwise you had better give it up.

Above:
Saffron Crusted
Salmon

Sage-stuffed
Cornish Hens with
Cranberry Syrup

Roasted Fennel,
Tomatoes
and Olives with
Rosemary

EVAN KLEIMAN

MARJORIE KLOSS

SUSAN MCCREIGHT LINDEBORG

SUSAN MENDELSON

SARABETH LEVINE

CARRIE NAHABEDIAN

DEBRA PONZEK

NANCY OAKES

Rustic Italian Supper

Spiced Broth with Chicken Breast

Grilled Marinated Veal Chop

Polenta with Pancetta and Sage

Braised Fennel

Ricotta Pudding

SPICED BROTH WITH CHICKEN BREAST

Yield: 4 servings

3 cups water

Salt

½ chicken breast, boned

4 egg yolks

½ cup dry Marsala

4 cups Spiced Chicken Broth

Freshly grated nutmeg

1. In a small saucepan, put water and salt. Bring to a boil, covered. Add chicken breast and cook until springy to the touch.

2. Remove chicken to a cutting surface and let cool 2 to 3 minutes. Remove skin and any traces of fat from the chicken. Cut breast into thin, 2-inch slivers, and put in a small bowl. Cover, and place in a warm spot on the stove.

3. Lightly beat together the yolks and Marsala. Add to cooled Spiced Chicken Broth and stir well.

4. Pour broth mixture into a cheesecloth-lined strainer placed over a soup pot and strain broth.

5. Slowly heat broth, stirring constantly, until mixture is hot but not boiling. Do not let broth boil or the eggs will curdle.

6. To serve, place a few slivers of chicken breast in the bottoms of shallow soup bowls. Ladle soup over chicken and sprinkle with nutmeg.

SPICED CHICKEN BROTH

Yield: 4 cups

1 medium stewing chicken

1 pound chicken backs and necks

Water

2 carrots, trimmed and peeled

3 celery stalks, washed and trimmed

3 sprigs Italian parsley with stems

2 garlic cloves, peeled

1 small onion, quartered

1 bay leaf

5-10 peppercorns

½ stick cinnamon

2 cloves

1. Wash the chicken carefully, rinsing out any blood that remains in the cavity, and gently pull off any extra fat attached to the breast and tail area.

2. In a large, heavy soup pot, put the whole chicken and backs and necks, and cover completely with water. Bring to a boil, partially covered. Skim off the foamy scum that rises to the top. When there is no more scum, add the carrots, celery, parsley, garlic, onion, bay leaf, and peppercorns, and lower the heat.

3. Barely simmer the broth, uncovered or partially covered, until there are 4 cups of strong broth, about 2 hours. During the last hour of cooking, add cinnamon and cloves.

4. Using a medium-mesh sieve over a large bowl, strain broth and refrigerate. Discard chicken parts and vegetables.

5. When broth is well chilled, carefully lift off the congealed chicken fat and discard it. Set aside to make Spiced Broth with Chicken Breast.

GRILLED MARINATED VEAL CHOP

Yield: 4 servings

8 garlic cloves, peeled

12 sprigs fresh rosemary

Extra-virgin olive oil

4 large veal loin chops, 1½ to 2-inches thick

Lemon wedges

Coarse salt

1. Smash each garlic clove with the side of a large knife.

2. In a glass or stainless-steel baking dish, place half the garlic and 6 rosemary sprigs. Lay the chops on top of the herbs. Cover chops with remaining garlic and 4 more sprigs of rosemary. Pour enough olive oil over the chops to just coat them. Cover and put in refrigerator. (see Note)

3. Remove chops from marinade and with paper towels, carefully wipe off oil.

4. Grill chops, placing them on a rack over hot, glowing wood charcoal, turning once. To cook the meat medium rare takes approximately 10 to 12 minutes total. Grilling produces the best flavor but chops can also be pan fried or broiled.

5. Remove chops to a serving platter and garnish with remaining rosemary sprigs and lemon wedges. Sprinkle coarse salt and drizzle a little oil over chops just before serving.

Note: If the meat is well covered with oil it can marinate for several days. The longer it marinates, the more intense the flavor of the rosemary becomes.

POLENTA WITH PANCETTA AND SAGE

Yield: 4 to 6 servings

½ cup unsalted butter, divided

¼ pound pancetta, cut into 3-inch lengths

1 bunch fresh sage, leaves only

6½ cups water

2 teaspoons salt

1½ cups imported polenta or coarse yellow cornmeal

6 tablespoons grated Parmesan cheese

1. In a medium-size sauté pan, put 4 tablespoons butter. Add pancetta and sage, and sauté over low heat until pancetta browns, about 10 minutes. Set aside.

2. In a large pot on high heat bring water to boil and add salt.

3. When the water returns to a boil, whisk in polenta, adding it in a slow, steady stream. Reduce heat to medium and, with a wooden spoon, stir continuously until polenta is thick and soft, about 30 to 40 minutes.

4. Stir in remaining butter and Parmesan cheese.

5. Pour polenta into a wet bowl and immediately invert it onto a serving platter. Pour juices from the sauté pan over the polenta, and garnish with pancetta and sage. Serve immediately.

BRAISED FENNEL

Yield: 4 to 6 servings

3 medium fennel bulbs

3 tablespoons extra-virgin olive oil

1 large onion, peeled and cut into medium dice

2 large tomatoes, peeled, seeded, and chopped

4 bay leaves

Salt and freshly ground pepper

1. Trim fennel stalks and root ends. Remove any wilted or bruised parts. Cut bulbs in quarters lengthwise.

2. In a medium-size braising pan, put olive oil. And onions, and over low heat, sauté until tender, about 12 minutes.

3. Add fennel and sauté over medium heat until lightly colored. Add tomatoes, bay leaves, salt and pepper to taste.

4. Cook until fennel is tender when pierced with a knife.

Evan Kleiman

ANGELI CAFFE

RICOTTA PUDDING

Yield: 8 to 10 servings

2 pounds ricotta

1 egg yolk

½ cup sugar

1 teaspoon vanilla

¼ teaspoon almond extract

¼ teaspoon cinnamon

2 tablespoons lemon zest

3 egg whites

Pinch of salt

¼ teaspoon cream of tartar

1. Place the ricotta in a cheesecloth or muslin-lined strainer and set it over the sink. Let drain overnight.

Preheat oven to 325 degrees.

2. Butter a medium-sized loaf pan. Set aside.

3. Prepare a water bath by half filling a rectangular baking tray with water. The loaf pan containing the pudding will be placed in it to bake evenly and gently.

4. Using a food processor or electric mixer, process or beat the ricotta, egg yolk, sugar, vanilla and almond extracts, and cinnamon until very smooth and light. Add the zest. Transfer ricotta mixture to a large mixing bowl.

5. In another bowl, whip egg whites with the salt and cream of tartar until stiff.

6. Beat ¼ of the egg whites into the ricotta mixture, then with a rubber spatula gently fold in remaining whites.

7. Gently pour mixture into prepared loaf pan, and set pan into water bath.

8. Bake pudding until a toothpick or thin knife inserted in the center is dry when removed, about 35 to 40 minutes. Remove from oven and let cool before serving. The pudding can be served with a simple raspberry purée.

South-of-the Border Lunch

Mixed Green Salad
with Lime Vinaigrette

Game Hen Pibil

Whipped Potatoes

Lemon-Chili Butter
Sauce

Onions
Escabechada

Sangria Poached
Pear with
Sangria Compote

MIXED GREEN SALAD WITH LIME VINAIGRETTE

Yield: 6 to 8 servings salad and dressing

THE DRESSING:

Juice from 2 limes, about ¼ cup

1 scallion, minced

1½ tablespoons honey

½ teaspooon oregano

½ teaspoon ground cumin

¼ teaspoon cinnamon

¼ teaspoon ancho chili powder

⅛ teaspoon allspice

1 clove garlic, roasted and mashed

6 tablespoons olive oil

6 tablespoons corn or peanut oil

Salt, optional

THE SALAD:

8 to 10 cups crisp salad greens such as romaine, frisée, Belgian endive, and radicchio.

4 radishes, greens removed and sliced

½ carrot, sliced

¼ jicama, julienned

¼ cup pumpkin seeds, toasted

THE DRESSING:

1. In a mixing bowl or food processor, combine lime juice, scallion, honey, oregano, cumin, cinnamon, chili powder, allspice, and garlic.

2. Whisk or process in the oils. Let the vinaigrette sit, unrefrigerated, for 1 or 2 hours to allow flavors to blend. Add a dash of salt if necessary.

THE SALAD:

1. Tear or cut greens. Put in a bowl.

2. Just before serving, toss salad with dressing.

3. Place on salad plates and garnish each with radishes, carrot, jicama, and pumpkin seeds.

GAME HEN PIBIL

Yield: 6 to 8 1/2-hen servings - ideal for lunch

3 to 4 game hens (see Note)

1 cup orange juice

1 cup grapefruit juice

¼ cup lime juice, about 2 limes

¼ cup achiote paste

2 tablespoons chopped fresh garlic

2 teaspoons salt

2 tablespoons ground black pepper

2 bay leaves

1 teaspoon ground allspice

1 teaspoon dried oregano

¼ teaspoon ground cumin

6 to 8 banana leaves, optional

6 to 8 mild chilies, such as banana, poblano or sweet Italian

1. With a cleaver or knife, split hens in half. Remove back bones and reserve for stock, if desired. Place hens in a baking dish skin side up. Set aside.

2. In a bowl, combine orange, grapefruit, and lime juices, achiote paste, garlic, salt, pepper, bay leaves, allspice, oregano, and cumin, and mix well.

3. Pour over hens and marinate overnight, covered, in refrigerator.

Preheat oven to 325 degrees.

4. Place each hen on a banana leaf or foil, and partially wrap hen. Before closing package, top each hen with a chili and add several spoonfuls of marinade to the package. Wrap banana leaf around hen tightly.

5. Place the wrapped hens in a baking dish, and bake for 1½ to 2 hours.

6. Before serving, open packages and put in hot oven or broiler to brown skin, about 3 to 5 minutes. Serve with Whipped Potatoes, Onions Escabechada and Lemon-Chili Butter Sauce. (Hens can be reheated and served the next day.)

Note: Hens need to marinate overnight.

WHIPPED POTATOES

Yield: 8 to 10 servings

3 Idaho potatoes, peeled

1 yam, peeled

1 ripe plantain or two ripe bananas, peeled

6 to 8 tablespoons butter

½ cup milk

Salt to taste

1. Cut potatoes, yam, and plantain into large chunks. Put in a pot and cover with cold water. Bring to a boil and cook covered, until tender, about 20 minutes.

2. Place a collander in the sink and drain vegetables. Put them in a bowl.

3. Using an electric mixer or potato masher, whip vegetables and add the butter, milk, and salt, mashing until smooth. Serve.

LEMON-CHILI BUTTER SAUCE

Yield: about 1 cup

1 tablespoon finely chopped red onions

¼ cup lemon juice

¼ cup white wine

1 jalapeño, serrano or habanero chili, finely chopped (see Note)

⅓ cup unsalted butter, softened

1. In a saucepan, put onion, lemon juice, wine, and chili. Simmer uncovered, until reduced to one-third, about 10 to 15 minutes.

2. Remove saucepan from heat and whisk in butter, 1 tablespoon at a time. Using a fine or medium mesh strainer over a bowl, strain. Keep sauce at room temperature.

Note: This sauce can be made as hot as desired, or chilies can be omitted.

ONIONS ESCABECHADA

Yield: about 4 cups

2 red onions, peeled and sliced thin

½ cup cider vinegar

½ cup water plus extra

1 jalapeño or serrano chili

1 bay leaf

1 clove garlic, peeled

½ teaspoon salt

¼ teaspoon cumin

¼ teaspoon oregano

Marjorie Kloss

ZOCALO

1. Place onions in a bowl and fill with water. Soak for 10 minutes. Remove onions and discard water.

2. In a saucepan, put vinegar, ½ cup water, jalapeño chili, bay leaf, garlic, salt, cumin, and oregano. Mix well and add onions.

3. Bring to a boil, covered. Reduce heat and simmer, stirring, and cook about 5 minutes.

4. Turn off heat and let sit covered until cool.

SANGRIA POACHED PEAR WITH SANGRIA COMPOTE

Yield: 6 to 8 servings

4 cups water

2 cups red wine

1 cup orange juice

1¼ cups sugar

½ cup blueberries, blackberries, or raspberries, optional for color

½ cup rum

1 cinnamon stick

4 whole allspice berries

Juice of 1 lemon

Juice of 1 lime

6 to 8 firm Anjou or Bosc pears, carefully peeled and seeded

1. In a medium-size pot, put water, wine, orange juice, 1 cup sugar, berries, rum, cinnamon stick, allspice, and lemon and lime juices. Bring to a boil, covered.

2. Add pears to the poaching liquid and cover. Lower heat and simmer pears until tender, about 20 minutes.

3. Turn off heat and allow pears to cool in poaching liquid, about 1½ hours.

4. While the pears are cooling, remove 2 cups of the poaching liquid and put into a saucepan. Add ¼ cup sugar and bring to a boil. Reduce flame, and simmer until reduced by half, uncovered.

5. Serve pears on a dessert plate with sauce drizzled over, and with either vanilla wafers, a sorbet or fresh fruit on the side.

New York Brunch

Perfectly
Scrambled Eggs

Goldilox

English Muffins

Scallop and
Shrimp Loaf

Yellow Peppers
and Onion Salad

Poached Pears
and Yogurt Parfait

PERFECTLY SCRAMBLED EGGS

Yield: 1 serving

2 or 3 large eggs (see Note)

2 teaspoons clarified butter

1. In a mixing bowl, with a fork or wire whisk, beat eggs until the yolks and whites are well incorporated, about 50 strokes.

2. Using a medium-mesh strainer, over another bowl, strain the eggs.

3. In a skillet on a medium flame, heat the clarified butter. When butter is hot, lower the flame and add eggs. Cook slowly and as eggs begin to firm up, stir them gently with a rubber spatula to keep them from sticking to the bottom of the pan. Be careful not to overcook or overmix.

4. Serve on a warm plate.

Note: When preparing larger quantities of eggs, beat eggs with an electric mixer at medium speed for 30 seconds. Use a large skillet and extra butter.

GOLDILOX

Yield: 1 serving

2 to 3 large eggs

2 teaspoons clarified butter

1 ounce Nova Scotia salmon, sliced

2 ounces cream cheese, cubed

1. Cook the eggs as directed for Perfectly Scrambled Eggs.

2. When eggs are almost done, evenly distribute salmon and cream cheese over eggs.

3. Remove pan from heat and gently fold salmon and cheese into eggs, taking care not to break up cubes of cheese.

4. Turn out on a warm plate and serve immediately

ENGLISH MUFFINS

Yield: about 14 muffins

1 cup milk

1 cup water

2 tablespoons sugar

½ teaspoon salt

2 ½ tablespoons sweet butter, melted

1 tablespoon active dry yeast

1 large egg

4 cups unbleached flour

Cornmeal for dusting

English muffin rings (see Note)

1. In a saucepan, put milk, water, sugar, and salt, and bring to a boil, covered.

2. Add butter and remove saucepan from heat.

3. Cool milk mixture to room temperature and pour into a large mixing bowl. Add yeast, egg, and flour.

4. Using an electric mixer or by hand with a whisk, beat at medium speed until batter is smooth and has a loose, sticky consistency.

5. Cover bowl with plastic wrap and place in refrigerator. Leave overnight.

6. Butter English muffin rings, dip these in cornmeal, and place rings on a baking sheet.

7. Take bowl out of refrigerator and with a rubber spatula, stir down batter until it is deflated. Fill muffin rings half full and sprinkle tops lightly with cornmeal. Cover loosely with a cloth and let dough rise to tops of rings, about 45 minutes to an hour.

Preheat oven to 450 degrees.

8. Bake muffins until golden, about 15 minutes. Remove from oven and lift rings off muffins. With a metal spatula, put muffins on a serving platter.

9. Enjoy muffins sliced in half and toasted.

Note: English muffin rings are available at specialty kitchenware stores. They are metal rings 1⅜ inches high and about 3 inches in diameter. As a substitute, use empty 7½-ounce tuna fish cans, tops and bottoms removed and any rough edges filed away.

SCALLOP AND SHRIMP LOAF

Yield: 12 servings

1½ pounds bay scallops

½ pound shelled shrimp, deveined

2 large eggs, separated, plus one egg white

2 teaspoons kosher salt

¾ teaspoon freshly ground pepper

1 tablespoon fresh lemon juice

1 tablespoon dry white wine

¼ cup chopped Italian parsley

2 cups heavy cream

Butter

Preheat oven to 325 degrees.

1. In a food processor, coarsely purée scallops and shrimp. Add egg whites, one at a time, and pulse until shellfish becomes a smooth purée.

2. Put purée in a sieve over a bowl. With the back of a wooden spoon or spatula, force purée through sieve. To the strained purée, add salt, pepper, lemon juice, wine, and parsley, and mix well. Stir in cream.

3. Butter a medium-size, enameled terrine and fill with shellfish purée. With a spatula, level the top of the loaf.

4. Fill baking dish with an inch of water and place terrine in this. Bake until firm, about 45 minutes.

5. Remove terrine from oven. Let cool.

6. Remove loaf from terrine. Cover with plastic wrap and chill until ready to serve. Carefully slice with a sharp serrated knife.

YELLOW PEPPERS AND ONION SALAD

Yield: 6 servings

8 yellow peppers

Boiling water

1 large Spanish onion, sliced thin

2 tablespoons rice vinegar

2 tablespoons apple cider vinegar

6 tablespoons olive oil

¼ cup freshly chopped parsley

Salt and freshly ground pepper

1. Wash peppers and cut in half. Remove stems and seeds.

2. Add peppers to boiling water, cooking just long enough to soften the skins, about 5 minutes.

3. Using a slotted spoon, remove peppers from pot and put into a colander. Place colander under running cold water to cool peppers.

4. Put pepper halves on paper towels to dry.

5. Peel skins and cut peppers into ¾-inch wide strips.

6. Put peppers in a stainless steel bowl and add onion, rice and cider vinegars, oil, parsley, salt, and pepper. Mix, cover and chill in refrigerator for 2 hours before serving.

Sarabeth Levine

SARABETH'S KITCHEN

POACHED PEARS AND YOGURT PARFAIT

Yield: 4 to 6 servings

1 cup water

½ cup sugar

1 tablespoon lemon juice

⅛ teaspoon salt

1 vanilla bean

6 sprigs of fresh mint

6 slightly under-ripe pears, peeled, cored, and cut in medium cubes

1 cup goat milk yogurt

1 tablespoon finely chopped crystallized ginger

½ cup sliced almonds, toasted and chopped

1. In a 2-quart stainless steel pot, put water, sugar, lemon juice, and salt, and bring to a boil, covered.

2. To the syrup mixture, squeeze in the vanilla from the bean and add the pod, 4 mint sprigs, and pears. Bring to a boil, covered, and reduce heat to simmer. Cook pears until al dente, about 10 to 15 minutes.

3. Using a collander in another pot, pour in the pears and syrup. Lift out collander and set aside. Bring syrup to a boil and simmer uncovered until reduced by one-third.

4. In parfait glasses, layer the pears and syrup, alternating with yogurt. End with a layer of yogurt. Sprinkle top of parfait with ginger and nuts, and garnish with remaining mint.

Sunday Dinner

Lemon Roasted Chicken

Maple Glazed Carrots with Tarragon

Fresh Green Beans with Bacon

Spoon Bread

Deep Dish Apple Pie

LEMON ROASTED CHICKEN

Yield: 6 servings

1 6- to 8-pound roasting chicken

2 small onions, finely diced

2 small carrots, finely diced

1 stalk celery, finely diced

6 lemons, peel grated

2 bay leaves, broken

4 sprigs parsley, coarsely chopped

Kosher salt and freshly ground pepper

4 tablespoons butter, room temperature

1 tablespoon oil

Preheat oven to 425 degrees.

1. Wash and dry chicken. Trim excess fat from neck and body cavity. Set aside on a board or tray.

2. In a bowl combine the onions, carrots, celery, half the peel, bay leaves, and parsley. Toss together and season with salt and pepper. Stuff cavity of chicken with mixture.

3. Divide the remaining lemon peel in half (about 1 teaspoon). In a bowl, add lemon peel, butter, salt, and pepper. Beginning at the neck end of the chicken, using your fingers, gently push skin away from breast meat, and into this pocket press butter mixture.

4. Truss and tie chicken. Rub outside of chicken with oil. Add salt and pepper to the remaining lemon peel and by hand, pat this mixture onto chicken skin.

5. In a roasting pan with a rack, put chicken. Roast for 15 minutes and reduce temperature to 350 degrees. Continue to roast chicken for an additional 1 to 1½-hours or until done. (The chicken juices will run clear and legs will move easily. If using a thermometer, the internal temperature of the thigh meat will be 180 degrees.)

6. Remove chicken from oven and let rest 15 to 20 minutes. (While chicken is cooling, leave oven on to bake spoon bread.)

7. Carve and serve.

MAPLE GLAZED CARROTS WITH TARRAGON

Yield: 6 servings

1 pound carrots with tops

Boiling water

1½ teaspoons salt

2 tablespoons butter

1 to 2 tablespoons maple syrup

1 tablespoon fresh tarragon, chopped

Kosher salt and freshly ground pepper

1. Remove carrot tops and discard. Peel carrots and cut in half lengthwise. Then cut crosswise into half moon slices.

2. In a large pot put water and salt. Add carrots and blanch until just tender, about 3 to 4 minutes. Drain carrots and cool in a bowl of cold water. Drain again, shaking to remove excess water. This can be done a day ahead.

3. In a sauté pan, over medium heat, melt butter and add blanched carrots and 1 tablespoon maple syrup. Stir until carrots are hot. If carrots stick to pan, add a table-spoon or two of water. Add tarragon, salt, and pepper. Taste and add more maple syrup, if desired. Stir briefly and serve.

FRESH GREEN BEANS WITH BACON

Yield: 6 servings

6 slices lean smoked bacon, cut crosswise in ¼-inch wide strips

2 small onions, diced

2 pounds tender fresh green beans, ends trimmed and beans snapped in half (see Note)

Water

Kosher salt and freshly ground pepper

1. In a large pot, over medium heat, slowly cook the bacon. When bacon begins to brown, add onions and sauté until soft, about 15 minutes.

3. Add beans and stir to mix. Add enough water to cover beans so they float a little. Bring to boil, covered, and reduce heat to low. Simmer until beans are very tender but have not fallen apart, about 1½ to 2 hours. Add additional water if necessary. Before serving, season with salt and pepper to taste.

SPOON BREAD

Yield: 6 large servings

3½ cups water (more as needed)

1 tablespoon kosher salt

1 cup yellow or white cornmeal

¼ cup non-instant grits

4½ tablespoons butter, room temperature

1 cup half-and-half

3 eggs, separated

1. In a 2-quart saucepan, boil water and salt, covered. Slowly whisk in cornmeal and grits, stirring constantly. Reduce heat to low, and cover. Stir frequently. (If texture looks dry, add a little water.) Cook until soft, about 30 minutes.

2. Grease a 2-quart baking dish with ½ tablespoon butter.

3. In a bowl, whisk together half-and-half and egg yolks.

Preheat oven to 350 degrees.

4. When cornmeal and grits are cooked, stir in remaining butter and half-and-half mixture.

5. Using an electric mixer, beat egg whites until stiff but not dry. Fold whites into cornmeal mixture.

6. Pour batter into baking dish, place in a water bath, and put in oven. Bake until puffed and light brown, about 30 minutes. Serve immediately, hot from the oven with your very best serving spoon!

DEEP DISH APPLE PIE

Yield: 1 10-inch deep-dish pie

THE PIE CRUST:

3¼ cups flour

2 tablespoons sugar, plus extra

1 teaspoon salt

10 ounces cold butter, cut into pieces

6 to 10 tablespoons cold water

THE FILLING:

4½ pounds mixed tart baking apples, (see Note)

3 tablespoons lemon juice

1 teaspoon vanilla

¾ to 1 cup sugar, depending on tartness of apples

4 tablespoons flour

1½ teaspoons cinnamon

½ teaspoon nutmeg

THE PIE CRUST:

1. In a bowl mix flour, sugar, and salt. Using your finger tips, work butter into flour mixture until the texture resembles coarse meal.

2. While fluffing the flour mixture with one hand, slowly add cold water until mixture is sticky enough to form a ball.

3. On a lightly floured board, place dough and knead briefly.

4. Shape the dough into a flat circle. Cover with plastic wrap and chill for one hour. (The dough can be held for 10 to 12 days in the refrigerator, and in the freezer for 2 to 3 months.) While the dough is chilling, prepare the filling.

THE FILLING:

1. Peel and core apples. Slice very thin and put into a large bowl.

2. Toss apples with lemon juice and vanilla.

3. In a small bowl mix ¾ cup sugar, flour, cinnamon, and nutmeg. Add to apples and toss. Taste and add more sugar, if needed.

Preheat oven to 350 degrees.

To assemble:

1. Cut pastry in half and on a floured board, roll out dough to ¼-inch thick. Roll larger than pie plate. Place dough in plate and leave excess untrimmed. Layer apples carefully to create a mound higher than the rim of dish.

2. Roll the remaining dough as before. Cut out small triangular holes in the center area and place crust on top of apples.

3. Trim dough edges to overhang ½-inch. Starting with the bottom crust, roll the two layers of dough upward and toward the center of the pie. Crimp edges together. Brush top crust lightly with water and sprinkle several teaspoons of sugar on top.

4. Bake until pie is bubbling from center, about 1½ to 2 hours. If crust is browning too fast, reduce heat to 325 degrees and cover pie with aluminum foil.

5. Remove pie from oven and place on a cooling rack. Cool to room temperature for easier cutting. Reheat slices if hot pie is desired.

Note: A mixture of apples gives the pie a depth of flavor that changes with the varieties. Good choices are Empire, Jonagold, Greening, Granny Smith.

Susan McCreight Lindeborg

MORRISON
CLARK
INN

Easy Elegant Dinner

Butter Lettuce Salad with Sliced Pears and Candied Pecans

Honey Mustard Salmon

Garlic and Sun-dried Tomato Mashed Potatoes

Green Beans Provençal

Lemon Lime Tart

Nanaimo Bars

BUTTER LETTUCE SALAD WITH SLICED PEARS AND CANDIED PECANS

Yield: 6 servings

THE PECANS:

½ cup pecans

4 tablespoons sugar

Salt and freshly ground pepper

THE SALAD:

1 large head Butter lettuce (10 cups)

2 to 3 Bosc pears, quartered, cored and sliced

½ cup Balsamic vinaigrette

5 tablespoons blue cheese

THE PECANS:

1. In a sauté pan, heat pecans on medium-high heat 2 minutes.

2. Add sugar, letting it melt and coat pecans. Season with a dash of salt and pepper. Toss until pecans are glazed.

3. Transfer pecans to a plate and let cool. Separate pecans, and set aside.

THE SALAD:

1. In a bowl toss together lettuce, pears, and candied pecans. Add Balsamic Vinaigrette to taste and toss again.

2. Divide salad among 6 salad plates. Crumble cheese on lettuce, and serve.

BALSAMIC VINAIGRETTE

Yield: about 1 cup

¾ cup olive oil

¼ cup balsamic vinegar

2 tablespoons minced garlic

2 tablespoons water

1. In a small bowl whisk together oil, vinegar, and garlic.

2. Boil water in a small saucepan and whisk into vinaigrette. Set aside.

HONEY MUSTARD SALMON

Yield: 4 to 6 servings

½ cup liquid honey

2 to 3 tablespoons hot water

2 tablespoons grain mustard

2 pounds farmed spring salmon fillets

1. In a saucepan combine honey, water, and mustard. Warm over medium heat.

2. Arrange salmon fillets in a non-glass baking dish and pour half of sauce over fish. Put under broiler and cook until just done, 10 to 12 minutes.

3. Remove dish from broiler and pour remaining sauce over salmon. Return dish to broiler and broil 30 seconds more. Serve.

GARLIC AND SUN-DRIED TOMATO MASHED POTATOES

Yield: 8 servings

1 cup reconstituted sun-dried tomatoes, chopped

2 tablespoons olive oil

6 cups water

¾ teaspoon salt

8 potatoes, peeled

6 cloves garlic

2 tablespoons butter

6 to 8 tablespoons heavy cream

Preheat oven to 350 degrees.

1. In a small bowl, combine tomatoes and oil and set aside to soak.

2. In a large pot put water and salt, and bring to a boil.

3. Add potatoes and cook until tender, about 30 to 40 minutes.

4. Meanwhile, put garlic on baking sheet and bake until soft, about 15 minutes. Remove from oven.

5. Drain cooked potatoes. Place on baking sheet along with garlic. Return to oven and roast vegetables 5 minutes.

6. In a large bowl, put potatoes, garlic, butter, and cream. Remove tomatoes from oil. Add to potatoes and mash together.

7. Return potato mixture to pot and heat thoroughly. Season to taste. Serve.

GREEN BEANS PROVENÇAL

Yield: 4 to 6 servings

2 cups water

1 pound green beans, ends removed

2 tablespoons butter

4 cloves garlic, crushed or minced very fine

1 Roma tomato, chopped (½ cup)

¼ teaspoon salt

Freshly ground pepper

1. In a medium-size saucepan bring water to boil. Add beans and cook until tender, about 3 to 4 minutes. Do not overcook. Drain and cover pot to keep beans warm.

2. In a sauté pan melt butter with garlic. Add tomatoes, salt, and pepper and stirring, cook 30 seconds. Add beans and toss to evenly coat beans with tomato mixture. Serve warm.

LEMON LIME TART

Yield: 1 pie filling

1 cup sugar

3 eggs

2 tablespoons flour

½ cup freshly squeezed lemon juice

¼ cup lime juice

Zest of 1 lemon, finely grated

7 tablespoons melted butter

10-inch prebaked Sweet Dough Pastry pie crust

Preheat oven to 325 degrees.

1. In a bowl combine sugar and eggs, mixing well. Stir in flour. Add lemon and lime juices, zest, and butter. Mix well.

2. Pour lemon-lime mixture into pie shell and bake for 30 to 35 minutes. Do not allow tart to brown. Serve warm.

SWEET DOUGH PASTRY

Yield: 1 pie crust

⅔ cup butter

¾ cup sugar

2 egg yolks, beaten

2 cups all-purpose flour

1. In a bowl or a food processor, cream together butter and sugar. Add egg yolks and flour, and mix until a ball forms.

2. Remove dough from bowl and cover dough with plastic film and chill 1 hour.

Preheat oven to 325 degrees.

3. On a floured surface, roll dough into a circle to fit a 10-inch pie plate. Place dough in pie plate, trim and crimp edges, and prick pastry with a fork.

4. Bake until golden, about 10 to 12 minutes.

Susan Mendelson

LAZY GOURMET

NANAIMO BARS

Yield: 16 to 20 bars

LAYER ONE:

½ cup butter

¼ cup sugar

1 egg beaten

1 teaspoon vanilla

1 tablespoon cocoa

2 cups graham cracker crumbs

1 cup coconut

½ cup chopped nuts

LAYER TWO:

¼ cup butter

3 tablespoons milk

2 cups powdered sugar

2 tablespoons ready-made custard mix

LAYER THREE:

4 ounces semisweet chocolate

1 tablespoon butter

LAYER ONE:

1. Using a double boiler, heat butter, sugar, egg, vanilla, and cocoa. Stir until slightly thickened.

2. Add graham cracker, coconut, and nuts.

3. Grease a 9-inch baking pan, and press in mixture with a spoon. Let stand 15 minutes.

LAYER TWO:

1. In a bowl mix together the butter, milk, sugar, and custard mix.

2. With a spatula spread over the first layer. Refrigerate for 15 minutes.

LAYER THREE:

1. In the top of a double boiler melt chocolate. Do not allow water to boil.

2. Very slowly and gently, stir in butter until it has just blended.

3. With a spatula, spread chocolate mixture over layer two.

4. Refrigerate until chilled, about 1 hour. Cut into squares.

Hollywood Star Dinner

Honey Glazed and Spiced Ranch Squab

Red Snapper Mediterranean

Three Flavors of Lemon

HONEY GLAZED AND SPICED RANCH SQUAB

Yield: 6 servings

6 squabs

2 tablespoons ground dried orange peel

½ teaspoon powdered cardamom

¼ teaspoon fennel seeds, crushed

¼ teaspoon anise seeds, crushed

⅛ teaspoon caraway seeds

Sea salt and freshly ground black pepper

16 tablespoons blossom honey

¼ cup molasses

1½ tablespoons green peppercorns, crushed

6 ounces port

2 cups plus 2 tablespoons chicken stock

24 white icicle radishes, peeled, stem on

2 tablespoons butter, room temperature

Freshly ground white pepper

18 Medjool dates, halved and pitted

6 fresh figs, cut in quarters

Preheat oven to 350 degrees.

1. Remove squab wing at first joint. Roast wing bones until golden brown, about 15 minutes. Reserve.

2. Combine orange peel, cardamom, fennel, anise, caraway, salt, and pepper. Season squabs inside and out.

3. In a shallow pan mix together 14 tablespoons honey, molasses, and 1 tablespoon green peppercorns. Dredge squabs in honey mixture, at all angles.

4. Heat a heavy sauté pan. Sear squabs. Put in a baking pan and spoon more honey mixture over birds. Roast breast side up. For medium rare, roast 15 minutes.

5. Remove breast meat from bone. Carefully remove leg and thigh from carcass. Remove bone from thigh. Chop carcass, wing, and thigh bones.

6. In a heavy sauce pan, place bones and quickly saute. Deglaze pan with 4 ounces port. Reduce liquid by half. Add chicken stock. Bring to a boil. Simmer uncovered for 15 minutes.

7. Cook radishes in 1 tablespoon butter without browning, about 4 to 5 minutes. Add salt and white pepper. Set aside.

8. Arrange squabs on platter. Garnish with radishes.

9. Strain squab jus into a saucepan, and return to heat. Add the remaining port, honey, and green peppercorns, and dates and figs. Stir in 1 tablespoon butter. Spoon sauce over squab and serve.

RED SNAPPER MEDITERRANEAN

Yield: 6 servings

1 lemon, rind peeled

½ cup sugar

2 tablespoons water

12 baby fennel, stalks trimmed

2 cups chicken stock

1 pound baby spinach

½ cup olive oil, plus extra

2 vine-ripe tomatoes, peeled, seeded and chopped

Salt and cracked black pepper

6 6-ounce red snapper fillets, with skin

1. Fill bowl with cold water and drop in rind. Let sit 1 minute and strain. Discard water. Repeat procedure with fresh water twice.

2. In a small saucepan, combine sugar and 2 tablespoons water. Add rind and cook, uncovered, over low heat, until thickened, 20 to 25 minutes. Chill lemon rind in sauce.

Preheat oven to 375 degrees.

3. Put fennel in a pot, cover with stock. Bring to a boil and then turn off flame. Transfer fennel to a baking dish and cover with oiled parchment paper. Braise in oven until tender, about 30 minutes. Set aside.

4. Bring 1 quart water to a boil. Add spinach, blanch and remove with slotted spoon. Set aside.

5. Coat bottom of sauté pan with oil and add tomatoes. Sauté over low heat, stirring occasionally, 10 to 15 minutes.

6. Julienne cooked fennel. Remove candied rind from sauce and julienne.

7. In another skillet, sauté spinach in some oil, for 2 to 3 minutes.

8. When tomatoes are cooked, add fennel and rind. Gently combine and keep warm.

9. In a bowl whisk 1 teaspoon lemon juice, ¼ cup oil, salt, and pepper. Brush fillets with mixture.

10. Score skin of fillets to insure even cooking. Sear on a hot grill or in a sauté pan, flesh side first and then finish cooking on skin side until skin is crisp and flesh moist, about 8 to 10 minutes. Place on a serving platter.

11. Put spinach around edge of platter. Spoon tomato mixture around fish. Serve with lemon sauce on the side.

THREE FLAVORS OF LEMON

Yield: 4 to 6 servings

The lemon confit:

1½ lemons

5 cups water

2 cups granulated sugar

The lemon granite:

¼ bunch mint (6 to 8 sprigs)

1 sprig thyme, plus extra for garnish

1 cup water, boiling

¼ cup plus 2 tablespoons fresh lemon juice (3 lemons)

½ cup sugar syrup at 30 degrees (see Note)

THE LEMON ICE CREAM:

¼ cup fresh lemon juice (1 lemon)

¾ cup sugar

1 cup milk

5 egg yolks

1½ cups heavy cream

THE LEMON TART:

4 tablespoons butter

3 tablespoons powdered sugar

Zest of ¼ lemon

½ cup plus 2 teaspoons flour

Pinch salt

1 egg, plus 1 egg yolk

2 tablespoon lemon juice

1½ teaspoons cream

The lemon confit:

1. With a paring knife, cut ½-inch wide strips of lemon peel without removing pith, the length of the lemon.

2. Put 1 cup cold water and peel into saucepan. Bring to a boil, covered, and boil 1 minute. Drain peel and rinse well in cold water. Repeat procedure two more times.

3. Put 1 cup sugar and 2 cups water in saucepan and add peel. Simmer uncovered 15 minutes. Add remaining sugar and continue to simmer another 15 minutes. Let peel cool in syrup overnight, covered.

Carrie Nahabedian

THE FOUR SEASONS HOTEL

THE LEMON GRANITE:

1. Add mint and thyme to water. Remove from heat and let steep for 20 minutes, covered. Strain infusion into a bowl. Add lemon juice and syrup. Freeze thoroughly, about 2 hours.

THE LEMON ICE CREAM:

1. In a saucepan, bring lemon juice and ⅔ cup sugar to a boil. Set aside.

2. Put milk and 1 tablespoon sugar in another pot. Bring to a boil. Set aside.

3. In a bowl, whisk together egg yolks and 1 tablespoon sugar until egg yolks form a ribbon. Slowly whisk into milk mixture. Cook until thickened, 185 degrees on a thermometer.

4. Put cream in a bowl, and pour egg mixture through a strainer into cream. Add juice mixture and stir to combine.

5. Using an ice cream machine, churn mixture according to manufacturer's instructions.

Preheat oven to 375 degrees.

THE LEMON TART:

1. In a food processor, blend butter, sugar, and zest. Add ½ cup flour and salt. Mix until a ball forms.

2. On a floured surface, roll dough to ¼-inch thick, and place in 8-inch tart pan. Bake until pastry is golden, about 15 minutes.

Lower heat to 325 degrees.

3. In a bowl, whisk together egg and yolk, 2 teaspoons flour, lemon juice, and cream. Pour onto prebaked crust. Bake until set, about 20 minutes.

To assemble:

1. Cut a wedge of tart and place on individual plate. Shave granite over tart. Top with ice cream, and garnish with lemon confit and sprig of mint.

Note: Make a heavy syrup by combining 1 part sugar with 1 part water, and put in saucepan to boil for 5 minutes.

California Dinner Party

Lobster Cocktail with Meyer Lemon Vinaigrette

Roasted Squab with Wild Mushroom and Asparagus Salad with a Warm Caramelized Onion Vinaigrette

Salmon with Summer Truffles and Leeks

Red Wine Risotto

Lemon Custard with Figs and Berries and a Lemon Vanilla Sauce

LOBSTER COCKTAIL WITH MEYER LEMON VINAIGRETTE

Yield: 6 servings

THE COCKTAIL:

3 Maine lobsters, cooked, shells removed

3 ears sweet white corn

3 tablespoons chopped chives

THE MEYER LEMON VINAIGRETTE:

3 Meyer lemons, zest and juice (½ cup juice)

1 teaspoon champagne vinegar

1 teaspoon white balsamic vinegar

3 shallots, finely minced

½ teaspoon fresh rosemary, finely minced

1 tablespoon mild flavoured honey

Kosher salt and freshly ground pepper

1 cup olive oil

To assemble:

½ cup ancho cress

½ cup baby mâche

6 tablespoons golden tobiko caviar

Heat oven to 400 degrees.

THE COCKTAIL:

1. Cut lobster meat into chunks and set aside.

2. Without removing husk from corn, open up husks and remove excess corn silk. Replace husk around corn. Place corn in oven on shelf and roast for 15 minutes. Remove from oven and set aside to cool.

3. Remove corn husks. Break corn in half. Using a sharp knife, cut kernels from the cob and put in a bowl. Add chives and mix. Set aside.

THE MEYER LEMON VINAIGRETTE:

1. In a bowl, combine lemon juice, and champagne and balsamic vinegars. Add shallots, rosemary, honey, lemon zest, salt, and pepper.

2. Whisk in the olive oil and set aside.

To assemble:

1. Select 6 spectacular Martini glasses! Put 2 spoonfuls of corn mixture in each glass and 2 or 3 tablespoons of vinaigrette, reserving some to drizzle on top of cocktail.

2. Divide lobster into 6 equal portions (1 claw and ½ tail per person) and add to each glass.

3. Drizzle with remaining dressing. Garnish with cress, baby mâche, and a tablespoon of caviar. Serve.

ROASTED SQUAB WITH WILD MUSHROOM AND ASPARAGUS SALAD WITH A WARM CARAMELIZED ONION VINAIGRETTE

Yield: 6 servings

1 ¼ cups olive oil

2 yellow onions, finely chopped

6 squabs

2 tablespoons chopped fresh thyme

Salt and freshly ground black pepper

1 cup chanterelle mushrooms, washed

2 tablespoons chopped garlic

½ cup aged balsamic vinegar

¼ cup good red wine vinegar

4 cups frisée, well picked, white parts only

2 cups asparagus, cooked and cut into 2-inch lengths

1. In a large skillet, put 2 tablespoons olive oil and onions. Cook over low heat, uncovered, until very well caramelized, about 1 hour. Set aside to cool.

Preheat oven to 450 degrees.

2. Using a sharp deboning knife, cut squab into quarters. Remove breast bones. Season with thyme, salt, and pepper.

3. Heat an iron skillet on a high flame until it is hot. Place squab breasts in skillet, skin side down and brown until well caramelized. Turn over and brown other side. Put squab in baking pan.

4. Deglaze skillet and drizzle the pan juice over squab and set aside.

5. In a large bowl put mushrooms, garlic, 2 tablespoons olive oil, salt, and pepper. Toss together. Pour over squab. Put pan in oven and roast for 7 minutes. Remove from oven and set aside.

6. In a large bowl, whisk together the vinegars and 1 cup olive oil. Add onions and mix well. Add frisée, asparagus, and baked mushrooms, and toss. Reserve some dressing for garnish.

7. Divide salad equally on 6 individual plates, and place squab on top. Drizzle salad with reserved vinaigrette.

SALMON WITH SUMMER TRUFFLES AND LEEKS

Yield: 6 servings

12 medium-size leeks

6 6-ounce salmon steaks, thick center cut

Salt and freshly ground pepper

1 large Summer truffle (Hazelnut truffle)

1. Cut leeks in half lengthwise and soak in water. Discard tough outer leaves. Chop leeks into ½-inch pieces. In a pot of boiling salted water, blanch leeks until tender, about 5 minutes. Put in a bowl of ice water.

2. Place each salmon steak on a piece of plastic wrap. Season with salt and pepper. Cover top of fish with a thin layer of leeks.

3. Using a mandolin, thinly slice truffles. Place 3 or 4 slices on top of leeks.

4. Wrap salmon tightly. Place in freezer until almost solid, about 20 minutes.

Preheat oven to 350 degrees.

5. Remove salmon from freezer and unwrap. Cook salmon on oiled baking sheet until medium rare, about 8 to 10 minutes. Do not turn over.

RED WINE RISOTTO

Yield: 6 to 8 servings

2 large red beets

1 cup red wine

3 cups port

2 tablespoons olive oil

1 large red onion, finely diced

1½ cups superfino arborio rice

1 tablespoon sweet butter

Salt and freshly ground pepper

Preheat oven to 400 degrees.

1. Put beets in a roasting pan and bake until tender, about 1 hour. Remove from oven and set aside to cool.

2. Peel beets and purée them.

3. Using a fine mesh strainer over a bowl, push beets through strainer to make beet juice. Set aside residual solids in strainer.

4. In a small pot, over medium heat, warm wine. Add beet juice.

5. In a separate pot, warm port and bring to a simmer.

6. Heat oil in heavy pot, over a medium flame. Add onion and cook until tender.

7. Turn heat to medium high and add rice. Stir until rice is well coated and begins to sizzle, about 3 minutes. Do not brown rice.

8. Add ¼ cup port, stir rice and cook. Let port evaporate, about 2 minutes. Slowly add 1 cup port, to cover the rice. Simmer uncovered. Shake pan and stir continually, about 3 minutes. Continue this process, adding the port, a half cup at a time. After about 12 minutes, stir in beet juice mixture. When all liquid is absorbed and rice is done, stir in butter, beet solids, salt and pepper.

LEMON CUSTARD WITH FIGS AND BERRIES AND A LEMON VANILLA SAUCE

Yield: 6 servings

THE CUSTARD:

2 sticks butter, plus extra

½ cup crème fraîche

5 large eggs plus 5 large egg yolks

6 to 8 Meyer lemons (2 tablespoons zest and 1½ cups juice)

1½ cups superfine sugar

6 fresh figs, sliced

1½ cups raspberries, blackberries, or blueberries

THE LEMON VANILLA SAUCE:

1 cup sugar

½ cup water

2 to 3 Meyer lemons (zest from 1 lemon and ½ cup juice)

1 vanilla bean

THE CUSTARD:

Preheat oven to 250 degrees.

1. Grease 6 3-inch round custard molds. Place on a baking sheet and set aside.

2. In the top half of a double boiler, put 2 sticks butter and crème fraîche. Heat uncovered, stirring frequently until warm.

3. In a bowl over a hot water bath, put eggs and yolks, and whisk together.

4. Pour eggs into a small saucepan and heat over medium flame, whisking constantly until warm.

5. Using an electric mixer, slowly beat the butter mixture into the eggs. Cook until steaming. Beat in lemon juice.

6. Place a clean double boiler top on work surface and place a fine mesh sieve in it. Strain egg and butter mixture through seive.

7. Add sugar and lemon zest and place top over boiling water. Stir until foam disappears and mixture is warm, about 4 to 5 minutes.

8. Pour into prepared molds.

9. Bake until custard is firm around edges and center is almost set, about 30 minutes. Remove and refrigerate until set, about 1 hour.

THE SAUCE:

1. In a saucepan, combine sugar, water, zest, lemon juice, and vanilla. Heat over moderate flame until sugar has melted.

To assemble:

1. Slide a knife around custard edge. Invert custard onto individual plates.

2. Spoon Lemon Vanilla Sauce over custard and accent with berries and figs.

Nancy Oakes

BOULEVARD

New England Fall Lunch

Creamless Butternut Squash Soup with Roasted Chestnuts

Roasted Duck Breasts with Wild Mushroom Risotto

Grilled Endive, Roquefort and Pear Salad

Fresh Fruit Rustic Tartlettes

CREAMLESS BUTTERNUT SQUASH SOUP WITH ROASTED CHESTNUTS

Yield:10 servings

THE SOUP:

1 medium butternut squash, halved and seeded

2 tablespoons butter

2 medium onions, thinly sliced

¼ teaspoon ground mace

¼ teaspoon ground cinnamon

Pinch of nutmeg

5½ cups chicken stock

Salt and freshly ground pepper

THE CHESTNUTS:

12 fresh chestnuts

1 1/2 tablespoons butter

Preheat oven to 400 degrees.

THE SOUP:

1. Place squash cut side up on a cookie sheet and bake until fork easily inserts into squash.

2. Remove from oven and cool slightly. Scoop out squash pulp. This should yield about 4 cups.

3. In a medium saucepan, melt the butter. Add onions and cook on medium heat, uncovered, until light brown, about 10 to 12 minutes. Add squash pulp, mace, cinnamon, nutmeg, and stock. On high heat, covered, bring squash mixture to a boil. Reduce heat to medium and simmer, about 15 minutes.

4. In a blender or processor, purée the squash mixture in batches until smooth.

5. Strain through a coarse strainer and season with salt and pepper.

Warm soup bowls.

THE CHESTNUTS:

1. Cut a small X on the flat side of each chestnut.

2. In a medium saucepan, put chestnuts and add cold water to cover. Bring to a boil, reduce heat and simmer chestnuts until softened, about 4 to 5 minutes.

3. Drain hot water from chestnuts and allow to cool slightly before handling. Using a sharp knife, peel off the shell.

4. In a small skillet over medium heat, melt butter and add chestnuts. Cook until golden.

5. Remove chestnuts to paper towels and when cool, chop into small pieces.

To serve soup:

1. Ladle hot soup into warm bowls. Garnish with a tablespoon of chopped chestnuts.

ROASTED DUCK BREASTS WITH WILD MUSHROOM RISOTTO

Yield: 4 servings

THE RISOTTO:

3¾ cups chicken stock

1 cup dry imported mushrooms, optional

12 shiitake mushroom caps, thinly sliced

3 tablespoons butter

1¼ cups arborio rice

3 cups oyster mushrooms or other wild mushrooms, thinly sliced

Kosher salt and freshly ground pepper

THE DUCK:

4 duck breasts, about 8 ounces each

Kosher salt and freshly ground black pepper

THE RISOTTO:

1. In a medium saucepan, covered, heat the chicken stock and dry mushrooms, until the stock is simmering and musrooms are soft, about 10 minutes. Add the shiitake and oyster mushrooms and simmer until they are soft, another 4 to 5 minutes. Reduce heat to low, cover, and keep broth at a low simmer.

2. In a medium saucepan, melt 2 tablespoons butter and sauté rice for 1 minute.

3. Add ½ cup broth and mushrooms. Bring rice to a simmer, continuing to stir until broth is absorbed, about 3 to 4 minutes. Stir, adding ¼ cup more broth at a time, until about half of broth is incorporated.

4. Still stirring, add broth in ½ cup amounts, allowing each addition to absorb before adding more. Continue until all broth has been used. Reduce heat to low and simmer risotto, uncovered, 5 minutes. Stir in additional stock or water if rice begins to dry.

5. Taste for doneness. Risotto should be al dente. Add remaining butter. Season with salt and pepper. Cover and keep warm.

Preheat oven to 400 degrees.

THE DUCK:

1. With a sharp knife, on the skin side of the duck breast, cut a shallow crosshatch pattern into the fat. Season with salt and pepper.

2. Heat a large skillet until very hot. Place duck in pan, fat-side down, and sear for 2 minutes. Place duck on baking pan and put in oven. Cook uncovered until duck is medium-rare, about 10 minutes. Turn duck over and cook 1 more minute. Remove from oven.

To serve duck:

1. Place a portion of risotto on serving plate. Cut each duck breast on the bias, making 8 to 10 slices, and fan these along side of risotto.

GRILLED ENDIVE, ROQUEFORT AND PEAR SALAD

Yield: 6 servings

4 tablespoons olive oil, plus additional

4 large endive

Salt and freshly ground pepper

1 head radicchio

2 large Bosc or Anjou pears, peeled and medium diced

¾ cup toasted walnuts, coarsely chopped

3½ ounces Roquefort cheese, crumbled

⅓ cup Mustard-Thyme Vinaigrette

Chill serving plates.

1. Prepare a charcoal or wood fire, and let fire burn down to embers. Heat the grill and lightly oil the grill rack.

2. Split endive in half lengthwise and loosen spears. In a bowl, toss with 3 tablespoons oil. Lightly season with salt and pepper.

3. Place endive on grill and lightly char, about 1 minute. Remove endive from grill.

4. Cut grilled endive on the bias into 1-inch pieces.

5. Split head of radicchio in half, remove core and loosen leaves. Coat with the remaining tablespoon of oil. Season with salt and pepper and lightly grill each half.

To assemble salad:

6. In a bowl, put endive, radicchio, pears, walnuts, and Roquefort cheese. Add vinaigrette and toss to combine. Serve on chilled salad plates.

MUSTARD-THYME VINAIGRETTE

Yield: about 1 cup

¼ teaspoon kosher salt

2 tablespoons good quality French Dijon mustard

3 tablespoons champagne vinegar

½ cup extra virgin olive oil

1 teaspoon chopped fresh thyme

Freshly ground black pepper

1. In a small bowl, put salt, mustard, and vinegar, and whisk until salt is dissolved. Slowly whisk in oil until dressing is emulsified.

2. Add thyme and pepper. Taste with an endive sliver and adjust seasoning.

FRESH FRUIT RUSTIC TARTLETTES

Yield: 6 tartlettes

THE DOUGH:

2 cups all-purpose flour

¼ teaspoon salt

1 teaspoon sugar

12 tablespoons cold butter, cut in pieces

½ cup ice water

THE FILLING:

4 tablespoons butter

¼ cup flour

¼ cup sugar, plus 2 tablespoons sugar

3 cups fruit of choice, diced

THE DOUGH:

1. Using an electric mixer or processor with a paddle attachment, combine flour, salt, and sugar.

2. Add 6 tablespoons butter and mix until fairly well incorporated, but not as fine as cornmeal. Add remaining butter. Mix again until pea-size pieces form. Do not overmix.

3. Add ice water and mix until dough just begins to come together.

4. Remove from bowl and gather loosely into a log. Divide dough into 6 portions and using the heel of your hand, press each into small disks, about 4 inches in diameter. Wrap each in plastic wrap. Refrigerate for about 3 hours.

5. Using a rolling pin, roll out each portion into an 8-inch circle about ⅛ inch thick.

6. Prepare two cookie sheets with parchment paper and place rolled pastry on these. Cover sheets with plastic wrap. Set aside, unrefrigerated, for one hour.

Preheat oven to 425 degrees.

THE FILLING:

1. In a small saucepan, melt butter.

2. In a bowl, combine flour and ¼ cup sugar, mixing well.

3. Place a piece of rolled pastry on work surface. In the center of each, sprinkle about 1 tablespoon flour mixture and ½ cup loosely packed fruit. Gather edges of dough around the fruit, making a pastry pouch.

4. Brush gathered edges of each pastry liberally with melted butter, brushing upward towards center of pouch. Sprinkle each tart with 1 teaspoon sugar.

5. Place pouches on a parchment-lined cookie sheet. Bake until golden brown and juices are bubbling, about 35 to 45 minutes. Remove from oven and serve.

Debra Ponzek

AUX DELICES

JILL PRESCOTT   PEGGY RYAN   LYDIA SHIRE AND SUSAN REGIS   NANCY SILVERTON

MOLLY SIPLE   KATELL THIELEMANN   SUSAN WEAVER   PATRICIA WILLIAMS

Jill Prescott

ECOLE DE CUISINE

"I believe in butter, cream, eggs and great ingredients."

When Jill Prescott was a child growing up in the Midwest, her parents were away for many weekends and she cooked with her grandparents, who lived next door. Frequently she was punished for efforts that led to a mess - such as a kitchen floor covered with sticky taffy. But she never lost her enthusiasm. Her German-born mother put traditional fare on the table, like dumplings, beef rouladen and glorious desserts. Her Danish father was fascinated with good food and fine restaurants. At Oshkosh State University, Prescott studied art and music. She liked anything hands-on, but eventually expressed her interest in people's welfare by working as a cardiac technician in a hospital. She was twenty-seven years old when her husband bought her a series of Cordon Bleu classes at Carson Pirie Scott. The experience dramatically changed her life. She found she had a real talent for cooking and fell in love with French techniques. When she decided to go off to France to get further training at several schools in Paris, including La Varenne and Lenotre, friends told her she would die of culture shock. She found just the opposite. Culture shock set in when she returned to Chicago. She was determined to teach Midwesterners what she had learned about good food. Prescott established Ecole de Cuisine - named out of

respect for all the schools she had been to in France - in Milwaukee in 1987. What started off with a small loan of $5,000 has grown into a thriving enterprise devoted to teaching home cooks how to succeed in the classic French culinary techniques. The school moved to Kohler, Wisconsin, in 1995 and has a staff of twelve, including six chefs. Word of her strong personality and passionate views led to the PBS-targeted cooking series 'Jill Prescott's Professional Cooking for the Home Chef,' with a companion cookbook. While visiting Chicago, Prescott voiced her opinions over lunch at one of the city's notable restaurants, Prairie.

Ecole de Cuisine

765 H. Woodlake Road
Kohler, WI 53044
Phone: 414 451 9151
Fax: 414 451 9152

Right:
Orange
Grand Marnier
Creme Caramel

Middle:
Warm Vegetable
Salad

I always wanted to cook but never knew about culinary schools. When I was in high school I was forced to do algebra, which never made sense to me. I always felt like a square peg that never found a square slot. I was more interested in home economics and how to make clarified butter. Not that I think home economics programs teach really good cooking skills. I strongly believe that we should set up an alternative educational system for children as they do in France - half a day of traditional school and half a day learning how to cook. Many children in our schools are bored to death. We know we are losing our children and how sad that is. Children with artistic talent should be allowed to express it in whatever avenue that is appropriate. I am sorry I had to wait until I was practically thirty to trek off to France and learn my culinary skills.

Right:
Rack of Lamb
with
Pommes Duchesse

I was the only woman at Lenotre, and everyone else spoke French. I could barely speak, so I put on a recorder and followed the chef around. They could see I was interested in learning and thought it was fascinating that a woman wanted to do it at all. I was warned that a bread baker should be at least five feet eight inches tall, I am only five feet six inches, and I felt it right in my back right away. But I never had any difficulties with French attitude. If you are there to learn, you go in and know nothing and learn their way. The more questions you ask, the more they will help you. You don't tell them how you do it in the United States. You ask and ask and ask, and soon the chef is in your pocket.

My French mentors told me not to Americanize French traditions. I reassured them I was going to do the opposite. I want to teach people how to cook good food with no chemicals, no preservatives. I believe in butter, cream, eggs and great ingredients.

I never wanted to be a restaurant chef, working long hours, extra-hard over all the holidays and never having a vacation. But the restaurants I respect most in France are the very little ones, serving really well prepared classic French cuisine. I am fortunate that I am able to teach those techniques. I love the response from people who come to my school. Many return again and again for getaway weekends, to learn something new. It's a great reward.

Peggy Ryan

"Historically women do the cooking but
when it comes time to be paid for it,
then the trouble comes."

Peggy Ryan was brought up on an Illinois dairy farm in Tonica, one hundred miles south of Chicago. She was one of six children and got up each morning at 5:30 to milk the cows, bale hay and pitch manure. Her mother, a grade school teacher, was a wonderful cook who made everything from scratch, including bread. Ryan was raised on just-picked ingredients from the garden, fresh cream and often made caramel fudge or canned fruit and vegetables. Her brothers brought home wild game, her grandfather went fishing and caught wild rabbit. As a teenager, she helped out in a local restaurant run by two women who cooked homestyle food and baked

Va Pensiero

1566 Oak Avenue
Evanston, IL 60201
Phone: 847 475 7779
Fax 847 475 7825

their own pies. She liked the work, and at the age of nineteen answered an ad in a Chicago paper for help in a restaurant kitchen. The job turned out to be an extraordinary opportunity - working for the late Leslee Reis, chef-owner of Leslee's, then a new Chicago restaurant. Later she pursued her apprenticeship with Joe Decker (now head of the Italian division of Lettuce Entertain You Enterprises) at Mallory's. She returned to work with Reis as sous-chef and later co-chef at Cafe Provencal and moved to Va Pensiero in Evanston in March 1989. As the only female executive chef-owner cooking Italian food on the North Shore, Ryan gets plenty of attention from food critics. Favored in Zagats Restaurant Survey, Va Pensiero (meaning "thoughts fly")

was awarded the Chicago Restaurateurs 1995 and 96 Silver Platter Awards. And in 1995, Ryan was voted North Shore Best Chef by Pioneer Press newspapers. She came out of the kitchen one lunchtime to talk in her soothing, peach and cream dining room, and give flight to her thoughts about becoming a chef.

Right:
Crispy Duck
Breast with
Carmelized
Lemon Sauce

Opposite Left:
Pasta
Handkerchiefs

Far Right:
Sauteed Shrimp
with
Pistachio Pesto
on a
Risotto Cake

I decided when I was thirteen what I wanted to do. I always enjoyed cooking. It was a necessity with a big family. When I found Leslee Reis it was a case of being in the right place at the right time. She had a knack for hiring people. She knew hard workers. She recognized people who were serious about the business. She had an eye. When I started working with her, I was learning a lot and making money, so I said, Why go to cooking school? I'll stick with this. It was just my luck and I have no regrets. Good cooking comes through constant repetition. You have to bone salmon every day to get that down. Practice every day comes from working in a restaurant. Leslee got me interested in Italian cooking. She would go off to Italy and bring back Italian recipes. That was when Italian food was not as popular as it is now in Chicago. We made incredible, wonderful Northern Italian dishes, and it really piqued my interest in that cuisine.

Now I go to Italy once a year and stay for two weeks, eating lunch and dinner every day. My husband and I go to different regions, testing the food and the wine. I like to cook homey, rustic dishes, homemade pastas, raviolis and tortellini. Every month at the restaurant, we have a special six-course dinner with four wines from a particular region in Italy. People say, "What's a girl named Ryan doing cooking Italian food?" I reply that I love all the regions of the country equally and don't have any prejudices. It's not going to make me a better chef if I come from Italy.

I attract women looking for a job because they know my kitchen will be woman-friendly. There is still a lot of sexism in the field, but I don't see it. That may be because I've got blinders on. I've had such good experience in the kitchens I have worked in. I have no real horror stories, because I've always ended up working for American chefs, who are lot less abusive than European chefs. The Europeans come from a background where abuse is more normal. Abuse was a standard at one time, but it's not allowed anymore - it's frowned on. I'm glad to see it is being swept away.

Historically, women do the cooking, but when it comes time to be paid for it, then the trouble comes. I try to keep a nice balance in my kitchen, about four women and four men. Women care more about pleasing people in the restaurant and less about their own egos. I am concerned about whether people like a dish, not about satisfying my own ego as a chef. Women are very good with responsibility. If you have a twenty-two-year-old woman and a twenty-two-year-old man, the woman will be more responsible in the kitchen, cleaning up and doing jobs. And they don't try to hide mistakes. Our culture allows for women to emote more. Women ask for help. That's a good thing when you need it. Men have to hide it.

Ryan

Lydia Shire & Susan Regis

BIBA • PIGNOLI

"Being on the edge is my signature."

Lydia Shire received her initial training in the culinary arts at the Cordon Bleu school in London. As she walked to class every day, she passed Biba, one of the fanciest boutiques in the city. With limited spending money in her student's pocket, she was only able to indulge in window-shopping. But Biba remained an elusive, glamorous destination in her mind, and Shire carried the image all the way back to her native Boston. After moving from job to job in some of the city's most celebrated kitchens - Maison Robert, Harvest, Cafe Plaza, Parker's and Seasons - Shire was invited to Los Angeles to open the Four Seasons Hotel as executive chef. One year later, in 1989, she was back in Boston, ready to open her own place. She called it Biba which friends took to mean Back In Boston Again. But to Shire the name represented the beacon of luxury and excitement she remembered in London. No effort was spared to make Biba exude a sense of modern opulence. Shire invited the celebrated New York City restaurant designer Adam Tihany to decorate the two-story space, which has one of Boston's prettiest park views. Biba picked up so many gastronomic awards and Shire received so many honors, including the James Beard Foundation's America's Best Chef in the Northeast, that she opened her second restaurant, Pignoli,

(another Tihany masterpiece), five years later. As chef-owner of both operations, Shire oversees the day-to-day running of the two establishments with a total of 160 employees. Meanwhile Susan Regis, who has worked with her for more than fifteen years since they cooked together at Seasons, masterminds both the kitchens as executive chef. "Susan and I are best friends. She is an amazing cook, a powerhouse, a great woman," Shire said one after-noon at Biba, as she discussed her career, and her way of writing descriptive menus, which are a legend in the business.

Pignoli

79 Park Plaza
Boston, MA 02116
Phone: 617 338 7500
Fax: 617 338 7691

Biba

272 Boylston Street
Boston, MA 02116
Phone: 617 426 5684
Fax: 617 426 9253

Being on the edge is my signature. No one expects the norm from me. When I started Biba, I set a new style in menu presentation. Our menus are always well written. The food is eclectic American - Chinese, Japanese, Italian. I was among the first to create fusion cuisine when I was at Seasons at the Bostonian Hotel. That does not mean a mishmash with lots of different things thrown in for shock value. I don't like that at all. But we challenge ourselves, Susan and I, to figure out how to come up with menu changes about three times a year. I am very particular about the way a plate looks. I hate things piled up in a mound. I like it to look slightly messy, off-center, off-kilter. Nature is messy. I can't stand anything that is too rigid.

Both my parents were artists and I love art. I applied to go to art school before I became a cook. My father was the best cook in the family. He used to read The New York Times columns by Craig Claiborne and Pierre Franey. I remember when I was eight years old, coming home from school and seeing my father pounding veal by hand and making veal marsala. He had a great way of doing things. When he was making chicken in sherry, the smell went right through the house, and it's still in my head. I learned to love to cook for people, to set the table, to have people over for dinner.

To get my first job at Maison Robert, I took a seven-layer cake over to the chef in an air-conditioned cab. It slid all over the place, but he was very impressed that I

Above:
Taramasalata
with
Shredded Lobster

Left:
Baby Rack
of Lamb
with Artichoke
and
Preserved Lemon

Lydia

would go to that length to make something. So I was put to work as a salad girl, making paté, and opening oysters. There were not many women working in restaurants then, in 1971. I was the only woman at Maison Robert. One day I quit. I didn't want to be on the garde-manger forever, so I went to the Cordon Bleu. Then I went back to Maison Robert and eventually became the chef of the fancy dining room. I had a great time. Those were the days when you could stay late if you wished and make a croquembouche on your own time. State laws have changed all that. People can't work more than an eight-hour shift, and no one is allowed to come in and work on their own time; it's against labor regulations.

When I started out people weren't talking about healthy food. We were still stuck in the French mode. I began making my fresh spring roll, tempura and vegetables - doing things differently. There have been changes for the better. Now we tend to take more chances. Bostonians are extremely adventurous - they like food in Boston. They trust you. I've never had a problem selling specials. We take ourselves very seriously, but we never lose sight of the fact that eating is pleasure. We want guests to have a relaxed and wonderful time.

Nancy Silverton
CAMPANILE RESTAURANT • LA BREA BAKERY

"I have always been treated with respect because I pulled my own weight."

Nancy Silverton has been acknowledged as one of the country's leading bread bakers. Her story is the stuff of legend. Starting out as a small retail bakery on South La Brea in Los Angeles, in seven years the La Brea Bread company grew to employ about a hundred bakers producing 20,000 baguettes a day and delivering its products all over Southern California and even to Las Vegas. Silverton's accolades are numerous: James Beard Pastry Chef of the Year, 1990; James Beard Who's Who in American Cooking 1990; Los Angeles Culinary Master of the Year, 1994; Southern California Restaurant Writers Restaurant of the Year and Restaurateur of the Year, 1995. She is the author of six cookbooks, including 'Breads from La Brea Bakery.'

The turning point in Silverton's career occurred after she completed a series of pastry courses at the famous Ecole Lenotre in France. She was hired by Wolfgang Puck as head pastry chef at Spago, where she created a highly acclaimed dessert menu. In 1985, Silverton and her chef-husband, Mark Peel, moved to Manhattan and spent six months revamping Maxwell's Plum restaurant, an East Side institution. Determined to have their own establishment, they opened La Brea Bakery in January 1989, and followed that with a small

Campanile Restaurant • La Brea Bakery

624 South La Brea Avenue
Los Angeles,
CA 90038
Phone: 213 938 1447
Fax 213 935 9849

but highly successful breakfast cafe. Six months later the couple opened Campanile, an adjacent upscale restaurant very popular with Hollywood celebrities. In the bar one afternoon, with a Mozart piano concerto playing in the background, Silverton traced the path to culinary fame

When I was in college I spent several summer breaks taking restaurant jobs, and I worked for free on all stations. I found I was capable and I enjoyed cooking and thought this was what I would like to do when I grew up. Of course, American kitchens are a lot more welcoming than kitchens run by Europeans. But as a woman I have always been treated with respect because I pulled my own weight.

My father signed me up for Cordon Bleu in London. When I came back to Los Angeles in 1979, the food movement was definitely centered around L'Ermitage and Ma Maison. I joined Michael's, which was a new restaurant, to operate the first computer system of its kind for food inventory and tickets. I was very bad at it, but it was a foot in the door. The head chef told me that the pastry chef was going to leave, and he asked me to be the pastry chef's assistant so that I could learn the job. Pastry frightened me, because it is so exact. In 1979, the dessert menu was classic, like Napoleon, but I wondered how much flexibility there could be in dessert making. I realized that you can taste and improvise. And it dawned one me that I like being in my little world in the kitchen. In desserts you have only yourself and one other person. Then I took some courses at Lenotre in France, and when I returned Wolfgang Puck asked me to be the pastry chef at Spago. It was a great career move that put me on the map. I wrote my first dessert cookbook.

When it was time for Mark and me to open our own restaurant, we had our own original thoughts. We went to Italy for a few months, and ate and cooked there. We like food simply prepared with fresh ingredients and strong flavors. We are enthused about raw ingredients, fresh produce from the farmer's market. We wanted to make sure that we had good bread, so we had to have a bakery. I wanted space, not a corner of the kitchen, and I wanted to make bread for the restaurant and retail. We chose La Brea Avenue, because there were big pieces of property and it was on the West Side. We went ahead with a bakery

Above:
Focaccia

Opposite
Left:
Chocolate
Almond
Pound Cake

Opposite
Right:
Proscuitto Pie

Right:
Pecan
Sticky Bun

Far Right:
Meringue

designed after the famous ACME Bakery in Berkeley, which was my inspiration. I didn't know how to make a loaf of bread, but I went back to France and learned baking at Lenotre. The most important thing in bread is flavor, what you might call the inner beauty of the loaf. I came to the conclusion that in order to become a baker I'd have to have my own sourdough starter and start baking every day. If you're not careful, the bread can take over your life. The bread essentially ruled me until I learned a few tricks. It takes time. It takes patience. But the rewards are great. Every loaf you bake is slightly different, but most of all, it is uniquely your own. Nothing you can buy at a store will give you as much satisfaction.

A few years ago there were no bakeries and morning cafes like ours in Los Angeles - not a thing. We have started a lot of trends. If somebody had told me that I was going to sell 20,000 baguettes a day, I would never have believed it. It's tough business, and you have to be there all the time. You must do it every day to be successful.

Molly Siple

MOLLY'S KITCHEN

"Food as it affects the body chemistry is the biggest change going on in our culture."

Molly Siple remembers serving butter on Ritz crackers to family guests at a cocktail party when she was about three or four years old. A few years later, her architect father built a full-scale hot dog stand for her to play with in the backyard in Los Angeles. She vividly recalls the smell of the redwood and the joy of growing vegetables - like Swiss chard and carrots - in her own plot. Her love of serving food to company has been a consistent thread in her life ever since.

Siple brings a long and varied string of experiences to the table. She served as table top editor at House Beautiful magazine in the '70s, creating table settings, designing table ware and interacting with top chefs such as Jacques Pepin, Leon Leonides and James Beard, whose meals and recipes were shown in the glorious color photographs on the feature pages. During the opulent '80s, Siple developed a Manhattan catering business serving clients such as the Maharajah of Jaipur, Lincoln Center, The Whitney Museum and the Asia Society, and authored "Food Style", one of the first cookbooks to explain the techniques of serving the "picture plate" in the Nouvelle Cuisine style, "putting the sauce under rather than over the food and making artistic patterns on the plate."

As the era of big-spending turned into a time of downsizing and

reevaluation, Siple closed her business and moved to Los Angeles, where she pursued studies for qualifications that she considers more appropriate for a food service consultant in the '90s. Today, as a registered dietician with a master's of science degree in nutrition, Siple focuses her attention on helping people lead healthy lives through good eating habits. Her philosophy is described in "Recipes for Change," co-authored with Lissa de Angelis. Siple talked in her stylish kitchen in Los Angeles furnished with a recycled 1930s gas stove and her own glowing, oil paintings of vegetables hanging on the walls.

Molly's Kitchen

2178 Moreno Drive
Los Angeles, CA 90039
Phone 213 660 4620
Fax 213 660 8503

When I started my own catering business, I got a great deal of excitement out of the experience of entertaining. The best party was always going on in the kitchen and not out front. Sometimes I had as many as twenty waiters and six to eight people in the kitchen. I loved it, because it was like putting on a show - a performance art, planning the decorations, positioning the buffet and tables, doing the flowers. You set the stage for the party and you direct the entire scenario. Even after working eighteen to twenty-two hours, you leave on a high, just like after the theater.

Far Right:
Black-eyed Pea
Viniagrette

My father taught me to respect good food and the art of the chef. When I was a little girl he would take me out to fine restaurants and he would stop me from adding salt and pepper to a dish until I had tasted it. My stepmother was a real Southern cook, cooking out of a cookbook. She used natural ingredients and raw milk, not pasteurized, and made wonderful biscuits and gravy. My father built a house like a Scottish castle with a great kitchen-dining room, which had a wood-burning hearth and a round table. That table still has a sacred place in my mind. There were seven sets of china, always real silver on the table. So the idea of having parties and entertaining and being a hostess came very naturally to me as a teenager.

Although I was involved in food service and presentation, when I went back to study nutrition, I had not realized the connection between food and healing. Then I found I wanted to contribute something to the world and in order to serve the world of health you need degrees. It was a long haul and involved medical internships at hospitals and hours of studying biochemistry, organic chemistry, anatomy, physiology and other difficult subjects. It took twelve years, ending in a five hundred-page thesis on how nutrition can be effectively used to help women counteract side-effects of menopause.

I have always been an outsider, a pioneer and a trailblazer but I feel that I have found my own sense of self worth. I am now on the cutting edge of the alternative field of medicine. The establishment is beginning to listen and to realize that good food is the foundation of good health. Food as it affects the body chemistry is the biggest change going on in our culture. Most diseases are triggered by poor diet. What is central to good nutrition is central to good health. I can make nutritional advice into usable information for daily cooking. What do you buy, what do you eat? I tell people how they can apply it on a day-to-day eating basis - and how to do it with style and flair. That is the challenge.

Above:
Crudités

Left:
Avocado-Orange
Salad

"I'm a little bit of a perfectionist and would go crazy if I could not control everything."

Katell Thielemann's father was chef-owner of a restaurant in a seaside town in Brittany, France when she was growing up. By the age of six, she was cleaning mussels; at ten, she graduated to washing potatoes. As a teenager, Thielemann worked with him in the kitchen when she came home from school and on weekends. She also learned restaurant serving skills from her mother, who took care of the front of the house. When she went to college in France, she earned a bachelor's degree in international business and languages and volunteered for an exchange program at the University of Towson in Maryland. While studying for her American degree in International Studies, Thielemann met Gino Troia, the owner of a small deli in Towson, who persuaded her to work for him as a cook. At that time, 1989, it was difficult to get a cappuccino, espresso or anything typically European in Towson. Thielemann called on her skills as a classically trained French chef, and three years later Cafe Troia had tripled in size. Seeking out a different lifestyle after this success - and having graduated with her second degree - Thielemann went into international importing and exporting and started traveling around the world. But

Troia at the Walters

after three years of living out of a suitcase, she found she missed the restaurant business. So she returned to the kitchen, eventually teaming up with her former partner to open a second Troia restaurant in Baltimore at the Walters Art Museum. The restaurant was used in the Clint Eastwood movie "Absolute Power," and has been reviewed favorably in local newspapers, magazines and TV stations. Thielemann talked one afternoon while Edith Piaf songs played in the background.

600 North Charles Street
Baltimore, MD 21201
Phone: 410 752 2887
Fax: 410 752 0498

I don't think there are too many people who have had the varied background that I have, but it's not something I stop to think about. I've always liked the restaurant business, because as a child it was the only way to be with my parents. I have always wanted to learn more, to expand my education and knowledge, and that was why I decided to come to America. Now I am studying law in the evenings. I thought a law degree would be helpful to me in the restaurant business, because there is always so much paperwork to do, people to be employed, suppliers to handle, and regulations to be dealt with. There are a lot of legal issues when you are an entrepreneur with your own business.

Above:
Linguine
with Seafood

Right:
Grilled Baby
Eggplant
and Roasted
Red Pepper

To run a restaurant successfully, you have to be able to jump into any position that needs to be filled that day. With twenty-eight employees, almost every day someone doesn't show up and we need to fill one job or another. There are days when I'm the bus girl or I join the line as a cook. You have to be flexible. Running a restaurant is a bit like running a theatrical production. There's a lot of work to be done before the curtain goes up. Our chef, Mark Dobak, was trained in Washington, D.C., but has worked in France and a number of places. I wish we had the classical French system of training in the United States. I have found that the schools here charge $30,000 and the first week the students start calling each other chef. It takes at least ten years in France to earn that title.

As a woman in the kitchen, you've got to do more. My father taught me the French system, which is basically military style. It's even

Right:
Ravioli
with Salmon
and Dill

Below:
Ossobucco
with
Gremolata

called a brigade. It's compartmentalized and very strict. You are shown how to do things the right way. We used to get up early in the morning and go down to the port to buy the fresh fish. You see all the fish and you learn what is fresh. Then we used to go to the produce market. It was hands-on experience; see, touch and smell. It is hard to duplicate that in the classroom. Being disciplined about doing everything the right way has shaped my whole life. You try everything until it becomes second nature. For every success there are so many failures. Some people want to be successful from the beginning. I would rather take on people with very little training and teach them how to do things the right way, otherwise it is very hard to maintain quality and a high standard of service and food. I am a little bit of a perfectionist and would go crazy if I could not control everything.

Susan Weaver

FOUR SEASONS HOTEL

"Push, push, push.

I learned endurance."

Susan Weaver's astonishing rise to one of the most coveted jobs in the hotel and restaurant industry - executive chef at the Four Seasons Hotel, New York City, where she presides over a kitchen staff of forty-five people - began at the Boston Park Plaza Hotel. Under the tutelage of world renowned chef Fernand Guitierrez she learned the basics of fine French cuisine.

After a spell in Paris to polish this training, she returned to the U.S. to embark on her remarkable career with the Four Seasons hotel group. First she was a saucier at the Four Seasons Inn on the Park in Houston. Then she moved on to the Ritz Carlton in Chicago, then back in Houston, then to Toronto, where she became the first woman in Canada to hold the executive chef's position at a major hotel. She took over her prestigious job at the Four Seasons Hotel on 57th Street in Manhattan in 1993, ten months after the opening of the opulent, I. M. Pei-designed sliver skyscraper.

In chef's whites, sipping a glass of mineral water, Boston-born Weaver talked about how she made it to the exalted level of gastronomic competitions like the Bocuse d'Or.

Fifty Seven Fifty Seven

Four Seasons Hotel
57 East 57th Street
New York, N.Y. 10022
Phone: 212 758 5757
Fax: 212 758 5711

Right:
Almond Crusted
Salmon,
Salad of Crunchy
Vegetables,
Spinach,
Mango and Citrus

After I finished high school I took off for Europe for two months and ended up staying two years, taking jobs in kitchens - as a dishwasher, a potato peeler, a garlic chopper. I spent a year in one kitchen and that was it! Once I had done that I knew there was no going back. I returned to Boston and apprenticed with Fernand Guitierrez who became my mentor - and still is today. He was very hard-driving in the classic French way. He would say: "This is the way to do it. Let 's go!" Push, push, push. I learned endurance with him. We begin with flavor. We think about it, we sort it out. We make it. Then I went to Paris and was in the kitchen under Gerard Poulard at the Hotel Lancaster, and Pierre Le Boucher at La Mairie restaurant. I have been working for the Four Seasons since I

was in my twenties, and I adore my job. I always wanted to work in Manhattan, and being in this beautiful hotel environment on East 57th Street in the greatest city in the world is the perfect combination for me. I feel very fortunate.

There are other women chefs in executive positions at the Four Seasons besides me. Sarah Stegner is in charge of the dining room at the Ritz Carlton in Chicago and Carrie Nahabedian is executive chef at the Four Seasons, Los Angeles. We all trained with Guitierrez and the company is proud of us. We have a lot in common. We share ideas, we share all that we do, and we give each other support. In our company, female chefs are on a par with male chefs. There is no distinction. Discrimination doesn't enter into anyone's mind. No one notices the difference. Personally, I think women chefs bring something new to the table - a level of nurturing. We think about how to care for guests and how to make food that is soothing to a particular party or meal. When I came to this hotel, I made some changes in the dining room, to make it a warmer and more inviting space for our guests. I work very hard, and I set the rules for myself that I expect my staff to follow. I'm for working effectively, about 10 to 12 hours a day, five days a week. This industry has changed. The old ways are going out. I believe that my staff are more productive and more creative if they have a normal life. I take Sundays and Mondays off. We work very hard all day...without balance, you get in trouble.

Everyone in my family loves to eat. We like home cooking and we like experimentation. When I was growing up my mom did lots of New England boiled dinners, and standard American meals, like roast beef and potatoes, macaroni and cheese, spaghetti on Wednesdays. She makes the best turkey dinner and chicken noodle soup. She is very proud of me today. My grandmother made Portuguese-influenced dishes. I learned by watching them both in the kitchen and making things like birthday cakes. I discovered early on that good food made people happy, and I found that very gratifying.

Below: Maryland Crabcakes with Red Pepper Aioli

All my vacations are food-related. I may go to Spain or Italy to see how people do things. I might go on a food tour, meeting chefs and enjoying the experience as a consumer. This way I regain a new freshness about hospitality, what it is and what works. What makes an impression when you see it. Cooking is always a work in progress, and it's about constantly going forward with the work.

Patricia Williams

CITY WINE AND CIGAR CO.

*"You strive for excellence.
You always try to do something
better than you did it before."*

Patricia Williams spent two decades twirling to the top as a ballerina culminating her career at the New York City Opera Ballet by dancing with Rudolph Nureyev. Upon retiring from dance, she began a second career as a chef after exploring the kitchens and vineyards of France. At the famous Quilted Giraffe restaurant in New York in the 1980s, Williams found her way into the kitchen as a dessert plater. With an instinctive knack for cooking, she was soon moving up the culinary ladder. At Arizona 206, she explored the food of the Southwest and her ancestry - she is half Mexican and half Cherokee. Her experience broadened as she moved through several other kitchens: Sarabeth's, 150 Wooster, Restaurant Charlotte at the Hotel Macklowe and the Supper Club, receiving accolades from the food critics wherever she went. Mega-restaurant owner Drew Nieporent recognized her star quality and helped steer her destiny as one of the top women chefs in New York. In 1997, when Nieporent decided to capitalize on the fashionable trend for cigar-smoking, and add a sophisticated new rendezvous to his roster of successful restaurants (Montrachet, Tribeca Grill, and Nobu in Manhattan, Rubicon in San Francisco), he turned to Williams to develop a new culinary style. As a complement to a cigar bar offering more than one hundred varieties of cigars along with private humidors

City Wine and Cigar Co.

and personalized wrapping papers to serious aficionados, Nieporent requested Cigar World Cuisine. Williams was given the task of creating innovative menus and dishes from the cigar- producing countries: Cuba, the Dominican Republic, Brazil, Costa Rica, Honduras and Holland. It was an appropriate challenge for someone with a Latino background, named as one of the Rising Star Chefs on PBS, and used to leaping high under the spotlight. Williams talked about this culinary venture at the wine bar of the new restaurant.

62 Laight Street
New York, N.Y. 10013
Phone 212 334 2274
Fax 212 334 2276

Below:
Guava Glazed
Cucumbers
with Cucumber
Fettucine

Below Right:
Barbecue Pork
with
Mustard Greens

This new restaurant is a perfect match for me. I love to smoke cigars myself - little cigarillos. Before I started developing the menu, I went down to Puerto Rico and took a cooking course, and I learned a lot about the cigar country culture. Cuban cigars are illegal in America, but somehow they find their way here, through Britain, Switzerland, Aruba. Cuban cigars are like French wines: they are still considered the best, although there are many other good cigars. Of course, we had to install a very heavy-duty, air-conditioning system in the restaurant to take out the smoke, and put in a non-smoking section designed like a chef's table for those people who don't want to smoke while they eat.

I come from a large family. I have thirteen aunts and uncles. I grew up in the great outdoors of Texas, learning to hunt buffalo and venison, fishing from the age of eight. As I started experimenting as a chef, I found I could be creative with Latin ingredients, using them in new ways. Take a mole sauce and refine it. Take Ibarra chocolate and make a pot de creme. Make a guava glaze. I am particularly keen on spices, cinnamon, cumin, coriander, dried and fresh chiles. I make my dishes mild, medium and hot. Not all the food in Mexico is hot.

My second career didn't start until I was over thirty. In the beginning, I had trouble breaking into the business and getting job interviews. But after dancing, I think anything is easy! I found the Rainbow Room was one kitchen that employed women without any prejudice. I was thirty-two when I fell in love with the energy and creativity in the kitchen at the Quilted Giraffe. All the activity that went into the preparation of exquisite food was carefully planned and orchestrated. I knew that this was the creative outlet I wanted to pursue.

Cooking is a bit like dance. You strive for excellence. You do something over and over again until you get it right. In a ballet movement, you try to do something better than you did it before. That is the only way to go. As I got to be an executive chef, the job became more managerial and I learned how to manage people. This was kind of hard for me at first, because I came to understand that some people are not used to seeking the highest standards of excellence. But in my kitchen, you must strive to do something better every time. You must strive for excellence.

Top:
Beggars Purse
with
Caviar

Center:
Chicken
with
Yellow Hominy
and Mole

Bottom:
Orange Salad
with
Arugula

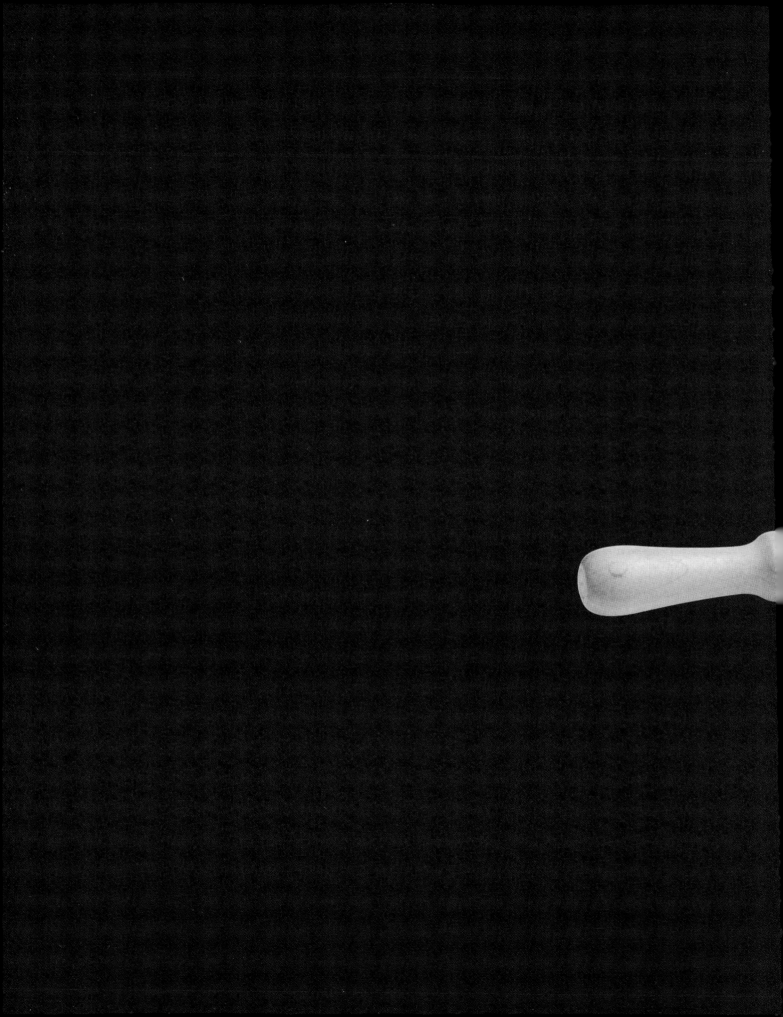

JILL PRESCOTT
PEGGY RYAN

LYDIA SHIRE & SUSAN REGIS
NANCY SILVERTON
MOLLY SIPLE
KATELL THIELEMANN
SUSAN WEAVER
PATRICIA WILLIAMS

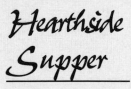

Hearthside Supper

Warm Vegetable Salad with Balsamic Vinegar and Honey

Pork Loin Chops with Caramelized Apples, Calvados, Cider and Cream

Green Beans in Hazelnut Butter

Grand Marnier Chocolate Cake with Shiny Chocolate Icing

WARM VEGETABLE SALAD WITH BALSAMIC VINEGAR AND HONEY

Yield: 6-8 servings

2 to 3 tablespoons olive oil

1 small head red cabbage, julienned

1 Belgian endive, julienned

1 bunch green onions cut into ½-inch diagonal pieces

½ pound pea pods

½ cup fresh watercress, stems removed

1 medium head Bibb lettuce torn into pieces, 6 to 8 leaves left whole for garnish

1 tablespoon balsamic vinegar

1 tablespoon honey

Salt and freshly ground pepper

1. In a large sauté pan, put olive oil. Add cabbage, endive, and green onions and sauté until just wilted, about 1½ minutes. Add pea pods. Heat for a few seconds. Add vinegar and honey and heat for a few seconds. Add watercress and Bibb lettuce.

3. Toss to coat the salad with vinegar and honey, adding more if necessary. Season with salt and pepper.

4. Place Bibb leaf on each plate and put salad on top, letting part of leaf show for presentation. Serve warm.

PORK LOIN CHOPS WITH CARAMELIZED APPLES, CALVADOS, CIDER AND CREAM

Yield: 6 servings

6 loin pork chops, ¾ to 1-inch thick, room temperature and patted dry

Sea salt and freshly ground pepper

Freshly ground nutmeg

¼ cup unsalted butter, more as needed

1 tablespoon vegetable oil

4 Golden Delicious apples

¼ cup Calvados

1 cup apple cider

½ cup heavy cream

1. Season chops with salt, pepper, and a few grinds of nutmeg.

2. Peel and core apples. Cut into quarters and then cut each quarter into 3 slices.

3. Heat butter and oil in a large sauté pan over medium heat. Add chops and cook for 8 to 10 minutes on each side.

4. Remove chops from pan to warmed serving platter, reserving all of the pan juices and fat in sauté pan. Place a sheet of foil over chops to keep hot.

5. Add apples to pan and sauté over medium-high heat, adding additional butter if needed. Turn once to lightly brown and cook through. Place cooked apples around chops.

6. Deglaze pan with Calvados. Add cider and scrape up all browned bits.

7. Transfer mixture to a 2-quart sauce pan. Reduce cider mixture to about ⅓ cup. Add cream and 2 or 3 grinds of nutmeg. Reduce cider mixture to thicken to a sauce consistency. Strain sauce and serve over chops.

GREEN BEANS IN HAZELNUT-BUTTER

Yield: 6 servings

1 pound fresh green beans, preferably haricots verts, trimmed

Sea salt

¼ cup unsalted butter

¼ cup hazelnuts, toasted, skinned and chopped

Freshly ground pepper.

1. Bring 2 quarts of water to boil in a saucepan. Add salt. Add beans to boiling water. Cook over moderate heat until beans are just tender.

2. Strain beans in a colander. Then run beans under cold water to immediately stop cooking. (see Note)

3. Melt the butter in a medium-size sauté pan. Add the nuts and heat briefly to develop flavors. Add beans and heat through. Stir to combine. Add salt and pepper to taste. Serve.

Note: Beans can be prepared one day in advance through step 2. Cover and store in refrigerator.

GRAND MARNIER CHOCOLATE CAKE WITH SHINY CHOCOLATE ICING

THE CAKE:

4 ounces bittersweet chocolate, finely chopped (see Note)

½ cup unsalted butter, room temperature

Zest of one orange, finely chopped**

½ cup plus 2 tablespoons sugar

3 eggs, separated and at room temperature

1 tablespoon Grand Marnier**

¼ teaspoon cream of tartar

Pinch of salt

½ cup sifted cake flour

½ cup grated chocolate for garnish

THE SHINY CHOCOLATE ICING:

7 ounces bittersweet chocolate, finely grated

⅔ cup heavy cream

7 tablespoons clarified butter

1 tablespoon Grand Marnier, optional**

Preheat oven to 325 degrees.

1. Prepare a cake pan by buttering the sides and bottom, placing a piece of parchment paper on the bottom and buttering the parchment. Set aside.

THE CAKE:

2. Melt 4 ounces chocolate in a small saucepan over very low heat.

3. Cream room temperature butter, orange zest, and ½ cup sugar in the bowl of an electric mixer until soft and fluffy. Beat in egg yolks and Grand Marnier. Add the warm (not hot) melted chocolate.

4. With clean beaters, whip egg whites until foaming. Add the cream of tartar and salt and continue whipping until soft peaks form. Add remaining sugar gradually and whip until stiff peaks form.

5. Stir a spoonful of whites into chocolate to lighten it.

6. Beginning with another scoop of whites and alternating with flour, fold both mixtures into chocolate until just blended.

7. Place batter evenly into prepared pan. Bake for 25 minutes. The center of the cake will be moist and damp crumbs form when pierced with a toothpick. The outside edge will be dry 2 to 3 inches from the edge of pan.

8. Remove pan from oven and allow to cool on a wire rack for about 15 minutes. Unmold on a wire cooling rack. Remove parchment paper. The bottom of the cake

Jill Prescott

ÉCOLE DE CUISINE

will become the top. After the cake cools, brush loose crumbs from the sides. Meanwhile prepare Shiney Chocolate Icing.

THE SHINY CHOCOLATE ICING:

1. Place chopped chocolate in medium-size bowl. Heat cream and pour over chocolate. Whisk together. Add butter and whisk together. Add liqueur, to taste.

To ice cake:

1. To glaze cake with icing, begin by pouring icing on top of cake. Spread with an icing spatula so that glaze runs down sides of cake.

2. Press grated chocolate onto sides of cake while icing is still soft. Allow icing to set in a cool room or in refrigerator.

3. Using a wide flat spatula, carefully move cake to a cake platter. Cake may be refrigerated in an airtight container but must be served at room temperature for full flavor.

Note: Valrhona chocolate, a very fine quality French brand, is preferred.

VARIATIONS:

Raspberry: Replace the Grand Marnier with Chambord in both cake and icing. Omit zest. Decorate top rim of cake with fresh raspberries. Melt together 2 tablespoons each red currant jelly and water. Brush raspberries with jelly mixture.

Hazelnut or Almond: In step 5 of making the cake, fold in ⅓ cup chopped toasted hazelnuts or almonds. Replace Grand Marnier with Frangelico or Amaretto. Garnish sides of cake with additional toasted and chopped nuts. Orange zest optional.

Coffee: Omit orange zest. Add 2 tablespoons coffee liqueur to batter and 1 tablespoon to icing. Garnish with grated chocolate on sides of cake and with a circle of chocolate/coffee beans around top rim of cake.

Plain chocolate: Add 1 teaspoon vanilla extract to cake batter. Do not add vanilla to the icing.

Extracts: If you prefer the use of extracts over liqueurs you may add almond, mint, or orange extracts instead. It is important to taste batter for depth of taste as every extract has a different strength.

Italian Shore Dinner

Sautéed Shrimp with Pistachio Pesto on a Risotto Cake

Grilled Salmon with Artichoke-Rosemary Sauce

Pasta Handkerchiefs

Warm Gratin of Raspberries and Amaretto Zabaglione

SAUTÉED SHRIMP WITH PISTACHIO PESTO ON A RISOTTO CAKE

Yield: 8 servings as an appetizer

THE RISOTTO CAKES:

2 tablespoons butter

4 tablespoons pure olive oil

½ cup diced onion

1 cup arborio rice

1 ½ cups chicken stock

Salt and freshly ground pepper

All-purpose flour

THE PESTO (makes 1 cup):

¾ cup shelled pistachios

Juice of 1 lemon

½ cup chopped parsley

2 cloves garlic

⅓ cup pure olive oil

1 teaspoon cumin

¼ teaspoon cayenne pepper

½ teaspoon salt

To assemble:

2 tablespoons pure olive oil

16 large shrimp, peeled and deveined

Salt and freshly ground pepper

THE RISOTTO CAKES:

1. In a heavy bottomed 2-quart saucepan, put butter, 1 tablespoon oil, and onion and sauté until transparent, about 10 minutes. Add rice to mixture and sauté for 5 minutes.

2. In a saucepan on high heat, covered, bring stock to a boil. Reduce heat and simmer.

3. Add hot stock to rice mixture, ¼ cup at a time. Cook on low heat, stirring constantly until liquid is absorbed. Repeat procedure until all liquid has been added. Season with salt and pepper.

4. Transfer risotto to a baking sheet to cool. Preheat oven to 250 degrees.

5. Divide risotto into 8 portions. Shape into flat cakes, pressing rice together.

6. In a 9-inch nonstick sauté pan, heat 3 tablespoons oil.

7. Lightly dust each cake with flour. Using a spatula, slide each cake into pan. Sauté 3 or 4 cakes at a time until golden, about 7 minutes on each side.

8. With a spatula, remove cakes and place on a baking sheet. Put in oven to keep warm.

THE PESTO:

Preheat oven to 350 degrees.

1. Scatter pistachios on a baking sheet and put in oven to toast for 6 minutes.

2. In a food processor or blender, put pistachios, lemon juice, garlic, oil, cumin, salt, and pepper. Blend until smooth. (Pesto can be made up to 3 days in advance and leftover pesto can be frozen.)

To assemble:

1. In a large sauté pan, heat oil. Sauté shrimp in batches until they turn opaque and pink. Set cooked shrimp aside.

2. Return all shrimp to pan and drain off excess oil. Add 1/2 cup Pistachio Pesto. Toss and coat shrimp thoroughly. Season with salt and pepper.

3. Place risotto cakes on individual plates and put 2 shrimps on each cake. Add additional pesto if desired. Serve.

GRILLED SALMON WITH ARTICHOKE-ROSEMARY SAUCE

Yield: 4 servings

1 tablespoon pure olive oil

2 large artichoke bottoms, thinly sliced

1 medium onion, peeled and diced

½ cup diced pancetta

2 cloves garlic, minced

1 teaspoon minced fresh rosemary

⅔ cup chicken stock

1 tablespoon lemon juice

Salt and freshly ground pepper

4 6-ounce salmon steaks

1. In a saucepan, put oil and add artichoke, onion, pancetta, garlic, and rosemary. Sauté until onion and artichoke are tender, 5 to 10 minutes.

2. Add stock and lemon juice, and uncovered, bring to a simmer. Season with salt and pepper. Remove from heat.

3. Preheat grill until very hot. Brush salmon lightly with oil and season with salt and pepper on both sides.

4. Cook salmon until grill marks appear, about 5 minutes, and then turn over and cook to medium, or desired doneness.

5. Warm sauce and spoon onto individual plates. Place salmon on sauce and serve immediately.

PASTA HANDKERCHIEFS

Yield: 4 servings as a main course; 8 as an appetizer

THE TOMATO SAUCE:

3 tablespoons olive oil

2 cloves garlic, finely minced

⅛ teaspoon hot pepper flakes

1 16-ounce can plum tomatoes, drained and coarsely chopped

THE PARMESAN SAUCE:

2 cups heavy whipping cream

½ cup. imported Parmesan cheese

Salt and freshly ground pepper

THE FILLING:

15 ounces ricotta cheese

1 cup grated Parmesan cheese.

1 cup steamed spinach, finely chopped and squeezed of extra water

1 teaspoon salt

Pinch of white pepper

Pinch nutmeg

THE PASTA:

3 ½ cups all-purpose flour

Pinch of salt

1 cup white wine

½ cup water

THE TOMATO SAUCE:

1. In a heavy bottomed saucepan over low heat, put oil, garlic and pepper flakes. Sauté until garlic is golden brown. Add tomatoes and cook over low heat for 20 minutes, stirring occasionally.

2. Remove from heat and purée in blender or food processor. Reserve.

THE PARMESAN SAUCE:

1. In a saucepan over low heat, put cream and reduce by half. Add cheese and season with salt and pepper. Reserve.

THE FILLING:

1. In a processor, put ricotta and Parmesan cheeses, spinach, salt, pepper, and nutmeg. Blend together. Remove to a bowl, and refrigerate covered for later use.

THE PASTA:

1. In a processor and using the dough paddle, blend flour and salt. Add wine and mix until smooth and elastic. Let rest 20 minutes.

2. Roll dough on pasta machine to finest setting. With a knife, cut into 8 squares.

3. Bring a large pot of salted water to a boil. (While water is heating, fill a large bowl with cold water.) Add 2 or 3 pieces of pasta to the boiling water and cook for 1 minute. With a slotted spoon, remove pasta and put in the cold water. Repeat procedure until all pasta is cooked.

Preheat oven to 400 degrees.

4. Place cooled pasta flat on work surface.

5. Divide filling into 8 portions and place in center of each pasta square.

6. To fold each square, select a corner and fold over the filling to meet the opposite corner, forming a large triangle. Then fold the two bottom corners of the triangle so that they slightly overlap in a 'crossed arms' style to make Handkerchiefs.

7. Place on a lightly-oiled baking sheet. Add ½ cup water. Cover with foil. Bake 20 minutes.

8. Place 2 Handkerchiefs on individual plates. Using a large spoon, drizzle tomato sauce over pasta, making a stripe. Then drizzle a stripe of Parmesan sauce over this. Serve immediately.

WARM GRATIN OF RASPBERRIES AND AMARETTO ZABAGLIONE

Yield: 6 servings

6 egg yolks

½ cup sugar

½ cup white wine

¼ cup amaretto liqueur

4 pints fresh raspberries

Preheat broiler 10 minutes before actual serving time.

1. In the top of a double boiler, put yolks, sugar, wine, and amaretto. Whisk together.

2. Place top of double boiler over simmering water and whisk egg mixture until light and fluffy, about 4 minutes. (The zabaglione can be made hours in advance and refrigerated.)

3. Put raspberries in a 10-inch gratin dish or quiche pan. Spoon zabaglione over fruit.

4. Place dish on an oven rack 5-inches below broiler flame and cook until zabaglione is dappled with brown, about 1 to 2 minutes. Serve immediately.

Peggy Ryan

VA PENSIERO

Midnight Supper

Charcoaled Loin
of Lamb with
Winter Honey,
Quince Tart
and Shaved
Sheepsmilk Cheese

Chilled
Mascarpone
Souffle

CHARCOALED LOIN OF LAMB WITH WINTER HONEY, QUINCE TART AND SHAVED SHEEPSMILK CHEESE

Yield: 6 servings

THE LAMB:

6 shallots, chopped

6 cloves garlic, chopped

1 seeded jalapeño, chopped

¾ cup olive oil

¼ cup pomegranate molasses

1 tablespoon coarsely ground pepper

2 sprigs rosemary, chopped

2 sprigs thyme, chopped

1 8-pound saddle of lamb (see Note)

THE TART:

4 quince, peeled and quartered

Pinch salt

Pinch sugar, optional

12 ounces paté brisée dough
(1½ ounces per tart)

THE SAUCE:

1 large onion, coarsely chopped

2 carrots, coarsely chopped

2 stalks celery, coarsely chopped

1 leek, washed and coarsely chopped

2 bay leaves

20 peppercorns

½ bottle white wine

½ bottle red wine

3 cups veal stock or water

½ cup crushed fresh tomato

2 sprigs rosemary or thyme

¼ cup mushroom trimmings

3 shallots, neatly diced

5 tablespoons butter

1 cup sauterne or other sweet wine

THE VINAIGRETTE:

1½ tablespoons good balsamic or red
wine vinegar

5 tablespoons top quality olive oil

½ teaspoon good Dijon mustard

1 sprig Italian parsley, minced

1 spring thyme, minced

6 small heads mâche

To assemble:

4 ounces Vermont aged sheepsmilk cheese

Coarse sea salt

1 tablespoon pomegranate seeds

1 tablespoon Hawaiian winter honey

THE LAMB:

1. Sauté shallots, garlic, and jalapeño in
oil until soft.

2. Add molasses, pepper, rosemary and
thyme. Mix and spread on lamb. Cover
and marinate refrigerated 6 to 8 hours.

Preheat oven to 375 degrees.

THE TART:

1. Wrap quince in cheese cloth and tie
closed. Put in saucepan and cover with
water. Add salt and sugar.

2. Simmer until very tender and water
has evaporated, about 1 hour.

3. Remove skins and purée quince.

4. Roll dough very thin and line 8 (to
insure against breakage) shallow
individual tart pans. Bake until golden
and crisp, about 15 to 18 minutes.
Remove from pans.

Lydia Shire & Susan Regis

BIBA AND PIGNOLI

Raise oven to 400 degrees.

THE SAUCE:

1. In a roasting pan, put lamb bones, onion, carrots, celery, leek, bay leaves and peppercorns. Roast until brown, but not burned, about 20 minutes.

2. Add both wines and deglaze pan.

3. Scrape wine mixture into a sauce pan. Add stock, tomato, thyme, and mushroom. Reduce to 3 cups. Strain and reserve liquid.

4. Sauté shallots in 2 tablespoons butter. Add sauterne and deglaze. Add reserved liquid. Simmer uncovered and reduce liquid to about 1½ cups

5. Stir in butter. Season to taste.

THE VINAIGRETTE:

1. In a bowl combine vinegar, oil, mustard, parsley, thyme, salt and pepper

To cook lamb:

1. Pat lamb dry and season liberally with salt and pepper.

2. In a very hot skillet, brown meat.

3. Place on a baking sheet and roast until rare. Remove from oven and let rest on a cooling rack.

To assemble:

1. On a plate place a pastry shell and fill with quince purée.

2. From the fat side of meat, through to bottom of meat, slice into 5 pieces. Arrange in a fan.

3. Toss mâche with vinaigrette. Season.

4. Spoon sauce around plate. Arrange mâche next to lamb and grate cheese over mache and meat.

5. Sprinkle lamb with salt and pomegranate seeds. Then drizzle each portion with ½ teaspoon honey. Serve.

Note: Ask butcher to remove most of the fat and heaviest piece of "strap." Keep the two loins in whole long pieces with some silver skin and some fat. Divide each loin into 3 7-ounce pieces. Also remove tenderloins and roughly chop bones for later use.

CHILLED MASCARPONE SOUFFLE

Yield: 10 4-ounce portions

2 sheets gelatin

1 cup granulated sugar

4 eggs, separated

1½ tablespoons vanilla

Pinch salt

1 cup heavy cream

¼ cup lemon juice

¼ cup dark rum

1 pound mascarpone cheese

1. Soften gelatin in cold water.

2. By hand combine ⅓ cup sugar, egg yolks, vanilla, and salt. Set aside.

3. Whip heavy cream until it begins to thicken and have a soft texture. Chill.

4. In a saucepan, combine lemon juice and rum. Heat and add gelatin to melt.

5. Whip whites with ½ cup sugar until they form soft peaks.

6. Fold gelatin mixture into mascarpone.

7. Quickly fold half the whites into cheese mixture to lighten and then fold in remainder.

8. Fold in whipped cream. Spoon into individual molds and chill.

Tea-Time Sweets

Ginger Cake
with Dried Fruit
Compote and
Applesauce

Strawberry
Rhubarb Cobbler
with Brown
Butter Biscuits

GINGER CAKE WITH DRIED FRUIT COMPOTE AND APPLESAUCE

Yield: 10 to 12 servings

THE CAKE:

2 sticks plus 2 tablespoons unsalted butter

3½ cups unbleached all-purpose flour plus 1 tablespoon

1 cup whole milk

4 eggs

1¼ cups packed, dark brown sugar

5 teaspoons baking powder

1 tablespoon ginger powder

¾ teaspoon white pepper

¼ cup molasses

2 tablespoons freshly grated ginger

THE COMPOTE:

1 cup granulated sugar

1¼ cups water

1 vanilla bean, split lengthwise

1 2-inch piece gingerroot, cut into 4 long slices

1 cup dried apricots, thinly sliced

1 cup dried Black Mission figs, quartered

1 cup fresh grapefruit juice

4 tablespoons champagne or white wine vinegar

¾ cup golden raisins

¾ cup dried sour cherries

8 tablespoons unsalted butter, cut into pieces

THE APPLESAUCE:

6 large, tart green apples, peeled, cored and cut into 1-inch chunks

4 tablespoons unsalted butter, cut into pieces

2 teaspoons fresh lemon juice

⅓ cup water

¾ cup granulated sugar

2 vanilla beans, split lengthwise

THE CAKE:

1. Melt 1 tablespoon butter. Using an 11 cup capacity decorative bundt pan, brush with butter and chill briefly to set. Dust pan with 1 tablespoon flour. Set aside.

Preheat oven to 350 degrees.

2. In a stainless steel saucepan heat milk and 2 sticks plus 1 tablespoon butter over medium heat until butter melts. Turn off heat and cool.

3. In an electric mixer fitted with whisk attachment, beat eggs and sugar on medium high speed until egg mixture is thick and pale, about 5 minutes.

4. Using a fine mesh strainer set over a bowl, combine flour, baking powder, ginger, and pepper, and sift. Set aside.

5. Change mixer to paddle attachment and add molasses and ginger to egg mixture and combine. Turn mixer to low and alternately add melted butter mixture and dry ingredients. Mix just until ingredients are incorporated.

6. Turn batter into prepared cake pan. Place on rack in bottom third of oven and bake until cake is springy to the touch, about 35 to 40 minutes.

7. Cool cake completely, about 1 hour. Unmold. Cake will have a very moist texture.

THE COMPOTE:

1. In a large stainless steel saucepan combine sugar and water, and bring to a boil over medium-high heat.

2. Use a knife to scrape out pulp and seeds of vanilla bean. Add scrapings plus pod to sugar mixture, and ginger.

3. Bring mixture to a boil and cook for 3 minutes. Taste to insure ginger flavor is strong enough. Remove ginger. Lower heat to medium.

4. Add apricots and figs. Cook covered, until fruit is softened, 4 to 5 minutes.

5. Add grapefruit juice, vinegar, currants, raisins, and cherries.

Stir well. Simmer compote, uncovered, about 20 minutes.

6. Remove from heat and discard vanilla bean. Whisk in butter. Serve warm.

THE APPLESAUCE:

1. In a saucepan combine apples, butter, lemon juice, water, and ½ cup sugar.

2. Scrape out pulp and seeds of vanilla beans, and add with pods to apple mixture.

3. Use aluminum foil to cover saucepan tightly. Crimp edges. Bring to a boil, and cook until foil has puffed, not more than 3 to 5 minutes.

4. Turn off heat and allow to sit, covered, for about 20 to 25 minutes.

To assemble:

1. Place a slice of Ginger Cake on an individual serving plate. Drizzle compote over cake and ladle about ⅓ cup applesauce next to cake. Serve additional compote and applesauce on the side.

STRAWBERRY RHUBARB COBBLER WITH BROWN BUTTER BISCUITS

Yield: 6 servings

THE COBBLER:

1 pound hothouse, thin, young, dark red stalks of rhubarb

¼ cup sugar

2 tablespoons water

1 cinnamon stick

3 to 4 grindings nutmeg

3 to 4 grindings fresh pepper

1 vanilla bean, split lengthwise

¼ cup Riesling wine

½ pound strawberries, stems removed and cut into ¼-inch slices

THE BISCUITS:

5 tablespoons unsalted butter

1 vanilla bean, split lengthwise

1¼ cups flour

2 hard boiled eggs, yolks only, cooled

¼ cup white cornmeal, plus extra

⅛ cup sugar, plus extra

2 teaspoons baking powder

¼ teaspoon salt

½ cup heavy cream, plus 2 tablespoons

THE COBBLER:

1. Discard rhubarb leaves. Cut stalks into 3-inch lengths and cut each length into pencil-size sticks. Set aside.

2. In a large stainless steel saucepan, over medium high heat, combine sugar and water. Bring to a boil, uncovered. Add cinnamon, nutmeg, and pepper.

3. Use a knife to scrape out pulp and seeds of vanilla bean. Add scrapings plus pod to sugar mixture.

4. When sugar mixture begins to brown, swirl pan gently to insure even color.

5. Add rhubarb and stir. Add wine and continue to cook over high heat, uncovered, until rhubarb just begins to soften, about 5 minutes.

6. Stir in strawberries. Cook until tender but still intact and mixture is slightly thickened, another 4 to 5 minutes. Remove vanilla bean and discard. Set aside to cool, about 1 hour.

7. When cool, transfer fruit mixture to an ovenproof 8 x 8x 2-inch baking dish.

Nancy Silverton

CAMPANILE

THE BISCUITS:

1. In a medium saucepan over medium-high heat, melt butter.

2. Use a knife to scrape out pulp and seeds of vanilla bean. Add scrapings plus pod to the melted butter.

3. Stir butter until it begins to brown and has a nutty aroma, about 2 to 3 minutes. Be careful it does not burn.

4. Remove vanilla bean and discard. Pour butter into a bowl and chill until firm, about 20 minutes. Set aside.

Preheat oven to 375 degrees.

5. In a food processor fitted with a steel blade, put flour, corn meal, sugar, baking powder, and salt. Process to combine.

6. Push yolks through a mesh strainer into flour mixture. Pulse to combine.

7. Cut chilled vanilla butter into chunks and add to flour mixture. Process until a fine meal. Add ½ cup cream and mix just until combined.

8. Turn dough out onto a lightly floured surface and knead gently 3 or 4 times until it forms a smooth ball. Don't over-work dough.

9. Roll out dough, fold and roll again a couple of times until smooth. For the final roll, leave dough ½-inch thick.

10. Using a 2 to 2½-inch biscuit cutter, cut out 6 biscuits. Place on top of fruit in a ring, with edges just touching. Keep biscuits at least 1 inch away from edges of mold. Brush tops of biscuits with 2 tablespoons cream and sprinkle with cornmeal and sugar.

11. Place in oven and lower heat to 350 degrees. Bake until browned, about 25 minutes.

12. Serve warm Cobbler with vanilla ice cream or slightly whipped cream.

California Plein Air Picnic

Salmon and Avocado Salad Sandwich

Grilled Chicken Sandwich with Fig Chutney on Whole Wheat Baguette

Red Bliss Potato Salad

Celeriac Slaw with Mustard Vinaigrette

Swords of Fruit with Almond-Raspberry Sauce

SALMON AND AVOCADO SALAD SANDWICH

Yield: 6 to 8 servings

THE SALMON SALAD:

1 ½ to 2 pounds fresh salmon fillet, poached

¼ cup extra virgin olive oil

¼ cup lemon juice

2 teaspoons capers, chopped

Sea salt and freshly ground white pepper

THE AVOCADO SALAD:

3 ripe Hass avocados, seeded and cubed, with seeds reserved

¼ cup fresh lime or lemon juice

1 small red onion, minced

3 cloves garlic, finely minced

1 tablespoon extra virgin olive oil

½ to 1 teaspoon sea salt

THE TRIMMINGS:

8 lettuce leaves

8 slices tomato

12-16 slices of hearty European bread, thickly sliced

THE SALMON SALAD:

1. Place fish on a flat tray and using a fork, flake fish, removing any bones and the skin.

2. Put flaked fish into a bowl. Add olive oil, lemon juice, capers, salt, and pepper. Toss gently. Cover and refrigerate at least 1 hour.

THE AVOCADO SALAD:

1. In a bowl, put avocado and sprinkle lime juice all over. Add onion, garlic, olive oil, and salt and toss to combine.

3. Place pits in avocado mixture to prevent browning. Place a piece of plastic film directly on mixture and refrigerate for at least 30 minutes.

To assemble:

1. Choose a traveling container that can be used for serving. Alternating the two salads, make 5 rows starting and ending with Salmon Salad.

2. Serve with bread, letting each person make their own sandwich using one or both of the salads, lettuce, and tomato. Pack in a picnic basket and enjoy later under the shade of a eucalyptus tree.

GRILLED CHICKEN SANDWICH WITH FIG CHUTNEY ON WHOLE WHEAT BAGUETTE

Yield: 6 to 8 servings

THE CHICKEN:

8 cloves garlic, minced

1 onion, minced

2 tablespoons extra virgin olive oil

1 teaspoon sea salt

½ teaspoon white pepper

4 to 6 boneless chicken breasts, organic or free-range preferred

THE CHUTNEY:

½ cup unsulphured black mission figs

½ cup chopped gingerroot

⅛ teaspoon sea salt

2 pears, ripe but firm

1 teaspoon lemon juice

2 whole wheat baguettes

6 to 8 green lettuce leaves

THE CHICKEN:

1. In a small bowl, mix together garlic, onion, oil, salt, and pepper. Wash and dry the chicken breasts and place in a flat shallow pan. Spread half the onion mixture on one side, turn chicken over and spread the remaining on the other side. Cover with plastic film and refrigerate 6 to 8 hours or overnight.

2. Heat a grill or broiler. Scrape onion mixture off chicken and discard. Place chicken on grill or under broiler and cook until done, about 5 to 7 minutes per side. Remove to a cutting surface and let cool a few minutes.

3. Slice chicken breasts into thin pieces.

THE CHUTNEY:

1. Remove tough stems from the figs.

2. Place figs, gingerroot, and salt into a blender or processor. Purée until well mixed. Add a little water, if needed.

3. Slice pears into quarters, core, and slice each quarter into 4 pieces. Put into a bowl and toss with lemon juice.

To assemble:

1. Cut each baguette into 3 or 4 pieces, and open to ready for sandwiches.

2. Spread chutney on one side and place a lettuce leaf on the other side of the bread, then the chicken slices, and several slices of pear. Cover with plastic film. Refrigerate until ready to pack picnic basket.

RED BLISS POTATO SALAD

Yield: 6 to 8 servings

3 pounds Red Bliss potatoes, small to medium size, washed

2 to 3 teaspoons sea salt

¾ cup extra virgin olive oil

1 box button mushrooms, sliced

Freshly ground black pepper

¼ cup balsamic vinegar

2 tablespoons cider vinegar

2 tablespoons grain mustard

2 anchovy fillets, pulverized or 1 table-spoon paste

1 small red pepper, minced

1 small yellow onion, minced

2 stalks celery, minced

1. In a large pot, put whole potatoes with skins, cover with water and add 2 teaspoons salt. Bring to a boil, covered and simmer 30 to 40 minutes. Do not over cook.

2. Heat a sauté pan, add 2 to 3 table-spoons olive oil and mushrooms. Sprinkle with salt and pepper, and cook uncovered for 5 to 7 minutes. Turn off flame, cover and set aside.

3. Put potatoes in a bowl of cold water, cool for about 2 minutes and remove.

4. Cut potatoes in quarters and put into a dry bowl.

5. In a small bowl or using a processor, put in balsamic and cider vinegars, remaining oil, mustard, and anchovies, and mix well. Pour dressing over warm potatoes.

6. Add mushrooms, red pepper, onion, and celery. Toss gently to keep potatoes intact.

7. Cover and refrigerate at least 1 hour before using. Adjust seasoning.

CELERIAC SLAW WITH MUSTARD VINAIGRETTE

Yield: 6 to 8 servings

½ cup extra virgin olive oil

⅓ cup cider vinegar

3 tablespoons strong Dijon mustard

Sea salt and freshly ground pepper

1 small red onion, finely minced

¼ bunch parsley, finely minced

2 celeriac roots, washed, peeled, and julienned

Molly Siple & Lissa de Angelis

MOLLY'S KITCHEN

1. In a small bowl whisk together oil, vinegar, and mustard. Add salt and pepper, to taste. Stir in onion and parsley.

2. Put celeriac in a bowl and add half of dressing. Toss. Drizzle on a little more dressing. Cover and let marinate, unrefrigerated, at least 30 minutes. Adjust seasoning before serving.

SWORDS OF FRUIT WITH ALMOND-RASPBERRY SAUCE

Yield: 6 to 8 servings

THE FRUIT:

¼ watermelon with rind

1 cantaloupe, seeded and peeled

12 to 16 beautiful strawberries, with greens

12 to 16 wooden skewers

2 6-ounce blocks raw goat milk cheddar

THE SAUCE:

½ cup almonds, roasted and finely ground

½ cup whole milk yogurt

½ cup raspberry all-fruit jam

THE FRUIT:

1. Cut watermelon into 1 by 2-inch triangular pieces with rind remaining on each piece. Cut cantaloupe into 2-inch chunks.

2. Starting at the rind end, thread watermelon onto the skewer, then a piece of cantaloupe, and then the strawberry, leaving the tip exposed. Set aside.

3. Cut the cheddar into 12 to 16 1-inch cubes. Thread one piece of cheddar onto the tip of each skewer.

4. Place in a container with a lid for travel. Serve with a bowl of sauce for dipping.

THE SAUCE:

1. In a bowl mix together the almonds, yogurt, and jam. Chill ½ hour before serving and pack next to the chilled drinks.

Gala Dinner

Roasted Red
Peppers

Grilled Baby
Eggplant

Linguine ai Frutti
di Mare

Ravioli with Sliced
Salmon Fillet

Ossobuco with
Gremolata Sauce

ROASTED RED PEPPERS

Yield: 6 to 8 as starter course

½ cup extra virgin olive oil, plus extra

3 cloves garlic, peeled and smashed

2½ pounds roasted red peppers, skins removed and quartered

½ lemon, juiced

1 tablespoon capers

2 tablespoons chopped calamata olives

Salt to taste

1½ teaspoons herbes de Provence

1 tablespoon bread crumbs

1. Coat a large pan with ¼ cup olive oil. On medium heat, sauté garlic until lightly browned.

2. Add peppers and another ¼ cup oil. Cook peppers on high heat for 5 minutes, stirring constantly.

3. Add lemon juice, capers, and olives. Cook for 3 minutes. Add salt, herbes de Provence, bread crumbs, and oil as needed to prevent sticking. Lower heat and simmer 10 minutes, stirring constantly.

4. Place pepper mixture in a large open container to cool. Serve Roasted Red Peppers chilled with Grilled Baby Eggplant.

GRILLED BABY EGGPLANT

Yield: 6 to 8 as starter course

5 small Italian eggplants, cut in 1/16-inch thick slices

Salt

½ cup oil

1 clove garlic, minced

1 tablespoon fresh mint, finely chopped

¼ teaspoon crushed chili

1. Heat a griddle and cook eggplant on it, turning to cook both sides. Repeat until all slices are cooked.

2. Line a collander with a layer of eggplant slices. Sprinkle liberally with salt. Repeat layering process until all eggplant has been used. Cover and place collander in a container to catch liquid. Refrigerate overnight, allowing salt to draw bitterness from eggplant.

3. Rinse eggplant slices. Using paper towels, pat dry. Layer a shallow pan with eggplant.

4. In a small bowl combine oil, garlic, mint, chili, and salt to taste. Pour oil mixture over eggplant.

5. Marinate eggplant until thoroughly chilled. Serve cold with the Roasted Red Peppers.

LINGUINE AI FRUTTI DI MARE

Yield: 6 servings

4 quarts water

4 tablespoons olive oil

4 cloves garlic, peeled and chopped

14 mussels, washed and beards removed

½ cup dry white wine

3 teaspoons salt

1 pound linguine

16 shrimp, shelled and deveined

¼ cup flour

3 calamari, cut into ¾-inch rings

½ cup fish stock or clam juice

1 tablespoon butter

1 tablespoon herbes de Provence

¼ teaspoon red pepper flakes

¼ cup chopped parsley

1. In a stock pot bring water to a boil.

2. In a saucepan, put 2 tablespoons oil, garlic, mussels, and ¼ cup white wine. Cover and steam on high heat until mussels open, about 4 minutes. Set aside and keep warm.

3. Add salt and linguine to boiling water. Cook uncovered, until al dente, about 11 minutes. Stir frequently.

4. Toss shrimp in flour to lighlty coat. Put 2 tablespoons oil in a large sauté pan and cook shrimp on medium-high heat until pink, about 3 minutes.

5. Add calamari, ¼ cup wine, stock, butter, herbes de Provence, pepper flakes, and parsley. Simmer uncovered until calamari is cooked, about 3 or 4 minutes.

6. Pour pasta into a collander and drain. Put pasta in a large serving bowl.

7. Stir steamed mussels and mussel pan juices into shrimp and calamari. Pour on pasta and toss. Serve immediately.

RAVIOLI WITH SLICED SALMON FILLET

Yield: 4 servings

4 quarts water

3 teaspoons salt

1 pound ravioli filled with a mild filling such as ricotta or ricotta and dill

2 tablespoons Dill Butter

8 thin slices fresh salmon fillet

6 stems fresh dill

Splash of heavy cream

Salt and freshly ground pepper

1. In a large stock pot bring water to a boil. Add salt and ravioli, and cook until al dente, about 6 to 8 minutes.

2. Meanwhile in a sauté pan, on medium heat, melt Dill Butter, being careful not to burn.

3. Add salmon and sauté, turning once, about 5 minutes per side.

4. Arrange fresh dill around border of a serving platter. Place salmon in center.

5. Drain ravioli in a collander and arrange around fish.

6. Add cream, salt, and pepper to sauté pan used for salmon. Heat briefly and spoon over salmon and ravioli. Serve immediately.

DILL BUTTER

Yield: 2 cups

1 pound butter, softened

1 cup loosely packed chopped fresh dill

1. In a food processor, cream together butter and dill.

2. Remove butter mixture from processor and place on parchment paper.

3. Wrap paper around butter and roll into a cylinder. Refrigerate. Dill Butter can be frozen for later use.

OSSOBUCO WITH GREMOLATA SAUCE

Yield: 4 servings

1 pound butter, cut into chunks

4 1-inch thick veal shanks

Flour

1 medium onion, chopped

½ cup dry white wine

1 carrot, peeled and chopped fine

1 celery stalk, chopped

6 fresh sage leaves, minced

TROIA

2 bay leaves

Salt and freshly ground pepper

½ cup tomato purée

½ cup Gremolata Sauce, warmed

3 to 4 cups cooked, warm risotto (see Note)

1. In a large skillet, melt butter until it sizzles.

2. Dust veal shanks with flour. Add to butter. Brown each side.

3. Add onions to veal and cook until translucent. Do not brown. Add wine and let simmer 3 minutes.

4. Transfer veal to a platter. To the pan add carrot, celery, sage, bay leaves, salt, pepper, and tomato purée. Simmer uncovered for another 3 minutes. Make sure no flour sticks to the pan.

5. Return veal to pan. Cook in sauce on low heat, covered, until meat is about to separate from bone, about 45 minutes.

6. Place 1 veal shank on plate with a serving of risotto next to it. Fill the center of the bone with 1 or 2 tablespoons Gremolata Sauce, and serve.

Note: Ossobuco is traditionally served with arborio rice risotto which is cooked with butter, saffron, peas, and the cooking juices of the Ossobuco.

GREMOLATA SAUCE

Yield: about ¾ cup

10 capers

6 sprigs fresh parsley

2 cloves garlic

2 anchovies

½ lemon, rind only

½ teaspoon freshly ground pepper

½ cup olive oil

1. In the bowl of a food processor, place capers, parsley, garlic, anchovies, lemon, pepper, and olive oil.

2. Process until creamy. Serve with Ossobuco. (Extra sauce can be frozen for later use.)

Nouvelle Lunch

Gazpacho Soup
with Vegetable
Rice Paper Roll

Tuna with
Provencale
Breadcrumbs
and Red Wine
Vinaigrette

Crumble Berry Pie
with Reduced
Orange Sauce

GAZPACHO SOUP WITH VEGETABLE RICE PAPER ROLL

Yield: 12 servings

THE SOUP:

10 Roma tomatoes

2 cucumbers, peeled

2 red bell peppers

3 shallots

½ cup fresh chervil, loosely packed

½ cup fresh cilantro, loosely packed

½ cup fresh basil, loosely packed

10 ounces olive oil

7 ounces white wine vinegar

Dash of Tabasco

½ carton of 35-ounce "Pomi" brand strained tomatoes

THE VEGETABLE ROLL:

¼ cup romaine, chiffonade cut

¼ carrot, julienned

¼ cup jicama, julienned

3 tablespoons basil, chiffonade cut

3 tablespoons mint, chiffonade cut

1 package rice paper (see Note)

THE SOUP:

1. Roughly chop the tomatoes, cucumbers, bell peppers, shallots, chervil, cilantro, and basil. Place in a bowl and combine. Add oil, vinegar, and Tabasco. Allow to marinate overnight, covered and refrigerated.

2. The next day, add Pomi tomatoes, blending with marinated mixture.

3. Pass through a coarse strainer. Adjust seasoning, if needed.

THE VEGETABLE ROLL:

1. Toss together romaine, carrot, jicama, basil, and mint.

2. In a bowl, soak rice paper in cold water for 2 minutes to soften. Remove rice paper and place on board.

3. Place 1 tablespoon of vegetable mixture on one half of rice paper. Tightly roll rice paper around mixture, leaving ends open. Continue until 6 rolls are made. To use as a garnish, slice each vegetable roll into 6 pieces, about ¾-inch thick.

To serve gazpacho:

1. Serve gazpacho in chilled soup bowls. Garnish each with 3 slices of vegetable roll.

Note: Rice paper is available in Asian markets. It is circular and comes in varying diameters. The 6-inch size is needed for this recipe.

TUNA WITH PROVENCALE BREAD CRUMBS AND RED WINE VINAIGRETTE

Yield: 4 servings

2 cups fresh bread crumbs (see Note)

2 tablespoons capers, finely chopped

2 tablespoons anchovies, finely chopped

12 to 16 cloves garlic, finely chopped (about 4 tablespoons)

4 tablespoons mixed fresh herbs, finely chopped (basil, tarragon, oregano, parsley)

4 Ahi tuna steaks, about 6 ounces each

1 cup flour, seasoned with salt and freshly ground pepper

2 eggs, slightly beaten

1 cup extra virgin olive oil

⅓ cup red wine vinegar

2 shallots, finely chopped (about 2 tablespoons)

4 cups baby salad greens

Preheat oven to 350 degrees.

1. In a bowl combine bread crumbs, capers, anchovies, 2 tablespoons garlic, and 2 tablespoons herbs, and set aside. Dredge tuna in flour to lightly coat, dip each in egg and then bread crumb mixture. Repeat with remaining pieces until all are coated.

2. In a nonstick pan with 1 or 2 teaspoons oil, lightly brown each piece of tuna, carefully turning once.

3. Place steaks in a shallow baking dish and put in oven, cooking until medium rare, approximately 4 to 5 minutes.

4. Combine vinegar, shallots, remaining garlic and herbs. Slowly whisk in the remaining olive oil. Season to taste. Place salad greens in bowl and pour vinaigrette over, tossing well. On each serving plate, make a bed of greens. Top with tuna and enjoy!

Note: Fresh bread crumbs can be made with 2-day to 4-day-old-bread. Using a fork, scratch and pull bread so that the crumbs retain a light texture.

Susan Weaver

THE FOUR SEASONS HOTEL

CRUMBLE BERRY PIE WITH REDUCED ORANGE SAUCE

Yield: 8 servings

THE PIE CRUST (see Note 1):

2 cups powdered sugar

3 cups cake flour

Pinch salt

2 sticks unsalted butter,
cut into small pieces

2 large eggs

THE CRUMBLE TOPPING (see Note 2):

2 sticks unsalted butter

1¼ cups granulated sugar

1½ teaspoons vanilla extract

1¼ cups cake flour

¾ cup all-purpose flour

THE ORANGE SAUCE:

1 quart orange juice

THE BERRY FILLING:

2 pints raspberries

2 pints blackberries

2 pints blueberries

2 cups sugar

½ cup corn starch

THE PIE CRUST:

1. Using a food processor, blend sugar and flour. Add salt and butter, pulsing to combine slightly. Add eggs and mix until dough forms a ball.

2. Dust pastry board with flour and place dough on it. Shape dough into a loaf. Wrap in plastic film and chill overnight.

Preheat oven to 450 degrees

3. On a floured pastry board, roll out refrigerated dough. Place in a 9-inch pie pan, trimming edges. Bake for 10 to 12 minutes, or until lightly browned.

THE CRUMBLE TOPPING:

1. Using a mixer with a paddle attachment, combine butter and sugar at low speed. Add vanilla extract. Scrape the sides and bottom of the bowl well. Add both flours at once and mix until dough comes together. Using a cookie sheet to catch dough, press the dough through a medium mesh strainer, a little at a time. Refrigerate for 2 hours.

THE ORANGE SAUCE:

1. In a medium saucepan, over low heat, reduce orange juice to 1½ cups. Strain through a fine sieve, and chill before serving, about 1 hour.

Preheat a convection oven to 300 degrees or a standard oven to 325 degrees

THE BERRY FILLING:

1. Rinse and combine all berries in a bowl. Add sugar and cornstarch, and toss together. Place filling in the pre-baked pastry shell so that fruit height is 1 inch above the sides. Cover with the chilled crumble topping and press down gently.

To bake pie:

1. Place in preheated oven for 20 to 30 minutes, until the topping is golden

2. Remove pie from oven and cool slightly. Dust top with powdered sugar and serve slightly warm with chilled orange juice.

Note 1: Prepare dough before using and chill overnight.

Note 2: Prepare topping 2 hours before final baking of pie to allow for chilling.

South West Dinner

Corn Crepes with Ossetra Caviar

Guava Glazed Tuna with Cucumber and Toasted Pumpkin Seed Vinaigrette

Sofrito

Ibarra Pot de Crème

CORN CREPES WITH OSSETRA CAVIAR

Yield: 20 crepes

4 eggs, room temperature

1½ cups milk, room temperature

½ teaspoon kosher salt

½ cup all-purpose flour

4 tablespoons masa harina

1 ounce warm clarified butter

1¼ cups Mexican crema pura

7 tablespoons Ossetra Caviar

20 chives

1. In a bowl, put eggs and with a whisk, lightly beat. Add milk and salt.

2. In another bowl, combine flour and masa harina. Slowly whisk in egg mixture, making sure there are no lumps.

3. With a medium sieve placed over a bowl, strain the batter. Let batter rest in a double bain-marie or double boiler with ice in bottom, for 20 minutes.

4. Whisk butter into batter.

5. Heat a nonstick frying pan and pour in just enough batter to coat the bottom. Drain any excess batter back into the bain-marie. Cook crepe until edges are slightly dry and begin to curl.

6. Using a paring knife or bamboo skewer, remove crepe and place on a parchment paper covered cookie sheet. Repeat process until batter is finished.

7. To assemble, put one crepe on a work surface. In the center, spoon 1 tablespoon of crema pura, then 1 teaspoon caviar.

8. Gather edges of crepe, folding to form a sack and tie with a chive. Repeat process until all crepes are assembled. Place 2 crepes on each plate. Serve.

GUAVA GLAZED TUNA WITH CUCUMBER AND TOASTED PUMPKIN SEED VINAIGRETTE

Yield: 10 servings

THE CUCUMBER AND TOASTED PUMPKIN SEED VINAIGRETTE:

1 cucumber, peeled, cored, and sliced lengthwise into thin ribbons

4 limes (about ⅔ cup juice)

4 tablespoons orange zest, plus extra for garnish

1 tablespoon cilantro

1 jalapeño pepper

3 tablespoons pumpkin seeds, toasted

½ cup plus 5 tablespoons olive oil

1 teaspoon powdered epazote

Kosher salt and freshly ground pepper

¼ chayote, peeled and julienned

THE GUAVA GLAZE:

Yield: 10 servings

1 ½ tablespoons olive oil

1 shallot, finely chopped (2 tablespoons)

1 ½ tablespoons finely chopped garlic

6 tablespoons dry sherry

1 ½ cups chicken stock

¾ cup guava jam

¾ cup "Pomì" brand strained tomatoes

¾ cup red wine vinegar

1 ½ tablespoons Colemans mustard

1 ½ teaspoons cumin seed, toasted and ground

1 ½ teaspoons chili powder

THE TUNA:

10 7-ounce tuna steaks

10 crispy tostadas, for garnish

THE CUCUMBER AND TOASTED PUMPKIN SEED VINAIGRETTE:

1. In a bowl combine cucumber, 2 tablespoons lime juice, zest, cilantro, and pepper. Set aside.

1. In a processor, grind seeds to a paste. Add 5 tablespoons oil and process to combine.

2. Place seed mixture in a bowl, add remaining oil, remaining lime juice, epazote, salt, and pepper. Whisk together. Add chayote.

3. Add vinaigrette to the cucumber mixture, combine and set aside.

THE GUAVA GLAZE:

1. In a large saucepan, put olive oil. Add shallot and garlic, and cook over medium heat, 5 to 7 minutes.

2. Add sherry and cook uncovered, reducing to a light syrup, about 5 minutes.

3. Add stock, jam, tomatoes, vinegar, mustard, cumin, and chili. Simmer 5 minutes to blend flavors. Remove from heat and set aside.

THE TUNA

1. On a grill, sear tuna and cook until rare.

2. Remove to platter and brush with Guava Glaze.

Patricia Williams

CITY WINE & CIGAR Co

To assemble:

1. On a plate, place about a ½ cup of Sofrito. On the Sofrito, place the glazed tuna.

2. Scatter cucumber mixture over tuna.

3. Garnish with a drizzle of guava glaze, zest, and crispy tostadas.

SOFRITO

Yield: about 4 cups or 10 servings

2 cups finely diced salt pork

1 onion, finely diced

2 tablespoons minced garlic

1 tablespoon minced ginger

5 tablespoons tamarind paste

2 cups hot water

3 tablespoons dark brown sugar

2 tablespoons achiote paste

2 tablespoons red wine

2 cups chicken stock

12 ounces "Pomì" brand strained tomatoes

2 jalapeño peppers, seeded and thinly sliced

2 carrots, finely diced

2 oranges, zest only

Kosher salt and freshly ground pepper

1. Cook salt pork and onions on medium heat, about 15 minutes.

2. Add garlic and ginger, and cook until golden, about 10 minutes.

3. In a bowl put tamarind paste and cover with hot water to soften. Using a wooden spoon, push through a sieve.

3. Add tamarind paste, sugar, achiote paste, and wine, and reduce uncovered, about 5 minutes.

4. Add chicken stock and tomatoes, and on medium-high heat, uncovered, reduce, about 20 minutes.

5. Add peppers, carrots, zest, salt, and pepper. Continue to cook on medium flame about 5 minutes. Set aside for use with Guava Glazed Tuna.

IBARRA POT DE CRÈME

Yield: 6 servings

2 cups heavy cream

4 ounces Ibarra chocolate (see Note)

4 ounces semi-sweet chocolate

1 cinnamon stick

6 egg yolks, beaten

3 capfuls Kahlúa

1. Put cream, Ibarra and semi-sweet chocolates, and cinnamon in the upper part of a double boiler. On medium-high heat, covered, melt chocolate, stirring occasionally to combine with cream, about 10 to 15 minutes.

2. Lower heat to medium and slowly whisk in egg yolks. Add Kahlúa and stir well. Cook until pudding thickens, stirring frequently, about 10 to 12 minutes.

3. Pour crème into molds of choice. Cover and chill in refrigerator until ready to serve.

Note: Ibarra or Mexican chocolate is chocolate mixed with cinnamon, sugar, and vanilla.

Index of

Recipes

Meat and Game

Charcoaled Loin of Lamb
with Winter Honey, Quince Tart
and Shaved Sheepsmilk Cheese, 196

Colorado Elk Loin in Swedish Lingonberry
and Cassis Sauce, 97

Grilled Marinated Veal Chop, 140

Grilled Tuscan-style Sirloin Steak
with Parmigiano-Reggiano, Lemon
and Truffle Oil, 39

Leg of Lamb Stuffed with Wild Rice
and Porcini Mushrooms, 36

Mandarin Pork
with Brandy-Infused Hoisin Sauce, 50

Ossobuco with Gremolata Sauce, 203

Pork Loin Chops with Caramelized Apples,
Calvados, Cider and Cream, 192

Rack of Lamb with Pesto Crumbs, 98

Wyoming Buffalo in
an Orange Curry Ragout, 96

Poultry and Fowl

Barbecued Duck, 88

Chicken Salad on Rosemary Crostini, 100

Duck Spring Rolls with Pineapple Citrus Sauce
and Sweet Thai Chili Sauce, 94

Game Hen Pibil, 142

Grilled Chicken Sandwich with Fig Chutney
on Whole Wheat Baguette, 201

Grilled Quail Salad with Avocado, Goat Cheese
and Croutons with Smoked Bacon Vinaigrette, 48

Honey Glazed and Spiced Ranch Squab, 150

Lemon Roasted Chicken, 146

Roasted Duck Breasts
with Wild Mushroom Risotto, 154

Roasted Squab with Wild Mushroom
and Asparagus Salad
with Warm Caramelized Onion Vinaigrette, 152

Eggs

Perfectly Scrambled Eggs, 144

Goldilox, 144

Fish and Shellfish

Alaskan Black Cod
with Clams, Chorizo and Orzo, 42

Grilled Atlantic Salmon
with Morels, Ramps and Pancetta, 49

Grilled Salmon
with Artichoke Rosemary Sauce, 194

Guava Glazed Tuna with Cucumber
and Toasted Pumpkin Seed Vinaigrette, 206

Fish Tostadas, 102

Honey Mustard Salmon, 148

Island Seafood Paella, 95

Mussels from Brussels, 98

Pan-Roasted Alaskan Halibut
with Morel Mushrooms, 46

Poached Arctic Char with Organic
Bean Salad and Red Ginger Essence, 40

Poached Halibut in Lemon Nage with Yukon
Gold Potatoes and Soup Vegetables, 91

Red Snapper Mediterranean, 150

Salmon with Summer Truffles and Leeks, 152

Sautéed Shrimp with Pistachio Pesto
on a Risotto Cake, 194

Spicy Steamed Littlenecks
with Toasted Angel Hair Pasta,
Slow Roasted Tomatoes and Basil Aioli, 38

Tuna with Provençal Bread Crumbs
and Red Wine Vinaigrette, 204

Grains

Cornmeal Shortcakes, 41

Polenta with Pancetta and Sage, 141

Red Wine Risotto, 152

Risotto Cakes, 194

Wild Mushroom Risotto, 154

Index of

Recipes

Baked Goods

Brown Butter Biscuits, 199

English Muffins, 144

Rosemary Crostini, 100

Spoon Bread, 147

Desserts

Blueberry Bread & Butter Pudding, 93

Blueberry Polenta Cake, 45

Buttermilk Ice Cream
with Strawberries in Grappa, 99

Chili Chocolate Truffles
and Pumpkin Seed Praline, 103

Chilled Mascarpone Souffle, 197

Chocolate Almond Biscotti, 92

Chocolate-Pistachio "Salami", 99

Chocolate Sour Cream Marble Cake, 92

Chocolate Sushi, 89

Corn Crème Brûlée
with Blueberry Polenta Cake. 45

Cornmeal Shortcakes
with Ontario Peaches in Late Harvest
Wine Syrup with Maple Lavender Yogurt, 141

Crème Brûlée Infused
with Verbena Leaves, 91

Crumble Berry Pie
with Reduced Orange Sauce, 205

Deep Dish Apple Pie, 147

Fresh Fruit Rustic Tartlettes, 155

Frozen Chocolate Charlotte Marquise, 37

Fruit Tart, 97

Ginger Cake with Dried Fruit Compote
and Applesauce, 198

Grand Marnier Chocolate Cake
with Shiny Chocolate Icing, 193

Grape Cobbler
with Rosemary Crème Anglais, 43

Ibarra Pot de Crème, 207

Lemon Confit, 151

Lemon Custard with Figs and Berries
and Lemon Vanilla Sauce, 153

Lemon Granite, 151

Lemon Ice Cream, 151

Lemon Lime Tart, 149

Lemon Tart, 151

Nanaimo Bars, 149

Pastry Cream, 97

Peppered Peach Tarts with Ginger Caramel
Sauce and Whipped Cream, 39

Poached Pears and Yogurt Parfait, 145

Poppyseed Short Bread Cookies, 92

Quince Tart, 207

Ricotta Pudding, 141

Sangria Poached Pear
with Sangria Compote, 143

Strawberry Rhubarb Cobbler
with Brown Butter Biscuits, 199

Strawberry Rhubarb Tarte, 47

Sticky Toffee Pudding, 93

Swords of Fruit
with Almond-Raspberry Sauce, 201

Three Flavors of Lemon, 151

Warm Gratin of Raspberries
and Amaretto Zabaglione, 195

Index to Photographers and Restaurant Designers

ALL PHOTOGRAPHS ARE THE COPYRIGHT OF THE INDIVIDUAL PHOTOGRAPHERS

Every effort has been made to obtain correct information for credits. Any omissions will be corrected in future printings.

Julia Child
Portrait: Jim Scherer

Andree Abramoff
Portrait: Richard Bowditch
Food: Richard Bowditch

Jody Adams
Portrait: Mark Ostow
Food: Zach Feuer
Restaurant Design: Peter Niemitz

Suzanne Baby
Portrait: Don Mackenzie/Andrew Prowse
Food: Don Mackenzie/Andre Prowse
Restaurant: Don Mackenzie/Andrew Prowse

Karen Barnaby
Portrait: Greg Athans
Food: Greg Athans
Restaurant: Greg Athans
Restaurant Design: Robert Le Dingham

Alison Barshak
Portrait:Courtney Grant Winston
Food: Bill Deering, Michael Mundy
Restaurant Design: Marguerite Rodgers

Ann Cashion
Portrait: Christine R. Schuyler
Food: Christine R. Schuyler
Restaurant: Christine R. Schuyler
Restaurant Design:Walter Gagliano

Suzy Crofton
Portrait: Mitchell Canoff
Food: Kathy Sanders

Susanna Foo
Food: Matt Wargo
Restaurant: Louis E.Wallach
Restaurant Design: Marguerite Rodgers

Renee Foote
Portrait: Christopher Campbell
Food: Christopher Campbell
Restaurant:Jeremy McCormack
Restaurant Design: Richard Eppstadt

Diane Forley
Portrait: Stephan Russell
Food: Tom Kirkman
Restaurant: Michael Moran
Restaurant Design:
Glenn Forley and Natalie Fizer

Gale Gand
Portrait: Tim Turner
Food:Jim Purdum,Tim Turner, Carin Simon
Restaurant: Steinkamp, Ballog
Restaurant Design:Warren Architects Limited

Beverly Gannon
Portrait: Steve Brinkman
Food: Steven Brinkman
Restaurant:
Steven Minkowski, Randy Hufford

Monique Gaumont-Lanvin
Portrait: Rosemary Carroll
Food: Rosemary Carroll
Restaurant: Rosemary Carroll
Restaurant Design:
Monique Gaumont-Lanvin

Rozanne Gold
Portrait Jill Levine
Food: Cole Rigg
Restaurant Design:
Hardy Holzmann Pfeiffer

Aliza Green
Portrait: Bill Deering
Food: Bill Deering

Josefina Howard
Portrait: Elena Garrison
Food: Debra Denker, Elena Garrison

Evan Kleiman:
Food:John Forsman
Restaurant: Paul Warchol
Restaurant Design: Morphosis

Marjorie Kloss
Portrait: Richard McMichael
Food: Ian Campbell
Restaurant: Stan Mallis
Restaurant Design: Blackney/Hayes

Sarabeth Levine
Portrait: Keith Trumbo
Food: Molly Siple

Susan McCreight Lindeborg
Portrait: Chris Kleponis
Food: Rei Taka
Restaurant: Glen de Pas
Restaurant Design: Maureen Daly

Susan Mendelson
Portrait: Hans Sipma
Food: Derik Murray

Acknowledgments

Carrie Nahabedian
Portrait: John Solano
Food: John Salano
Restaurant: Jaime Ardiles-Arce
Restaurant Design: Intradesign

Nancy Oakes
Portrait: Joshua Ets-Hokin
Food: Joshua Ets-Hokin
Restaurant: Evan Jay Pilchik
Restaurant Design: Pat Kuleto

Debra Ponzek
Portrait: Tom Kirkman
Food: Tom Kirkman
Restaurant: David Barnum
Restaurant Design: Birch Coffey

Jill Prescott
Food: Jill Prescott

Peggy Ryan
Portrait: Randy Tunnell
Food: Randy Tunnell
Restaurant: Randy Tunnell
Restaurant Design:
Jerry Brennan/Barbara Gorham

Lydia Shire and Susan Regis
Portrait: Eric Roth
Food: Carl Tremblay
Restaurant: Peter Paige
Restaurant Design: Adam Tihany

Nancy Silverton
Portrait: Barry Michlin
Food: Barry Michlin
Restaurant: Barry Michlin
Restaurant Design: Peter Jennings

Molly Siple
Portrait: Anthony Peres
Food: Molly Siple
Interior: Anthony Peres

Katell Thielemann
Portrait: Steven Meltzer
Food: Steven Meltzer
Restaurant: Steven Meltzer
Restaurant Design: Rita St. Clair

Susan Weaver
Portrait: John Uher
Food: John Uher
Restaurant: Peter Vitale
Restaurant Design: I.M. Pei, (architect),
Chhada, Siembieda & Partners (interior design)

Patricia Williams
Portrait: Steven Freeman
Food: Steven Freeman
Restaurant Design: Chris Smith, CMS Design

Many friends contributed to the final realization of this book. Hanna Liebman worked as an initial researcher, identifying notable women chefs worthy of inclusion. Georgia Tetlow also acted as a researcher and identified further chefs for me. I am indebted to Molly Siple who took on the job of testing all the recipes and writing them up using quantities and language that are appropriate for home cooks. She was assisted by Lissa De Angelis, an independent food consultant, who checked the recipe copy and gave her invaluable professional critique. Molly's friend, Helen Bernstein was an early supporter of this book idea and was instrumental in bringing it to the attention of the publishers. Sally Beaudette was the influential liaison with Julia Child. Anne McGruder, a cookbook specialist, acted as copy editor. Amla Sanghvi performed the role of photo researcher and coordinator - as she has done so expertly for several of my previous books. I am very grateful to the Wiley team, including Senior Editor Claire Thompson, for piloting this book through from start to finish. Finally, I salute Gillian Redfern Rones who literally put the icing on the cake with her spectacular graphic design which sets this book apart as an inspiration and benchmark for others to follow. My sincere thanks to all these people.

Chefs Talk

BEVERLY RUSSELL INTERVIEWS WITH WOMEN OF TASTE CHEFS

7/7/96 Evan Kleiman, at Caffe Angeli, Los Angeles.

8/10/96 Rozanne Gold, at her office, New York.

8/27/96 Suzy Crofton, at the Four Seasons Hotel, Chicago.

9/3/96 Diane Forley, at Verbena, New York.

9/3/96 Josefina Howard, at Rosa Mexicano, New York.

9/5/96 Marjorie Kloss, at the Four Seasons Hotel, Philadelphia.

9/18/96 Ann Cashion, at Cashion's Eat Place, Washington, D.C.

10/3/96 Susan Weaver, at the Four Seasons Hotel, New York.

10/8/96 Debra Ponzek, at Aux Delices, Riverside.

10/17/96 Susan McCreight Lindeborg, at the Morrison Clark Inn, Washington, D.C.

11/17/96 Gale Gand, at Brasserie T, Northfield, Chicago.

11/19/96 Alison Barshak, at the Four Seasons Hotel, Philadelphia.

11/19/96 Susanna Foo, at Susanno Foo's, Philadelphia.

11/20/96 Aliza Green, at the Four Seasons Hotel, Philadelphia.

11/20/96 Monique Gaumont-Lanvin, at the Sign of the Sorrel Horse, Doylestown.

12/4/96 Sarabeth Levine, at her home, New York.

1/7/97 Renee Foote, at Mercer Street Grill, Toronto.

1/7/97 Susan Baby, at Gallery Grill, Toronto.

1/8/97 Lydia Shire, at Biba, Boston.

1/8/97 Jody Adams, at Rialto, Boston.

1/9/97 Patricia Williams, at City Wine & Cigar, New York.

1/24/97 Carrie Nahabedian, Four Seasons Hotel, Los Angeles.

1/24/97 Nancy Silverton, at Campanile, Los Angeles.

1/27/97 Nancy Oakes, at Boulevard, San Francisco.

1/29/97 Susan Mendelson, at the Lazy Gourmet, Vancouver.

1/29/97 Karen Barnaby, at The Fish House in Stanley Park, Vancouver.

2/14/97 Molly Siple, in New York.

3/20/97 Peggy Ryan, at Va Pensiero, Evanston.

3/22/97 Jill Prescott, at Prairie Restaurant, Chicago.

4/1/97 Beverly Gannon, by phone to Maui.

4/9/97 Katell Thielemann, at Troia, Bistro at the Walters, Baltimore.

5/2/97 Andree Abramoff, by phone to Cafe Crocodile, New York.